AI for the Rest of Us

AI for the Rest of Us

An Illustrated Introduction

Sairam Sundaresan

BLOOMSBURY ACADEMIC
NEW YORK • LONDON • OXFORD • NEW DELHI • SYDNEY

BLOOMSBURY ACADEMIC

Bloomsbury Publishing Inc, 1359 Broadway, New York, NY 10018, USA
Bloomsbury Publishing Plc, 50 Bedford Square, London, WC1B 3DP, UK
Bloomsbury Publishing Ireland, 29 Earlsfort Terrace, Dublin 2, D02 AY28, Ireland

BLOOMSBURY, BLOOMSBURY ACADEMIC and the Diana logo are trademarks of Bloomsbury Publishing Plc

First published in the United States of America 2025

Copyright © Sairam Sundaresan, 2025

Front cover illustration provided by the author
Front cover background © IStock / Fourleaflover

All rights reserved. No part of this publication may be: i) reproduced or transmitted in any form, electronic or mechanical, including photocopying, recording or by means of any information storage or retrieval system without prior permission in writing from the publishers; or ii) used or reproduced in any way for the training, development or operation of artificial intelligence (AI) technologies, including generative AI technologies. The rights holders expressly reserve this publication from the text and data mining exception as per Article 4(3) of the Digital Single Market Directive (EU) 2019/790.

Bloomsbury Publishing Inc does not have any control over, or responsibility for, any third-party websites referred to or in this book. All internet addresses given in this book were correct at the time of going to press. The author and publisher regret any inconvenience caused if addresses have changed or sites have ceased to exist, but can accept no responsibility for any such changes.

Library of Congress Cataloging-in-Publication Data Available

ISBN: PB: 979-8-8818-0795-5
ePDF: 979-8-8818-6745-4
eBook: 979-8-8818-0796-2

Typeset by Deanta Global Publishing Services, Chennai, India
Printed and bound in the United States of America

For product safety related questions contact productsafety@bloomsbury.com.

To find out more about our authors and books visit www.bloomsbury.com and sign up for our newsletters.

To He who must always be remembered for his eternal guidance and grace.
To my best half and our girls for their infinite patience and love. I promise I'll have more time now.
To my parents and sister, who've always believed in me more than I ever did.
And finally, to you, dear reader, for picking this book up. It means the world to me.

Ella Pughazhum Iraivanuke.

Contents

Preface viii
Acknowledgments xii

1 The AI Revolution 1
2 The Fundamentals of AI 11
3 A Few Good Algorithms 37
4 Neural Networks 61
5 AI That Reads and Writes 79
6 Transformers and Large Language Models 99
7 Machine Vision 125
8 Generative Models 157
9 AI That Recommends Stuff 185
10 Building Intelligence: The Complete AI Project Guide 203

Closing Thoughts 223

Notes 225
Index 232
About the Author 240

Preface

We're living through an AI revolution. Artificial intelligence transforms how we live, work, and interact with the world every day. AI has touched everything, from the phones in our pockets to the cars we drive. Yet, for most of us, AI remains a black box: powerful but mysterious. This book will change that. It's not just about machines learning; it's about us learning together.

Yet Another Book?

Why another book on AI, you ask? Why is this one different? The answer lies in how most AI literature is written. On one side of the coin, you have books that assume you know how to code. Conversely, you have books that require an intricate understanding of mathematics and statistics.

This book assumes neither. In fact, it assumes you have almost no knowledge of machine learning, coding, or any other technical prerequisite. Its ambition (and mine) is to make the complex world of AI accessible to those without a technical background.

Through a potent combination of illustrations, humor, and storytelling prose, we'll dive into the fundamental concepts and work our way up to more complex ideas. Both timeless algorithms and modern blockbusters are covered so that you have the context of what was (and on occasion still is) used and what powers the many applications we love and use today.

Prerequisites

Let's be clear about what you need for this journey. The good news? It's surprisingly little. While other books might require programming expertise or advanced mathematics, we'll use something more powerful: visual thinking and intuition. Yes, some basic high school math will help— simple algebra and probability. But fear not. We'll explain everything step by step using illustrations and real-world examples. This book is for the thinkers, the dreamers, and those eager to understand the world of AI and its potential.

This book is for the rest of us.

Outcomes

So, what can you expect from this book? By the time you turn the last page, you will have a solid understanding of key AI concepts, from Machine Learning (ML) and Natural Language Processing (NLP), to Neural Networks, Computer Vision, and Recommender Systems. You will know how these technologies function, their practical applications, and have a clear intuition of how they work. Most importantly, you will have the tools to navigate and understand the AI world, whether you're discussing it with colleagues for a project, considering it for a business venture, or simply pondering its implications on a lazy Sunday afternoon.

Roadmap

The book follows a carefully planned roadmap, starting with the basics and building up to the more advanced. The book can be thought of as having two parts. Part one sheds light on the basics of AI and its history. We explore machine learning, the heart of AI, before moving on to deep learning and neural networks. This includes Chapters 1 through 4. In particular, most modern algorithms are based on deep learning. So,

Chapter 4 covers the fundamentals of neural networks to help you make sense of the rest of the book.

Part two builds on this and explores areas of AI application like Natural Language Processing, Computer Vision, and Recommender Systems. This includes Chapters 5 through 9 and focuses on the use of deep learning and neural networks to solve problems in these areas.

Chapter 10 is reserved to give you input on planning your own AI projects and what it takes to make them successful.

By the end of the book, you'll understand how AI works and when to apply it in your work.

How Do I Read This Book?

In terms of how to read this book, it's designed to be flexible. While you can certainly read it cover to cover, each chapter is also intended to stand on its own, allowing you to dip into specific areas of interest.

With that said, if you're new to AI, I recommend following the book sequentially from start to finish to build a solid foundational understanding before tackling more complex topics.

Contact

I welcome your thoughts and questions along the way. To reach me with any queries or feedback, you can connect with me in the following ways:

- Email: sairam@artofsaience.com
- X: https://www.twitter.com/DSaience
- YouTube: https://www.youtube.com/@artofsaience
- LinkedIn: https://www.linkedin.com/in/sairam-sundaresan/
- Newsletter: https://newsletter.artofsaience.com

I hope this book will illuminate your path in the fascinating world of AI, making it less daunting and more accessible, regardless of your background or experience level.

I promise you that learning AI has NEVER been this fun. Our journey begins here. Let's get started!

Acknowledgments

This book exists because of two events. First, I kept annoying friends and guests at dinner parties, trying to explain AI so they would understand. When one guest (perhaps out of exasperation and needing a quick getaway) said, "You helped a non-coder like me understand this," the first seed was planted. Second, I made the questionable decision to check my email at 5 a.m. Through under-caffeinated, bleary eyes, I read, "Would you be interested in writing a book?" Thanks, Dr. Christin Chong, for both the email and your support.

Preethi, my brilliant wife and favorite biotech scientist: you've endured more neural network analogies than any marriage should require. While you're actually finding cures for diseases, I've been trying to explain why computers are good at recognizing cats. When I hit walls, you asked the perfect questions. When I overthought everything, you brought me back to earth. When I celebrated tiny victories at midnight, you celebrated with me. Thank you for your (infinite) patience, your wisdom, and for only occasionally reminding me that you actually help people. This book exists because you believed it should.

Sai Urmila and Sai Keerthi, who've grown up alongside these chapters: Urmi, you were two when this started. Now you're five and asking whether robots dream. Your curiosity shaped how I explain everything. Keerthi, you arrived mid-manuscript and immediately taught me that the best explanations are the simplest ones. Watching you both discover the world reminded me daily why making knowledge accessible matters. You're both in here, not by accident but by necessity. You're why I write.

My parents, sister, brother-in-law, and in-laws, who put up a brave smiling face whenever I launched into another explanation about diffusion models. I commend you and thank you for your support and patient listening, even when it felt like I had come from an alternate reality. Jokes aside, you've always indulged and encouraged my curiosity. I don't take that lightly and owe you a great debt of gratitude.

To my office colleagues, who transformed our coffee breaks into inspiring conversations about AI's possibilities and pitfalls: your diverse perspectives and thoughtful questions helped me see beyond my assumptions. The hallway debates, whiteboard sessions, and those moments when someone would say "but what if . . . " pushed me to think deeper and explain more clearly. Thank you for creating an environment where curiosity thrives.

To my mentors (you know who you are), who first lit the spark of teaching in me: you showed me that the greatest joy in understanding something comes from helping others understand it too. Your patience with my early attempts at explanation and encouragement to keep simplifying complex ideas planted the seeds that grew into this book. Thank you for believing that teaching is not just about what you know, but about how deeply you care that others learn.

Coffee deserves co-author credit. My coffee grinder and filter witnessed my transformation from "I'm writing a book!" enthusiasm to deadline-driven desperation. I've been through more cups of coffee these past few years than I can remember. To every barista who's ever made me a 6 a.m. double shot, you're doing sacred work.

My friend Chris Wong, your calm demeanor and excellent feedback on my "AI stuff explained good" draft helped me see through the chaos to find clarity. Thank you for believing AI education needed disrupting.

Hasan Kuba, thanks so much for helping me assemble a coherent book proposal that didn't sound like a collection of buzzwords.

Jason Bartholomew, agent extraordinaire: you took my stream-of-consciousness about "making AI less scary" and transformed it into something tangible. You protected the book's mission while navigating the business side I barely understand.

My publishing team at Bloomsbury deserves special thanks: Jacquie Flynn for believing in the book's vision, Mikayla Lindsay for editing the manuscript and preserving the core ideas, and the cover-design and copy-editing team for turning a collection of pages into a set of flowing ideas. You all made this book infinitely better than I could have alone.

My dear beta readers, the heroes who suffered so others wouldn't, thanks for keeping me honest. Special thanks go to the technical reviewer and friend I don't deserve but needed, Dr. Cameron R. Wolfe. Your attention to detail and encouraging feedback on every misstep and mistake remade this book. I can't thank you enough.

To everyone I missed by accident, I appreciate you, and each of you contributed something specific and irreplaceable. You kept me human while writing about machines, clear-headed while swimming in complexity, and hopeful while explaining technology that often sounds terrifying. I'm profoundly grateful.

To anyone who's ever felt like AI is a party they weren't invited to, this book exists because of you. We will understand this together, with plenty of coffee and zero judgment.

Finally, to you, dear reader: you holding this book validates a lifelong dream of mine. Thank you from the bottom of my heart.

(Every error is mine, likely made after too much caffeine. Every moment of clarity came from someone above. If I forgot you, find me. I owe you coffee and better thanks.)

Chapter 1
The AI Revolution

In 2020, an AI system called AlphaFold solved one of biology's greatest challenges: predicting protein structures with incredible accuracy. This breakthrough, which earned the Nobel Prize in Chemistry four years later, is accelerating drug discovery and our understanding of diseases. Meanwhile, different AI systems help us with simpler day-to-day tasks, from filtering spam in our emails to enhancing our smartphone photos.

Consider a common example that you might have encountered too. While trying to log into a social network site, the website demands I prove that I'm a human—welcome to today's world of artificial intelligence.

To prove my humanity, I need to complete a simple test. I have to select all the tiles in a grid that contain a traffic light. This is what's known as a Turing test, or more commonly as CAPTCHA (Completely Automated Public Turing test to tell Computers and Humans Apart). It's easy for humans to figure out but hard for machines to understand and solve.[1] By passing this test, I've just labeled some data that might be used to train an AI model somewhere.

Talk about crowdsourcing data collection and annotation. Using this simple test, companies can collect high-quality data annotations from people around the world who are none the wiser.

Look at how far AI has percolated into our lives. Like water from a stream that finds its way into every nook and cranny between tiny pebbles, AI has touched almost everything we interact with. Just think about our everyday life. Whether it is the smart speaker that controls the lights and devices in our home, our car that learns to avoid collisions and warns us of our blindspots, the chatbot that cracks dad jokes and answers questions (sometimes dubiously), our phone with its whip-smart camera, or even our email that completes text and filters spam, AI is everywhere.

These recent breakthroughs in AI are remarkable, and some of the hype is justified. In healthcare, AI can help doctors diagnose diseases early, helping save lives. AI coding assistants can assist programmers and engineers in implementing their ideas in a fraction of the time. AI has also managed to solve complex problems including math questions that haven't been solved for over half a century. Speaking of math problems, kids nowadays use AI to finish their homework for them.

Yet these advances also raise important questions. When students use AI to complete their homework, are they learning? When doctors use AI for diagnoses, who's responsible for the decisions? The implications of these technologies stretch far beyond their immediate applications.

How Did We Get Here?

To a lot of us, it can seem like the AI train has appeared from thin air in the last few years. Nothing could be further from the truth. Recent advances are built on nearly a century of research. The seeds were planted in 1943 when researchers Warren McCulloch and Walter Pitts first proposed a mathematical model for how neurons might work. Why start with neurons? Because understanding how the brain processes information seemed like a good first step toward building intelligent machines.

The human brain has millions of neurons that are intricately interconnected. They pass information to each other and help us perform so many complex tasks instantaneously. Inspired by this, McCulloch and Pitts showed that a simplified mathematical model of a neuron could perform basic logical operations. While modern AI systems still use the term "neural networks," they've evolved far beyond these humble beginnings. But getting here wasn't smooth or quick. In fact, early AI researchers were famously optimistic, hoping to create machines with general intelligence before the turn of the eighties. More than fifty years later, we're still far from that goal.

However, there were some practical successes. By the 1990s, neural networks were reading handwritten checks for the US Postal Service. So, why didn't we *see* the explosion until recently?

The answer lies in two crucial missing ingredients: computing power and data. While the core ideas existed, the computers of those times were too slow to run complex neural networks effectively. Imagine having to wait for weeks on end to see if your experiments worked.[2] This computational barrier, combined with a lack of large-scale datasets to train these models, meant that neural networks remained more theoretical than practical.

The field went through what researchers call "AI winters"—periods where interest and funding dried up because the technology couldn't deliver on its promises. Even in the early 2000s, with faster computers, AI systems still relied heavily on human experts' hand-crafting rules about what features to look for in data. For instance, to recognize faces in images, researchers had to explicitly tell the computer to look for specific patterns like edges, corners, and shapes. These systems improved with more data but only up to a point.

In 2009, a team of researchers, led by Dr. Fei Fei Li at Stanford, released ImageNet,[3] a massive collection of over fourteen million categorized images. Imagine having a visual dictionary with thousands of categories, from everyday objects like a coffee cup to specific dog breeds. Along with the dataset, the team also launched an annual competition, challenging researchers worldwide to build AI systems that could correctly identify objects in these images.

In 2012, the breakthrough arrived. For the first time, a neural network called AlexNet shattered all previous records and scored an impressive 15.3 percent top-5 error rate.[4] The runner-up that year was a whopping eleven percentage points behind. But didn't neural networks need a lot of computing power?

While ImageNet solved the availability of large data, GPUs or Graphical Processing Units solved the problem of computing horsepower. Historically, GPUs were used for rendering and other graphics-intensive applications. GPUs excel at accelerating mathematical operations like matrix multiplications. As it turns out, training neural networks requires exactly this kind of parallel processing power. What might have taken months on traditional computers could now be done in days or even hours.

Thus, modern AI as we know it was born. Soon, AI systems were translating languages, understanding speech, playing complex games, and even generating art. We're living through the results of that revolution today. We've covered a lot of terminology, and there's more to come. Let's start breaking it down. What better time to start than now?

So, What Is AI?

Like the tale of the blind men and the elephant, AI means different things to different people. A doctor might think of AI as a diagnostic tool, while a gamer might think of AI as the computer-controlled characters in their favorite game. There's also the free interchange[5] between the terms AI, Machine Learning (ML), Deep Learning (DL), and Data Science (DS) in the media and the tech industry. Let's untangle all this jargon and understand what AI really means.

Artificial Intelligence is a field that focuses on building machines that can perform complex tasks that would normally require human-level intelligence, like problem-solving, reasoning, and decision-making.

Despite recent advances in chatbots, robotics, and AI-generated content, we're still far from the dystopian future you might be imagining. To understand why, let's first look at the broad classification of AI.

- *Artificial Narrow Intelligence (ANI)*: These are AI systems designed for specific tasks. Your phone's facial recognition, spam filters, recommendation systems, and industrial defect detection systems are all examples of ANI. They excel at their specific jobs but can't transfer that intelligence to other tasks. Almost all AI systems today fall into this category.
- *Artificial General Intelligence (AGI)*: This is the class of AI systems that possess general reasoning and thinking abilities as humans do. In other words, this is the class of AI you see in movies that can do everything from pirouetting while baking a pie to taking over the world. Before you get nightmares, let me make this clear: This currently does not exist. Most narrow AI systems are often misinterpreted as AGI systems.

Now that we understand what AI is, let's explore a key part of it—machine learning.[6]

Machine learning is a subfield of AI that deals with developing systems that learn directly from data, rather than following pre-programmed rules. Instead of telling a computer exactly what to do in every situation, we show it examples and let it figure out the patterns.

What do I mean by "learning from data"? In traditional rule-based systems, we give the computer a step-by-step instruction guide on what to do with the input it receives. We write down what to do in every scenario we can think of and then let it meticulously follow these rules. Let's take an example. Say we want a computer to look at a picture and tell us if it is a picture of a dog or a tree. We know that the dog has four legs and a tail and usually has its tongue sticking out. It also usually is wider than taller.[7] The tree, on the other hand, has leaves, usually green, a brown trunk, and is much taller than it is wide. Let's build a rule-based system to teach the computer these differences.

Easy, right? Now, what if we have to differentiate between a dog and a cat instead? Our rules—check for four feet, whiskers, and a tail—go out the window. We'd have to get really granular with our rules, like "If the ears are this particular shape," or "The paws are smaller," and so on.

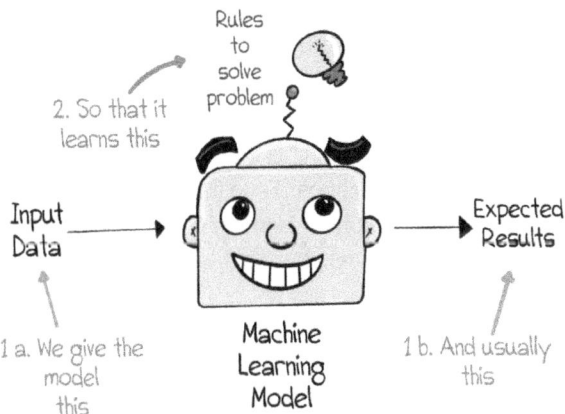

Figure 1.1. We let the machine learn the rules from data instead of giving it the rules directly.

But this is bound to fail. Imagine we juxtapose a Chow Chow and a cat next to each other. Both rules we set above would fail.

Another challenge with traditional rule-based systems is handling unexpected situations. Even domain experts might struggle to weave a series of rules to account for every possible situation. Not fun, right? Now, what if we need to identify not just whether the picture is of a cat or a dog but the exact breed? Imagine writing rules to tell a Golden Retriever from a Labrador or a German Shepherd from a Siberian Husky!

Writing rules for every possibility gets complicated really fast. This is where machine learning comes in. Instead of giving the computer rules and asking it to follow them meticulously, we can show examples. Just like you might learn to recognize dog breeds from a book, we show the computer thousands of pictures of cats and dogs with labels: "This is a Golden Retriever," "This is a German Shepherd," and so on.

Over the course of this process, the computer *learns* the rules from the *data* we provide (Figure 1.1). It identifies subtle cues in the image to inform its decision. The advantage of this process is that we don't need to hand-code every edge case. Plus, it scales really well when we need to build a system for thousands of categories. Can you imagine writing rules for differentiating one thousand categories?

Machine learning systems can find patterns we humans might miss. For instance, they might notice subtle combinations of shapes, colors, and textures that consistently appear in certain dog breeds. And unlike in rule-based approaches, adding more categories doesn't mean writing exponentially more rules.

Data science is the field that deals with extracting insights and knowledge from data. These insights then empower a business to make better decisions and predictions. Data science is an interdisciplinary field and overlaps with machine learning. A data scientist's goal is to suggest actions to make a business better based on insights they extract by analyzing data.

Deep learning is a subfield of machine learning that uses artificial neural networks to solve complex problems. These artificial neural networks are *loosely* inspired by the human brain. The "deep" in deep learning comes from the many layers of artificial neurons stacked together, each layer learning increasingly sophisticated patterns.

The AI systems making headlines today, like Midjourney and ChatGPT, are based on deep learning.

What makes these networks special?

Each of the layers in a deep network extracts specific informative patterns from data called *features*. These features are passed from one layer to the next. Earlier layers in a deep network extract simple patterns from the data while deeper layers use these simple features to build more complex and abstract representations. This ability of neural networks unlocks incredible solutions to a variety of problems. But, in order to learn these unique and powerful representations, these networks need a lot of data. A lot of data.

We've covered several interconnected fields—AI, Machine Learning, Deep Learning, and Data Science. Figure 1.2 shows how these fields overlap and relate to each other. Notice how deep learning is a specialized type of machine learning, which in turn is a subset of AI, while data science intersects with these fields but also extends beyond them.

Naturally, the next question that comes to mind is: Can AI do everything?

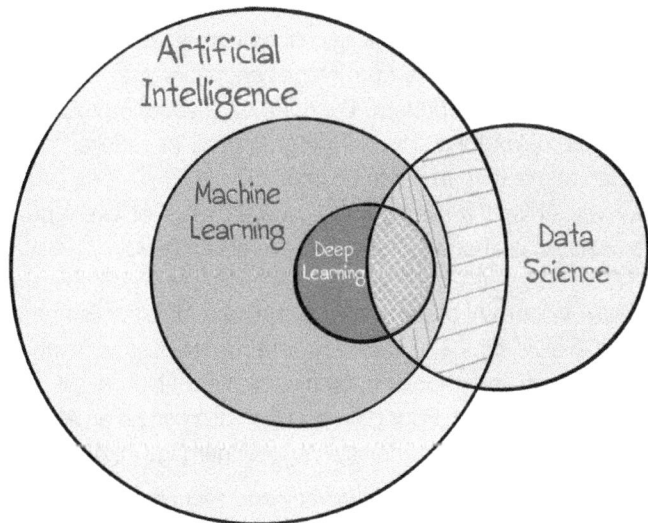

Figure 1.2. The intersection of different fields.

When Should I Use AI?

Despite its remarkable achievements, there are still many things that remain beyond its grasp. Creativity and innovation are distinctly human capabilities, as are emotional intelligence, ethics, and morality. AI can't handle tasks that require common sense reasoning[8] and contextual understanding beyond what it learns in its training data.

So where should we use AI? Let's look at three key areas where it shines:

- *Complex Problems:* Sometimes, finding ways to solve a problem might be impossible with traditional approaches. As new data arrives, patterns might change. In these scenarios, AI can adapt and find patterns that humans might miss.

- *Automation*: Using AI, we can process large volumes of data efficiently and automate mundane and repetitive tasks. This frees up our time to pursue more complex and creative endeavors.

- *Specialized Tasks*: The phrase riches are in the niches applies to AI too. The narrower and more specific the scope of a problem, the better AI is at solving it.

While looking at successful AI applications from speech recognition to autonomous driving systems, from image generators to recommendation engines, we can see a pattern. Each solves a specific problem that's either too complex for traditional programming or requires repetitive processing of massive amounts of data.

However, AI isn't a magic wand we can wave at every problem. Before using AI, we need to consider several factors:

- *Data*: Modern AI systems are data-hungry beasts.[9] But quantity isn't everything.[10] The quality of data matters just as much, if not more. First, ask yourself if you have sufficient high-quality data to train the model. Poor data or a lack of it can kill an AI project before it takes off. As the saying goes: garbage in, garbage out.

- *Privacy and Security*: User privacy and security can't be afterthoughts in AI development. Just because we can collect and label large volumes of data doesn't mean that we should. Respecting a user's right to privacy and protecting sensitive information should be at the forefront while building an AI solution.

- *Bias and Ethics*: AI is only as good as its training data. So, if the training data has biases baked in (which it will), so will the AI system that uses this data. This can lead to unfair discrimination against certain individuals or groups. Building a diverse and representative dataset is one of the many important steps we must take while building an AI solution. But just considering the bias issues in the data is not enough. We must evaluate the ethical implications of the solution we are building. Is it explainable? What impact does it have on the environment? Can it be used for malicious purposes? Answers to these questions require dialogue and collaboration between stakeholders, researchers, policymakers, and users.

- *Cost-Effectiveness*: Deploying AI systems can be expensive. So, here's a quick check to see if AI will be cost-effective for you. Can your problem be solved well with heuristics? Yes? You don't need AI. A lot of folks want to use AI for the sole reason that they market their wares as "AI solutions." Stop. You don't need the Ninja Turtles to tackle a pesky cockroach.[11] So, consider the cost-effectiveness of building and deploying your AI system. Measure twice, and cut once.

- *Human-Centric Problems*: If the problem you are solving needs human expertise, empathy, emotional intelligence, or subjective judgment, then AI isn't the right tool for it.

In conclusion, generally avoid using AI when high-stakes decisions are involved. It won't help when there's insufficient data or when human judgment is crucial. Remember: the more focused your problem, the better AI can help. It excels at automation, solving specialized problems, and finding hidden patterns in data. Use it wisely.

Next up, we're going to cover fundamentals that will help you understand the rest of the book better. See you there!

Chapter Summary

In this chapter, we explored the fundamentals of artificial intelligence and dispelled common myths. We learned that today's AI systems are narrow specialists rather than the general-purpose thinking machines often portrayed in science fiction. While these systems can outperform humans in specific tasks, they remain far from matching human-level general intelligence.

We discovered how modern AI works through machine learning by finding patterns in data rather than following predetermined rules. This approach proved particularly powerful when combined with deep learning, which uses layers of artificial neural networks to discover increasingly complex patterns. The recent AI breakthroughs came from combining these techniques with two crucial ingredients: massive amounts of data and powerful computers.

Next, we learned that AI excels in specific, well-defined problems with clear goals and abundant data. It's particularly effective at automating repetitive tasks, finding hidden patterns, and handling complex calculations. However, it struggles with tasks requiring human judgment, emotional intelligence, or common sense reasoning.

Finally, we explored crucial considerations before implementing AI solutions such as the need for high-quality data, privacy and security implications, potential biases, and cost-effectiveness. Sometimes, simpler solutions might be more appropriate than sophisticated AI systems.

Chapter 2
The Fundamentals of AI

In the previous chapter, we established that machine learning (ML) involves computers learning rules directly from data. Great! But how does a computer learn rules from data? To understand this, we need to look at the different types of ML algorithms.

Machine learning systems can be categorized in a number of ways. We'll look at two types of categorizations next. First, we'll look at the types of algorithms based on how they learn (how they are trained). Then, we'll check out how these algorithms can be grouped depending on how they make predictions.

Learning Approaches in ML

Broadly speaking, ML algorithms fall into five buckets based on how the training process works: Supervised learning, Unsupervised learning, Semi-supervised learning, Self-supervised learning, and Reinforcement learning.

Let's start with supervised learning, one of the most widely used approaches in machine learning today.

Supervised Learning

Let's assume that you're a robot designer. A local baker approaches you and asks you to design a robot to manage the front of the store.[1]

The expert designer you are, you build one in no time. Here's how it works: A customer asks for a baked good or two. The customer pays for the requested baked goods. The robot provides the appropriate baked goods to the customer. Everything seems to be going smoothly until one day when the baker comes to you red-faced and vexed. She tells you that the robot is a piece of junk and has been stealing muffins from her shop. She further accuses you of programming the robot to steal muffins for you. Affronted by this accusation, you promise to get to the bottom of this.

While combing through the surveillance tapes from the store, you discover something unexpected. Every day at lunchtime, muffins mysteriously disappear while your robot diligently cleans the store.

On zooming into this paranormal activity, you spot a dog that unmistakably looks like a blueberry muffin stealing muffins (Figure 2.1).

Your robot, designed to manage inventory and serve customers, couldn't tell the difference between the dog and the baked goods it was supposed to protect. But, if *you* couldn't tell the difference, how can the robot? Having figured out the problem, you decide to program the robot to classify dogs and muffins.[2] You painstakingly collect images of similar dogs and muffins from the store. You then label each image as either "dog" or "muffin." Finally, you provide these

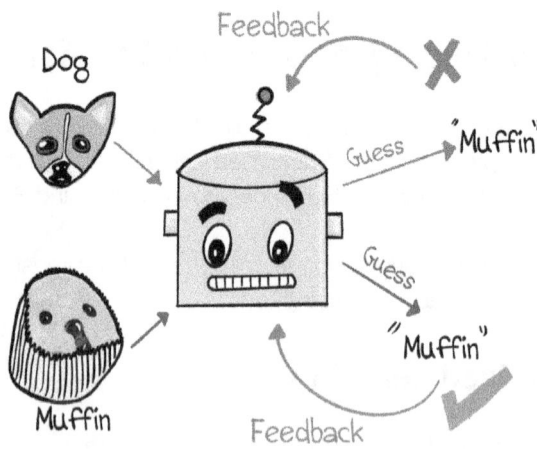

Figure 2.1. An overview of supervised learning.

labeled images to your robot and ask it to learn the difference. Initially, the robot struggles. It makes several incorrect guesses, and you have to tell it the correct answer. The eyes and nose of the dog look like blueberries on the muffin. But, after it has seen the images a few times, it learns that muffins don't have ears and dogs don't have liners. It's finally got it!

With this newfound ability, your robot successfully thwarts the dog's attempts to score free muffins. Each time the dog approaches the counter, your robot spots it coming and throws a ball for the dog to chase after. The local baker thanks you for saving her muffin empire, and all is well.[3]

This story actually illustrates supervised learning, one of the most powerful approaches in machine learning. Just like you taught the robot to distinguish between dogs and muffins by showing it examples, supervised learning works by providing models with labeled examples to learn from.

Let's break down how this works:

- *Collect Training Data*: First, we gather examples (like our images of dogs and muffins).

- *Label the Data*: We mark each example with the correct answer.

- *Train the Model*: The model makes predictions and learns from its mistakes through feedback.

- *Iterate and Improve*: Through repeated exposure and feedback, the model improves its accuracy.

This same approach powers many critical applications today. Email systems use it to protect you from spam by learning from millions of labeled emails. Doctors use models trained in this way to spot diseases in X-rays and scans. Self-driving cars use it to recognize traffic signs, and voice assistants use it to convert your speech to text.

Supervised learning is like having a very patient teacher who shows examples, checks answers, and provides feedback until the student (our model) gets it right. We provide both the input (like our images) and the expected output (dog or muffin labels). The model learns to map between them, getting better with each attempt. Just like training a new employee, we show it what to do in different scenarios until it can handle similar situations on its own. Hence the name supervised learning.

Unsupervised Learning

Word of your ML skills spreads far and wide, and you've been hired to be a part of the code-cracking team in the world's largest space organization. On a Tuesday morning, you receive some data from your new boss. It is a set of audio files that have a mix of high-pitched shrieks, unusual reverberations, and sounds resembling static interference.

Your team believes these signals might be of extraterrestrial origin, possibly a response to the various messages and recordings humanity has sent into space over the years. But there's a challenge—no one knows what these sounds mean or how they should be interpreted.

Unlike our muffin problem from earlier, we don't have any labeled examples to learn from. We just have raw data that we need to make sense of. Without any preexisting patterns to guide us, you decide to let an ML model analyze the sounds and see what it discovers. The model sorts the sounds into distinct clusters: high-pitched shrieks group together, reverberations form another cluster, and the static-like sounds form a third. Within each cluster, the model identifies specific patterns and characteristics that make these sounds similar to each other.

With these clusters in hand, you work with expert linguists to figure out the meaning of the alien signal. This is *unsupervised learning* in action. Instead of learning from labeled examples, the model discovers hidden patterns and structures in the data on its own. We can use this to make decisions, gain insights, or use it as input for other models.

If I gave you a box of crayons that were all jumbled up and walked away, what would you do? You might group the crayons by color (clustering). You might find that there are duplicate crayons of the same color and reduce the crayons down to one of each color (dimensionality reduction). You might find a crayon that is broken (outlier detection). Or, you might just build a tower of crayons. In this scenario, I didn't tell you what I expected. You looked at the crayons and found underlying patterns yourself. Since there isn't a supervisory signal (expected output) for this task or the alien language decoding task, these are called unsupervised (Figure 2.2).

The Fundamentals of AI

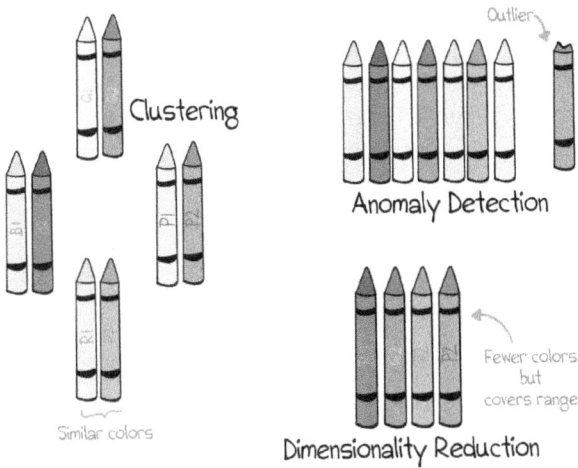

Figure 2.2. Unsupervised learning in a nutshell.

There are many types of unsupervised learning problems. Let's look at some of the popular ones below.

- *Clustering*: Clustering, as the name suggests, involves grouping similar things together. The clustering algorithm can spot commonalities in the data that aren't obvious to us and use these patterns to group similar data points together. Recall that in our alien language problem, the model grouped similar sounds together for further analysis. In the real world, clustering helps retailers group customers with similar shopping habits to personalize recommendations, streaming services group similar songs or shows to create better playlists, and social networks might use this to group similar news stories or posts together.
- *Dimensionality Reduction*: Imagine trying to describe a person. You could list hundreds of characteristics, but you might focus on just height, weight, and age to give a reasonable summary. Dimensionality reduction works similarly. It finds the most important characteristics in complex data while dropping less important ones. This helps us to visualize complex data in 2D or 3D graphs, speed up other ML algorithms by removing

unnecessary information in our data, and reduce noise in data while keeping important patterns.

- *Anomaly Detection*: This is the equivalent of spotting the odd man out. When a model learns what "normal" looks like, it can spot things that don't fit the pattern. This has a few crucial applications. Credit card companies can detect fraudulent transactions by learning your normal spending patterns. Manufacturing companies leverage this to spot defective products on assembly lines. Network security systems can identify unusual activity that might indicate a cyber attack, and medical devices flag irregular heartbeats or other concerning patterns.

Coming back to our alien story, the linguists leverage these techniques to identify distinct "words" or "phrases." In case you're wondering, the aliens either invited us to an intergalactic buffet or asked us to keep it down and stop waking them up.

Semi-supervised Learning

An SOS arrives from home. It's your grandmother. Age and illness have wreaked havoc, and it's not looking good. No, no, before you worry, she's fine. It's her plants that aren't.

She asks if you can help her ailing plants. After all, she thinks you're a rocket scientist. Given that you're working on mission-critical projects, you can't just catch a flight back home. You ask her to send you pictures of the plants. Gran was an ace photographer back in the day. She sends over hundreds of pictures that show her plants when they were healthy as well as their diseased state now. Unfortunately, she doesn't know what kinds of diseases these are, and neither do you. To help identify the diseases, you collect images of healthy and diseased plants off the web. Luckily, these images have labels clearly indicating the type of disease each plant has. However, there are far fewer labeled images available.

How will you train a model with so little labeled data? Given your day job, there's no way you can label all the images Gran sent you.

Enter *semi-supervised learning*. Semi-supervised learning typically combines unsupervised learning and supervised learning. By grouping together similar examples and using a few labeled examples to guide us, we can make a guess on the labels for the unlabeled ones. This allows us to *learn* labels for unlabeled examples from a limited set of labeled examples.

Here's how it works with Gran's plants:

- *Gather Data:* Combine Gran's unlabeled plant photos with the labeled disease examples you collected.
- *Group Similar Images:* A clustering model groups photos showing similar symptoms together.
- *Use Known Labels:* In each cluster, look at the labeled examples we have.
- *Assign Labels:* Apply the most common disease label to all unlabeled photos in that cluster.

So, let's say we have a bunch of images of plants that look like they are affected by rust. Our clustering algorithm might group all these images together because they look similar. Now, say that in this cluster, we have ten labeled images, that is, we have actual labels for the disease affecting each of these ten plants. Of these images, let's say seven of them are affected by rust, and three are affected by something else. We can use the majority label (rust) to assign the label "rust" to all the unlabeled examples in this cluster.

When we do this for all the examples we have, we end up with a large corpus of data to train and evaluate our model. This approach is widely used in:

- *Medical imaging:* Labeling large datasets of medical scans using a small set of expert-verified examples;
- *Speech recognition:* Improving accuracy using both labeled professional recordings and unlabeled user conversations;
- *Content moderation:* Identifying inappropriate content using a few clear examples to categorize many borderline cases.

Since there is a small amount of supervision involved in this approach, it's called *semi*-supervised. Semi-supervised learning is great when you have a limited amount of labeled data. Using just a few examples, you can "label" a large number of unlabeled examples in a pinch (Figure 2.3).

With your model trained and ready to go, you find out the diseases affecting Gran's plants and recommend the remedies she could use. Rest assured, someone's getting those patented oatmeal raisin cookies in the next goodie bag.

Self-supervised Learning

After a grueling summer of work, you return home for some well-deserved R&R. You meet your childhood friend Rico for coffee. While you pursued a career in the sciences, he chose literature and writing. After many false dawns, he finally made it big as a songwriter. He wrote the lyrics of the chart-topping song "Prompt Me Baby One More Time" for a major artist, and that album went platinum. Calls started rolling in from major artists and producers. Unfortunately for Rico, the next few

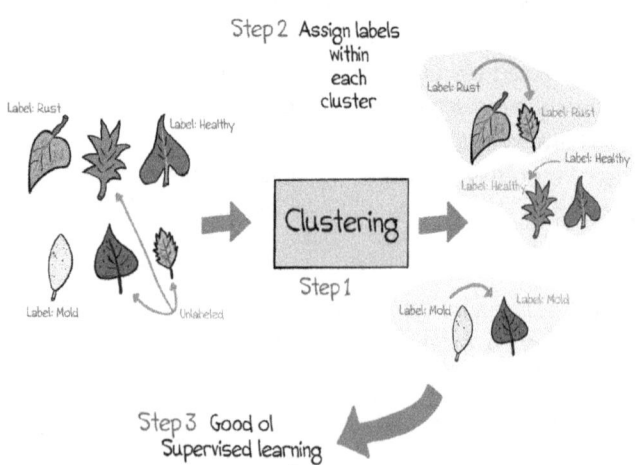

Figure 2.3. Semi-supervised learning can help us label unlabeled examples and create a larger dataset than we might have.

songs he wrote were duds. Inspiration left him. He's now on his last couple of projects, and work is beginning to run dry.

Thinking about your recent successes with ML, you suggest that you might be able to build a lyric generator to inspire him. He can't wait to learn more. Unfortunately, you don't have a large dataset of music lyrics to use. After thinking for a while, you realize that you could first teach your model English. Once it's learned the language, you can then use Rico's own work to fine-tune the model to produce songs of different moods and genres.

First, you take a large corpus of text (several books worth and then some) and give the model sentence fragments from these sources at random. You ask the model to guess the next word in each sentence fragment. With practice, the model learns to guess what these words are. But, more importantly, it learns the grammar, structure, and semantics of the English language.

Next, you take this model and show it some of Rico's best work. For each example, you show a phrase from the song and also provide information about the genre and emotion of the song. Using the limited collection of Alyrico's best work, you fine-tune for the task you *actually* want it to solve—Writing inspired lyrics.

Soon, the model begins to grasp Rico's sense of rhythm, rhyme, and structure. As a test, you ask it to write lyrics for a hip-hop song. You provide the phrase "This wired wordplay" and watch with bated breath. The model returns the following verse:

> *This wired wordplay, got me spinnin' like a top,*
> *I'm tossin' out these lines, ain't no way I'm gonna flop.*
> *I'm jugglin' metaphors, got these similes on lock,*
> *I'm like a linguistic acrobat with my verbal pop and rock.*
> *I'm mixin' highbrow slang with lowbrow for the masses,*
> *I'm a Shakespeare in disguise, with my funky fresh new glasses.*

Thrilled with the outcome, you show Rico what your "magic quill" has come up with. He can't believe it. He tries to see if the lyrics change when the genre of the song changes. This time he gives the same phrase, "This wired wordplay," but switches the genre to disco. The model doesn't even blink and responds with:

This wired wordplay, got me groovin' on the floor,
My funky rhymes are spinnin', got you beggin' me for more.
I'm glidin' on the beat, like a roller-skatin' queen,
In my disco ball of lyrics, find the fun you've never seen.
Mirror balls and platform shoes, my verses bring the vibe,
With my bell-bottom lyrics, it's a trip to '75.

Your model becomes Rico's secret weapon. Anytime he needs inspiration, he calls on the magic quill to suggest options for him to explore. He's now one of the top songwriters in the country.

Clever you! You made use of *self-supervised learning*. Here, we generate labels from fully unlabeled data. In the example above, we took full sentences and cut off the end to make the model guess. Thus we created labels (the correct word that follows each sentence fragment) from unlabeled data (the entire corpus).

Oftentimes, people confuse unsupervised learning with self-supervised learning. The key difference is that in unsupervised learning, there is no supervisory signal. The model just learns to extract underlying patterns and trends in the data. In self-supervised learning, on the other hand, the model uses part of the input as labels and thus has some "supervision." This type of learning algorithm is great when you have no labeled data or very limited labeled data.

Note that the model we get from using self-supervised learning is pretty nifty. But that by itself is not the goal. Once a model has been trained using self-supervision, we can use a small labeled dataset to fine-tune the model on the task we actually care about.

Take our example from above. We took a large corpus of text that wasn't labeled in any sort of way and created sentence fragments for the model to learn from. The model trained on this data by itself is pretty cool. It works like an autocomplete system. But that wasn't our goal. The model was tricked into thinking it had to complete these partial sentences. This first stage is often called the *"pretext task"* — What the model thinks we want it to learn.

Once the model could efficiently fill in missing words, we then fine-tuned it on a small dataset of song lyrics that had labels (genre, sentiment, etc.). This is called the *"target task"* — What we actually want the model to learn. Since we don't have sufficient data to train the model directly on this, we use the pretext task as a way to prime the model (Figure 2.4).

How can a model trained on one task do well on a completely different one? To understand, think about something you've learned in your life. If you took tennis lessons as a kid, would you not find ping pong easier to learn compared to someone who has never learned either? In our example, the model learned grammar and sentence structure and expanded its vocabulary thanks to the pretext task (auto-completing sentences). When it came to generating new lyrics, it could transfer this knowledge over and add new skills on top of this.

This idea is called *transfer learning*. We "transfer" the knowledge the model has gained in one task to another. This technique is very powerful and is used extensively in modern AI.

Reinforcement Learning

You've transformed your local bakery, pacified aliens from outer space, played the role of a plant doctor, and revived a songwriter's career. While you might be tempted to hang up your problem-solving boots, there's

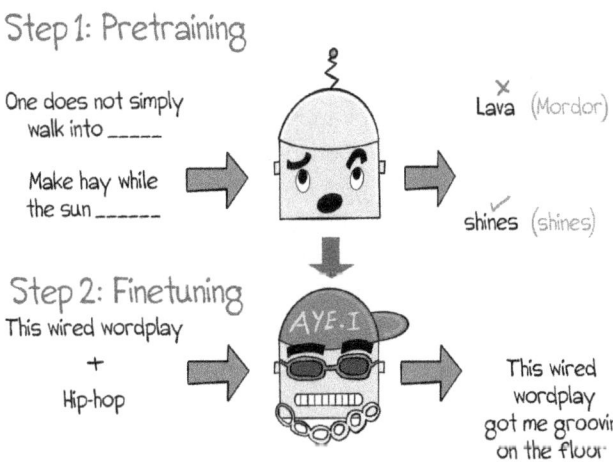

Figure 2.4. Self-supervised learning works in two stages: The pretext task and the target task.

always another project around the corner. A popular dance school contacts you and asks for your services. You're surprised since you have three left feet but speak with them anyway. The school wants to expand its services nationwide. However, there's a shortage of qualified dance teachers,[4] and the school wants to know if you can help provide a fleet of robots that can teach dance in institutes across the country.

After thinking through the problem, you come up with a plan. The dance school has given you access to its entire catalog of lessons. Armed with this and a ridiculously expansive DVR collection of every talent show ever telecast, you begin to teach a robot to dance. Out goes all the junk in your garage. In its place come stereo speakers, a giant mirror, a projector, and a robot. A dance instructor from the school is seated in another room, watching the robot. She'll be evaluating it as it learns to dance and providing feedback by rewarding or penalizing it. You blast music through the speakers, and the bass makes the roof wobble. The projector shows a dancer moving to the music. The robot stares at this odd collection of items and wonders what it's supposed to do.

Initially, it flounders. It tries walking forward and backward, but nothing happens. It sits down, and instantly a boo emanates from the speaker.[5] It also loses some battery power. Aah, so sitting idle is bad. It gets back up and tries walking around. Nothing happens. After a while, it realizes that there's a pattern to the music and starts tapping its feet. A small cheer plays through the speaker, and the robot gains five battery points back. Oooh! So this tippy-tappy movement helps me.

The robot tries to get more battery points back and keeps tapping its feet. Eventually, it neither gets cheers nor battery points. Hmmm, I guess I need to do something else. Its eyes then spot the projector and a dude in said projector moving around. It starts mirroring the movements of the dancer. At first, it sucked. In fact, it was so bad at dancing that you felt like an accomplished freestyler.

But this robot doesn't know how to give up. It keeps trying out moves that the dancer does and slowly starts getting better. Cheers start erupting from the speaker, and it gets generous helpings of battery points. The robot realizes that it needs to mirror the moves of the human in the projector and focuses entirely on that. Soon it can do all kinds of moves like the moonwalk or the infamous cabbage patch.

For the next part of the training, you turn the projector off and only play the music. The robot is confused and waits for something to show up on the projector. Nothing happens. Eventually, boos start playing through the speaker. Aware that its battery points will be next in line, the robot starts helplessly looking around. It remembers that tapping its feet helped the last time around. But it also remembers mirroring the movements of a dancer on the projector. Then something clicks. It moves to the song, and the boos are replaced with cheers. It realizes that every time it moves properly to match the song, it gets rewarded. Over time, the robot learns to combine dance moves and comes up with clever choreography that stuns the dance school instructor (Figure 2.5).

This is an example of *reinforcement learning*. Like a parent teaching a child through rewards and punishments, reinforcement learning involves an agent learning to solve tasks through trial and error. The agent isn't given any information to begin with but can perform certain actions. Every action the agent takes receives either a reward (positive feedback) or a penalty (negative feedback). The goal of the agent is to maximize the reward it receives. It learns a set of rules called a *policy* through this feedback process. To maximize its rewards, it needs to

Figure 2.5. Do you know that move called the robot?

learn a good policy through a combination of trying new actions (called exploration) and repeating previous actions that delivered rewards (called exploitation).

In our example above, the garage is the environment, and the robot is the agent. It performs dance moves (actions) which result in it getting a reward (the cheers and battery points) or a penalty (the boos and a deduction in battery points). Over time, it learns through feedback and performs actions to maximize its reward.

Unfortunately, our circuited choreographer never made it big on the national scene. The project was shuttered due to protests from a group called the Choreographica Collectif (yes, with an f) about AI taking jobs away and the fact that our robot wanted to only teach headspins to bare beginners.

Before we move forward, let's break down the key components of reinforcement learning:

- *Agent*: The learner or decision-maker in the process. In our example, the robot is the agent and tries to learn to dance.
- *Environment*: The setting or world within which the agent interacts and learns. The garage is the environment where the robot learns to dance.
- *State*: The current situation the agent is in. For our dancing robot, a state could be its position or the dance move it's currently performing.
- *Action*: The choices or decisions the agent can make. In our example, these are the different dance moves the robot tries.
- *Reward*: Positive feedback or reinforcement the agent receives when it performs a desirable action. For our robot, rewards are cheers and battery points gained when the robot performs a good dance move.
- *Penalty*: Negative feedback the agent receives when it performs an undesirable action. The boos and battery point deductions our robot receives for making a poor dance move are the penalties here.
- *Policy*: The strategy or set of rules the agent follows to decide which action to take in a given state. In our example, the policy

could be the set of rules that the robot uses to determine which dance moves to perform based on the music and past rewards.

- *Exploration*: The process of trying out new actions to discover their effects and potential rewards. In the example above, exploration is when the robot tries different dance moves to see which results in rewards.
- *Exploitation*: The process of using the knowledge gained from exploration to select actions that maximize rewards. For our dancing robot, exploitation is when the robot chooses dance moves it knows will result in rewards.

So far, we've explored different ways machines learn: through labeled examples (supervised), finding patterns (unsupervised), combining both approaches (semi-supervised), creating their own learning signals (self-supervised), and through trial and error (reinforcement). But how do these models make predictions once they've learned? There are two fundamental approaches that we'll cover next.

How ML Models Make Predictions

When we train a machine learning model, our ultimate goal is for it to perform well on new, unseen examples. This capability is called *generalization*. A model that "generalizes well" can effectively handle situations it hasn't encountered during training.

There are two types of approaches here: instance-based and model-based systems.

Instance-Based Systems

Ever had one of those classmates in school who could memorize anything and everything thrown their way? Instance-based systems are like those classmates. These systems build a vast library of experiences they can reference when faced with new situations. Thus, when a new example is presented after training, the system compares it to all the stored examples in its memory bank. It then makes a prediction based on the most similar examples.

Let's see how an instance-based system might distinguish apples from oranges. During training, it simply stores every apple and orange image it sees. When a new fruit image is shown, it compares it to all stored examples, looking for the closest matches. If the five most similar images in its memory are mostly oranges, it predicts "orange." How does it know how close each of the examples is? The comparison leverages similarity measures like matching colors between images (Figure 2.6).

Instance-based systems have a fascinating speed paradox. They're incredibly quick to train since they just memorize examples. However, making predictions can be painfully slow—imagine comparing each new case against thousands of stored examples. Plus, they need enormous memory to store their entire "library" of examples, which becomes problematic as datasets grow.

Model-Based Systems

On the other hand, model-based systems learn a mathematical model to represent the underlying patterns in the data. Thus, instead of blindly

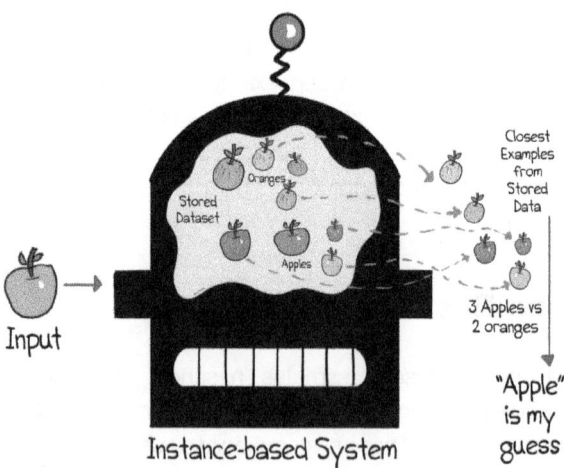

Figure 2.6. I'm willing to bet that instance-based models would crush any quiz contest.

memorizing data, think of these systems as chess grandmasters who study countless games to uncover patterns in the data they see. Once they've learned these rules during training, they use them to make predictions on unseen data. Let's look at what these "rules" are and how they are learned.

These systems are essentially building a model of the data they see. A model has a set of knobs called *parameters*. During the training phase, these systems tweak these knobs so that they can model[6] the patterns in the data they see. In our fruit example, these patterns can be the color of the fruit, its texture, size, shape, and so on. Each of these attributes the model learns to identify is called a *feature*.

To understand parameters, think of how the FM radio in your car works. When you want to hear the jazz station, you keep pressing the next station button on the console until you hear the right music. Behind the scenes, the radio is tweaking some knobs so that the antenna is tuned to the correct frequency. In our case, the model tweaks its knobs called parameters to make the correct predictions. In the previous section on the different training approaches, we saw how it learns from feedback to make these updates (error signals, reward functions, etc.).

Unlike their instance-based cousins, model-based systems invest more time training to discover these patterns. However, once trained, they make predictions quickly since they only need to apply the rules they have learned. They're also more memory-efficient, storing only their discovered patterns rather than entire datasets. Simply put, instance-based systems are like students who memorize every example in their textbook, while model-based systems are like students who learn the underlying principles and can apply them to new situations (Figure 2.7).

Now that we understand how models learn and make predictions, let's focus on something equally crucial—the data they learn from. After all, even the most sophisticated learning approach is only as good as the data it trains on. When working with data, we must be careful about how we use it. Let's explore how to prepare and use our data to build reliable models properly.

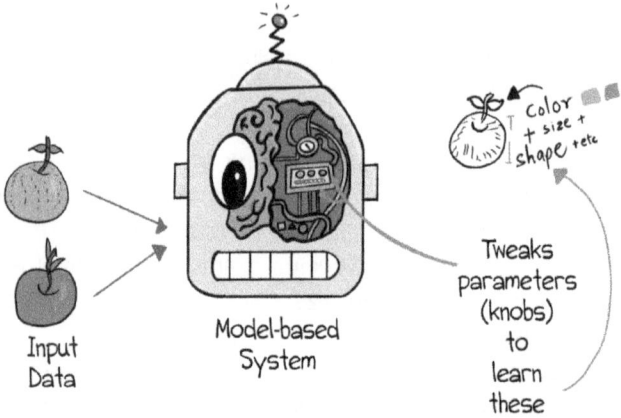

Figure 2.7. Instead of memorizing, model-based systems build a mathematical representation of the data.

The Lifeblood of AI

Regardless of the categorization of machine learning systems, there is a common thread connecting all of them.

Data

As these systems learn to make predictions from data, the quality and quantity of data at our disposal become critical. It's safe to say that, without good data, there's no point in using machine learning.

If you skip the prep work when you cook, even the best recipe will fail. In machine learning, rushing to model building while skimping on data analysis often creates a cascade of puzzling problems. Like a Rube Goldberg machine gone wrong, finding and fixing these issues becomes increasingly complex.

Here are key data challenges that, if ignored, can take a machine learning project from champ to chump.

Insufficient Data

If you have insufficient data to train and evaluate ML models, it's safe to say that your efforts are unlikely to succeed. It's like trying to learn a language from a single page of text. Collecting and curating large datasets is a time-consuming and often expensive process. This is why pretrained models are so valuable. You can transfer their knowledge to the task you care about with a significantly smaller amount of data.

Imbalanced Data

One of the most common issues that plague machine learning projects is imbalanced data. Let's say you are building a pet photo stylizer. Your app adds filters and touchups to pictures of dogs and cats so that they become social media-worthy.

Now, you need to build a model that can distinguish cats from dogs so that the app can apply the right set of filters for each animal. However, in a haste to get the app shipped, you collect as many images as you can.

You train the model with this data. After this, you quickly check how well the model did. It scores a whopping 90 percent accuracy on classifying cats versus dogs. Seems good enough to ship, right? Thinking so, you release the app.

Soon, users flood your app's review page with snarky comments that it doesn't work well for dogs. You're flummoxed. After all, you evaluated your model. It didn't have any issues. Or did it?

After exhausting all the possibilities you can think of, you turn to the data. On inspecting it, you realize you have ninety images of cats and ten of dogs. So, if your model just guessed "cat" as its prediction every time, it would score 90 percent accuracy. Your model simply refused to identify dogs, thus incurring the wrath of dog owners everywhere. See how easy it is to be fooled by this?

This situation is called a data imbalance. When this happens, the model you train using this data is heavily skewed toward a particular class or category. This, in turn, leads to biased models that are terrible at recognizing underrepresented categories. Returning to our example, you collect many more dog images and balance the number of images in each class. When you train the model now and redeploy the app, the users get a much better experience. Finally, dogs are recognized properly!

Noise and Missing Data

No data is perfect. It's bound to contain errors, inconsistencies, or even irrelevant information. Using data like this directly to train machine learning models only leads to pain and suffering. The model will find it harder to spot underlying patterns. Let's say I show you a picture. But every square inch of it is covered with a thick layer of dust and scuff marks. You'd find it ridiculously hard to tell me what the picture is, even if it was of the most famous celebrity in the world.

Data visualization and analysis are critical steps in a machine learning project. They allow us to inspect the data and spot obvious and sometimes not-so-obvious issues. It's during these steps that we can spot outliers and missing information. This, in turn, allows us to make appropriate decisions on what to do before jumping into modeling.

Irrelevant Data

Irrelevant data needs to be managed as well. Feature engineering is the process we use to identify which parts of the data are relevant to the model. Depending on the problem, finding the right features (called feature selection) might require domain expertise. For example, say that you are a data scientist who's trying to help identify credit card fraud. You get raw data that contains the transaction amount, the transaction date, the color of the credit card, the gender of the user, and their location. The card's color is irrelevant to the model in determining whether fraud has occurred or not.

On the other hand, the transaction amount and location are very critical. You could potentially create new features by manipulating the raw data, too. In our example above, you can count the number of transactions a user has made on the last day. You could compute the average transaction amount for the last month or use the distance between a transaction location and the user's home location. You can use these new features to give the model more context and valuable information and empower it to make better predictions.

Note that feature engineering is less critical for deep learning-based solutions. The main advantage of deep learning models (a.k.a. neural networks) is that they learn to extract meaningful features from raw data. But that isn't to say that feature engineering won't help.

Generalizability

Another crucial aspect is that the model is trained on the type of data it can expect to see in the real world. This ensures that it will generalize to the actual problem we want to solve. Going back to our pet-styling example, if you trained the model using high-quality, professional, studio-style photographs of cats and dogs, you'll be in for a big shock when you ship the app. Most, if not all, customers will use their mobile camera. The images they send to the app will be as far removed from studio quality as you can imagine. In this scenario, the model will struggle to classify dogs and cats in those images since it's used to getting high-quality professional photographs as input. Thus, it's paramount that you try to train the model on data that is as close as possible to what the model will see in the real world.

The Trinity

There's one more thing you need to know before we jump into the types of AI models.

We don't use the entire dataset to train a model. Wait, what?

Yes, you've spent a ton of time collecting the dataset. You've spent even more time inspecting it and ensuring that you have data that generalizes well, has most outliers and noise removed, and has the right features for the model to use. After all that effort, this news feels like a bombshell dropped on you.

There's a method to this madness. Regardless of what model we use, we need to keep one key objective in mind. At the end of the day, the model should make good predictions on unseen data. It shouldn't simply memorize the data it's trained on. Such a model would be useless.

That's why we split the dataset into three parts: The training, validation, and test sets. The training set is what we show the model. It learns to extract patterns from this subset of data. The model isn't allowed to learn from the other two subsets.

In simpler terms, the training set is like the prep material you get to learn a subject at school. The validation set is like the exercises at the back of each chapter that you can use to check your understanding. The test set is like the exam you take at the end of the course, where you must use what you've learned to solve new but similar problems.

After we train a model on the training set, we can evaluate how it performs on unseen examples. We use the validation set for this. Why not the test set? For that matter, why even have a test set if the validation set gives us an indication of the model's ability to generalize?

Great question. We use the validation set to help us choose the right type of model for the problem. Secondly, we use it to tune this model so that it gives the best possible results. By the end of the modeling process, we'd have a model that does well on the validation set. Thus, reporting results on this model would be an exercise in showing off.

We use the test set to report results and indicate how the model performs on unseen data. This is the result that is published in research papers, shared with clients to get their go-ahead, and provided to your colleagues who put the model into production.

There are no hard and fast rules regarding the sizes of the three sets. However, as a rule of thumb, 80 percent of the dataset is used as the training set, 10 percent as the validation, and 10 percent as the test set. At least, this is the convention for old-school models (non-neural network models). In this modern age, datasets have several million examples. Modern AI models need a lot of this data to train on. Therefore, 97 percent of the data is used for training, 1.5 percent for validation, and 1.5 percent for testing. If you'd like to trigger a fight between data scientists, just ask them how they'd split a dataset. Don't tell them I told you to ask.

A Model Befitting the Dataset

We saw how the validation set helps to identify the right model for the job. It also helps with another important aspect. It helps us figure out if the model is learning to generalize properly.

There are two issues to be aware of. The first is called *underfitting*. A model that underfits struggles to solve the problem. Such a model makes a ton of mistakes on the training data itself! This can happen

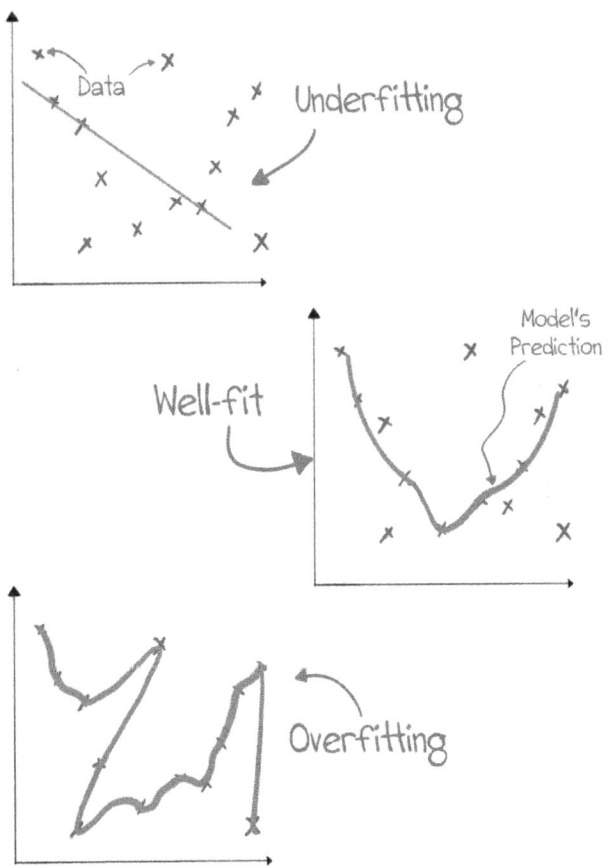

Figure 2.8. The Goldilocks problem. Notice how overfitting models try to fit every point, while underfitting models hardly fit any.

if the model you chose is too simple for the data you have. This is like sending a four-year-old to an art contest focused on recreating legendary Renaissance paintings.[7] The data or the features you provide the model might be terrible. In both cases, the solution is to try the opposite of what you've done. Try a more complex model and extract more useful features from the data.

The second issue is called *overfitting*. This is the inverse of the first problem. In this case, the model memorizes the training set completely. It loses the ability to generalize. Like a student who's committed every line of a textbook to memory, it can predict anything from the training set. But give it something new, and it will flounder. Overfitting occurs when the model is too complex for the data. Imagine wearing a full suit of armor to a pillow fight. Overfitting also occurs if you have insufficient data. The remedies for overfitting are usually to try a simpler model, add more training data, or a set of techniques broadly called regularization. We'll briefly touch on regularization later, but this is good enough to know for now (Figure 2.8).

We've covered a lot of ground so far. You might be feeling overwhelmed. That's perfectly normal. In the next chapter, we finally move from talking terminology to exploring some really cool models. Let's go!

Chapter Summary

In this chapter, we explored the fundamental approaches in machine learning. We examined five distinct learning paradigms. In supervised learning, models learn from labeled examples. Unsupervised learning discovers patterns in unlabeled data. Semi-supervised learning combines both labeled and unlabeled data, while self-supervised learning creates its own learning signals. Finally, reinforcement learning teaches models to learn through feedback and rewards.

We then investigated how models make predictions through two main approaches: instance-based systems, which compare new cases against stored examples, and model-based systems, which learn mathematical patterns and rules. Each approach has distinct tradeoffs in terms of training speed, inference time, and memory requirements.

We emphasized the critical role of data quality and preparation in machine learning and covered major data challenges, including insufficient data and techniques to handle limited datasets, imbalanced data and its impact on model performance, noise and missing data management, feature engineering and the importance of relevant data, and ensuring models work in real-world conditions through proper generalization.

We explored the process of splitting datasets into training, validation, and test sets and the specific role of each set: training data for learning patterns, validation data for model tuning and selection, and test data for final performance evaluation. We examined different splitting ratios for traditional and modern AI applications.

Finally, we discussed two fundamental challenges in model performance: underfitting, where models are too simple to capture underlying patterns, and overfitting, where models fail to generalize beyond their training data. These concepts provide the foundation for understanding model selection and optimization, which we'll explore in the next chapter.

Chapter 3
A Few Good Algorithms

From understanding what AI is, we now turn to how specific AI algorithms learn. How do patterns become predictions and data transform into decisions? Just as we learn from experience, AI models learn from examples. The key difference is that while we might need just a few examples to understand a concept, these models often need thousands or, in some cases, millions of examples to learn effectively. Why?

AI models use math to build an understanding of the world. From the examples we provide, they discover patterns and help us make sense of data, find hidden relationships, predict future outcomes, and make informed decisions. Without these models, we'd be drowning in numbers, words, and images with no way to connect the dots.

In this chapter, we will explore various algorithms, starting with the classic linear models—the simplest of them all. These models learn to draw lines through data points, much like you might have done in your high school math class. However, they find these lines automatically from examples. From there, we'll discover decision trees that make yes/no choices and clustering algorithms that learn to group similar things together. Don't worry if these terms sound complex now. We'll break down how each model learns and why it's useful.

By the end of this chapter, you'll have a solid understanding of these models, their applications, and how they bring us one step closer to making AI work for us. Despite the excitement around deep learning and large language models, these fundamental algorithms remain invaluable. They're faster to train, easier to interpret, and more efficient for many day-to-day problems, whether you're forecasting sales or detecting suspicious transactions. You don't need a flamethrower to light a candle, after all! So, let's roll up our sleeves and dive into the fascinating world of machine learning models.

Linear Models

Imagine you're a pirate holding a treasure map with a scattering of dots. Each dot marks where previous treasure hunters found gold. Some found more, and some found less. Your task is to find the pattern of where the treasure tends to be found. Once you draw a line through these dots, you can predict how much gold might be buried at any spot on the map, even where no one has dug before. Congratulations! You've just visualized a simple linear model.

In the context of AI, we're looking for different kinds of patterns. The dots are our data points, and instead of connecting them like a path, we draw a line that best represents their overall trend. This line becomes the model's way of understanding the relationship in our data. Just as your "treasure line" might help predict the value of treasure based on location, a linear model uses its line to predict new, unseen cases. These models look for patterns that can be described by a straight line or its higher-dimensional cousins.[1] When we feed in information (called independent variables), the model uses its line to make predictions (called dependent variables). This simple idea is surprisingly powerful. The line acts as a mathematical summary of the relationship between our inputs and outputs. To understand how these models find the "best" line automatically, let's look at our first algorithm, Linear Regression.

Linear Regression

Imagine you're a real-estate agent and need to predict the selling price for a house.[2] You know that larger houses generally cost more than smaller ones. But how much more? You have various facts and figures about the house, like its size in square feet, the number of rooms, the amenities, and the neighborhood. Rather than guessing, you could look at recent house sales in your area and try to find a pattern between these features and the price. This is exactly what linear regression helps us do. Each of these inputs, like size and square footage, is an independent variable. The dependent variable would be the house's selling price because that's what we are trying to predict based on the house's features.

Before we dive in, let's understand what "linear" means. A linear relationship is one where changes in one variable lead to proportional changes in another. For example, if you're buying tomatoes at $10 per pound, each additional pound adds exactly $10 to your total cost. This creates a straight-line pattern when graphed. However, not all relationships are linear. For example, the area of a square increases by four times when doubling the length of its side, not two. So, linear regression works best when we believe there's a roughly straight-line relationship between our variables.

How does it work?

Suppose each house becomes a point on a graph, with square footage on one axis and price on the other. Our goal is to find a line that best represents this data. This line has two important components: the bias (also called the intercept) and the slope. The intercept tells us where the line starts. Think of it as the baseline price you'd expect for any house, regardless of its features. The slope tells us how much the price changes when we increase the square footage. Together, these are called coefficients, and finding the right values for them is key to making good predictions (Figure 3.1).

If house prices were perfectly linear with size, all these points would fall exactly on a straight line. But in the real world, data is messy. Two houses of the same size might sell for different prices due to location, upgrades done to them, or market timing.

This is where the "regression" part of linear regression comes in. Instead of trying to connect all points perfectly, we look for a line that best captures the overall trend. But what makes a line best? For each house in our data, we can measure how far off our line's predicted price is from the actual price. These differences are called residuals. A positive residual means our line predicted the price too low. A negative residual means it guessed too high (Figure 3.2).

We could try to minimize these residuals, but there's a catch. If we simply add up all residuals, positive and negative values would cancel each other out, tricking us into thinking we have a good line when we

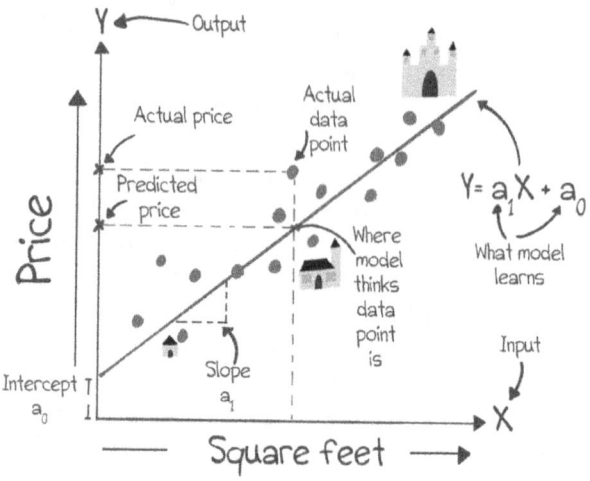

Figure 3.1. An overview of linear regression.

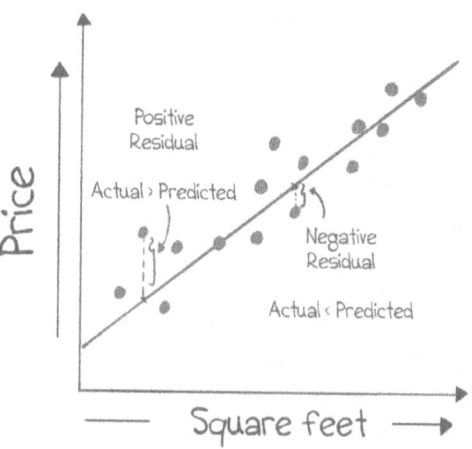

Figure 3.2. Residuals represent the difference between truth and prediction. See how the positive and negative residuals can cancel each other?

don't. Instead, we square each residual before adding them up. This approach, called the "least squares method," has two clever effects. It makes all residuals positive (so they can't cancel out), and it penalizes large errors more heavily than small ones. After all, being off by $100,000 in a house price prediction is worse than being off by $10,000 (Figure 3.3).

So, while there might be different lines that can pass through our points, only one of them minimizes the overall error in residuals. That is the solution that the least squares method finds. There are different ways to find these best coefficients and bias terms. The least squares method is one approach. Another important method, gradient descent, that can be used for this task will be covered in the next chapter. Both methods aim to minimize prediction errors, just in different ways.

In practice, predicting house prices isn't just about square footage. We might also consider the number of bedrooms, the age of the house, the location, and many other factors. Each factor becomes another dimension in our analysis. While we can't visualize these higher dimensions easily, the same principles apply—we're still looking for the best way to predict prices based on all these features together.

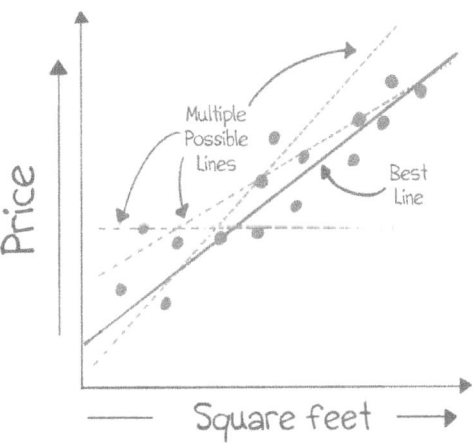

Figure 3.3. There are many lines that fit a subset of points. Only one of them, however, gives us the best results.

Once we've found our best fit, we can use it to make predictions. For a new house, we'd plug its features (the size, number of rooms, etc.) into our equation and predict a price.

But how do we know our model is any good? To understand if our predictions are reliable, we need ways to measure our model's performance. That's where evaluation metrics come in.

Evaluating Linear Regression

When we use linear regression, we want to be confident that our model makes good predictions. That's where regression metrics come into play. They provide us with a quantitative way to measure our model's performance. Let's look at three key metrics: Mean Absolute Error (MAE), Mean Squared Error (MSE), and R-squared.

Mean Absolute Error

Think of MAE as the average "miss" our model makes in its predictions. In the context of our house price prediction example, if the MAE is $40,000, our predictions are, on average, $40,000 away from the actual house price. The MAE is calculated as the average of the absolute differences between the predicted and actual values. The lower the MAE, the better our model is doing.

Mean Squared Error

MSE is similar to MAE, but we square the differences instead of taking the absolute value before averaging them. This means larger errors are punished more, making MSE sensitive to outliers. If our model predicts a house price that's way off, the MSE will capture this more than the MAE.

R-squared

Unlike MAE and MSE, which are error metrics, R-squared is a goodness-of-fit metric. It gives us a measure of how well our model's predictions fit the actual data. An R-squared of 100 percent means our model captures all the variability in the data—a perfect fit. In reality, we won't achieve this, but the closer our R-squared is to 100 percent, the better our model fits the data.

These metrics allow us to evaluate our model, understand its strengths, and identify areas for improvement.

In practice, we could use linear regression to predict temperature changes, estimate furniture sales, or measure recovery times for athletes. The key is identifying situations where one or more measurable factors might have a roughly linear relationship with what we're trying to predict. Remember: while linear regression is powerful, it's not magic. It works best when there's a genuine linear relationship between variables, when we have good quality data, and when we understand that predictions aren't perfect but educated estimates based on patterns in our data.

Logistic Regression: From Numbers to Categories

Every day, your email inbox makes dozens of quick decisions. Is this message from your boss important? Should that promotional offer go straight to spam? While these might seem like simple yes/no choices, they're actually part of a fascinating type of prediction problem called classification. We need algorithms that help classify things.

Hang on. We glossed over what regression and classification are. Let's briefly cover that before jumping into logistic regression.

Classification and Regression

In machine learning, there are two main types of tasks: regression and classification. The difference between these tasks lies in the kind of output or prediction they make.

Regression

Regression tasks are about predicting a continuous output. Imagine trying to predict the temperature for the next week, the price of a house, or the sales of a product for the next quarter. All these tasks require you to predict a number that can range anywhere along a continuum. You're not trying to categorize or classify the output into distinct groups but rather estimating a quantity. This is what we refer to as regression.

Classification

On the other hand, classification tasks are about predicting which category, class, or group an observation belongs to. Let's say you're trying to predict whether an email is spam, whether a tumor is malignant or benign, or whether a customer will churn. These predictions aren't continuous numbers but are one of several distinct categories. This is the essence of classification.

Simply put, regression is about predicting a quantity, while classification is about predicting a category. Remember how linear regression helped us predict house prices by finding patterns in data? Logistic regression does something similar but for yes/no decisions. Let's see how this works with our spam example.

How Logistic Regression Works

Imagine you're building a spam filter. You have thousands of emails, and you know which ones are spam and which aren't. This requires us to classify our input into two categories—"Spam" or "Not Spam." Thus, we need a classification model. Here's where logistic regression comes in. Logistic regression gives us the probability of an input belonging to a particular category—it helps classify the input into categories.

So how does it work?

Remember our trusty line equation from linear regression? Well, logistic regression uses a similar equation but with a twist. Unlike the problem of house prices, we can't just draw a straight line to get results. The outcome we are trying to predict isn't a price but a category. Thus, we need to use an algorithm that will give us a probability between 0 and 1. The higher the probability score, the more likely the email is spam. We can use information like the frequency of certain words, random capitalization of letters, the length of the email, and the number of recipients as features to help us. Just like we found patterns between house features and prices, we're now looking for patterns between email features and spamminess.

So, we take these features and compute the slope and intercept as we did before in linear regression. But then, logistic regression uses a special S-shaped curve called the sigmoid function to convert this output into a probability score (Figure 3.4).

The sigmoid[3] function has a gentle slope that gradually flattens at both ends. At very high and very low values, the function approaches but never quite reaches 1 or 0, respectively. This means that no matter how convincing or dubious a message may look, our model will never be 100 percent certain of its classification but will get very close. For example, when our model is very confident an email is spam, it might give a probability of 0.98 (98 percent). When it's very confident it's not spam, it might give 0.02 (2 percent). For borderline cases, it might give probabilities closer to 0.5 (50 percent).

The beauty of this approach is that we can choose how cautious we want to be. Should we mark an email as spam if we're 90 percent sure? 80 percent? 50 percent? This threshold can be adjusted based on what's more important, such as not missing any important emails (being conservative) or not letting any spam through (being aggressive) (Figure 3.5).

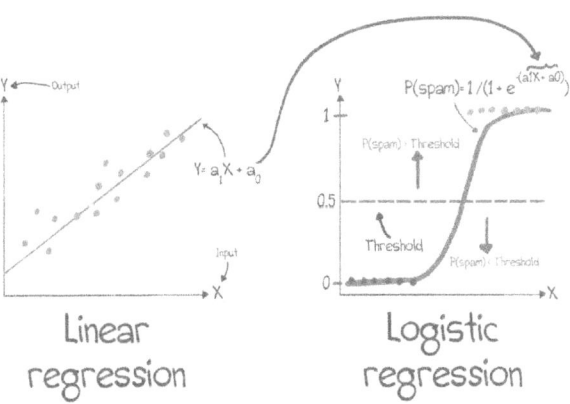

Figure 3.4. Logistic regression vs linear regression. Some of the calculations are still the same.

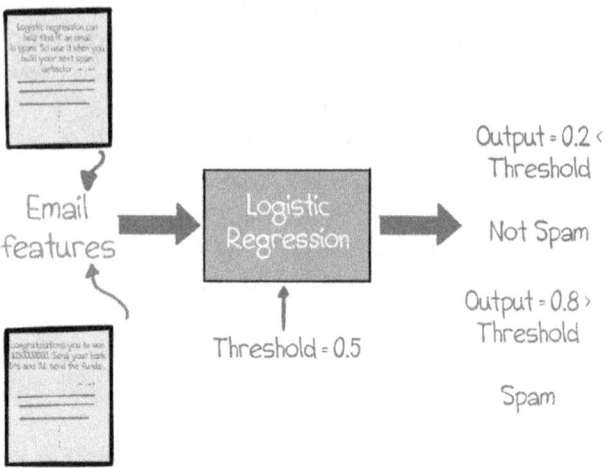

Figure 3.5. Filtering spam with logistic regression.

But how do we know if our spam filter is doing a good job? With linear regression, we could measure how far off our price predictions were in dollars. But with classification, being wrong by a little is the same as being wrong by a lot. An email is either spam or it isn't. This is where we need different ways to measure success.

Evaluating Logistic Regression

Think about it like this: our spam filter can make two types of mistakes. It might mark a legitimate email as spam (called a "false positive") or let a spam email through (a "false negative"). Which is worse? That depends on what you care about more. Do you not want to miss important emails or not see any spam? This leads us to three important measurements.

Accuracy

This is the proportion of predictions our model got right. But be wary. Accuracy can be misleading if our classes are imbalanced, as discussed in the previous chapters.

Precision and Recall

Precision measures how good your model is when it says an email is spam. In other words, if your model flags an email as spam, how often is it right? So, if your model has high precision, that means when it flags an email as spam, it's very likely that the email is indeed spam. On the other hand, recall measures how well your model catches all the spam emails. So, if there were one-hundred spam emails in your inbox, recall tells you how many of those your model successfully identified. A high recall would mean your model is good at catching spam emails, and they are less likely to land in your inbox.

Depending on our problem, we might care more about one than the other. We'll look at precision and recall in depth later in the book.

F1-Score

We often want to balance these measures, so we sometimes combine them into a single score called the F1-score. This single metric combines precision and recall using the harmonic mean. It's beneficial when we care about both precision and recall.

Understanding and applying these metrics allows us to evaluate and tune our logistic regression model for better performance.[4]

Just like linear regression, logistic regression works best when there are clear patterns in our data. If spammers keep changing their tactics, or if legitimate emails start looking like spam, our model needs to adapt. However, logistic regression provides a powerful and interpretable solution for many real-world problems where we need to make yes/no decisions based on data.

Whether it's detecting spam, predicting customer behavior, making medical diagnoses, or detecting fraudulent transactions, the principle remains the same. We find patterns in the features of known cases, use those patterns to calculate probabilities for new cases, and make decisions based on those probabilities. Next, we'll be venturing into a forest of decision trees, another set of powerful models for both regression and classification problems.

Decision Trees

Imagine playing twenty questions with a computer that's trying to guess your favorite restaurant. "Is it Italian?" "Does it serve breakfast?" With each question, it gets closer to the answer. This is exactly how decision trees work—they make predictions by asking a series of clever questions about our data. While linear and logistic regressions draw lines through our data, decision trees split it into smaller and smaller groups until they can make confident predictions (Figure 3.6).

Structurally, the decision tree looks like an inverted real-world tree.[5] The root is at the top, and the leaves are at the bottom. In a decision tree, each internal node represents a "test" or decision on an attribute or feature of the data (e.g., "Is the cuisine Italian?"), each branch represents the outcome of the test ("Yes" or "No"), and each leaf node represents a class label (a final decision like the chosen restaurant).

The decision process begins at the root node, where the algorithm evaluates a condition or question about the input data. Based on the answer, it follows the corresponding branch to the next node and asks another question. This continues until we reach a leaf node,[6] which provides the final decision or prediction. This systematic approach

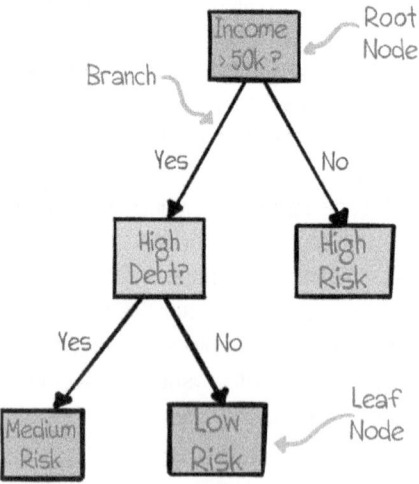

Figure 3.6. How a decision tree looks like.

makes decision trees uniquely transparent among machine learning models. You can literally trace the path of any prediction, making them invaluable in situations where we need to explain our model's decisions.

Node Impurity and Decision-Making

So, we've understood that decision trees are excellent at breaking down our data by making decisions based on certain conditions. But how exactly does a decision tree make these decisions? They rely on a concept called node impurity.

Think of organizing a library. If you separate books first by genre, then by the author's last name, you're creating increasingly "pure" groups. Each decision makes the groups more organized and less "messy." This is exactly what node impurity measures in decision trees—how well are our questions organizing the data.

The algorithm will evaluate the impact of a decision at each node and measure its impurity—or, in simple terms, its messiness. It evaluates every possible question it could ask at each step and chooses the one that creates the most organized (or pure) groups. For example, consider that we need to train a decision tree that efficiently separates apples and oranges. The decision "Is it orange?" will split the fruits into two groups, one mainly containing oranges and the other mostly containing apples. The decision "Is it round?" will lead to a more messy set of groups.

Node impurity measures how mixed the classes within a node are. If a node is pure (impurity is 0), it contains only one class, while a node with high impurity contains a mix of different classes. Impurity is typically calculated with criteria such as Gini Impurity or Entropy.[7] Think of these as scoring systems that give better scores to questions that create cleaner groups. The ultimate goal of the decision tree is to make decisions that decrease impurity within the groups. The more homogeneous the groups are after a decision, the better (Figure 3.7).

Decision Trees in Action

To see the power of decision trees, let's consider a practical use case: determining credit risk for loan applicants.

A financial institution that provides loans wants to minimize risk. One of the most significant risks is the possibility that the borrower will default

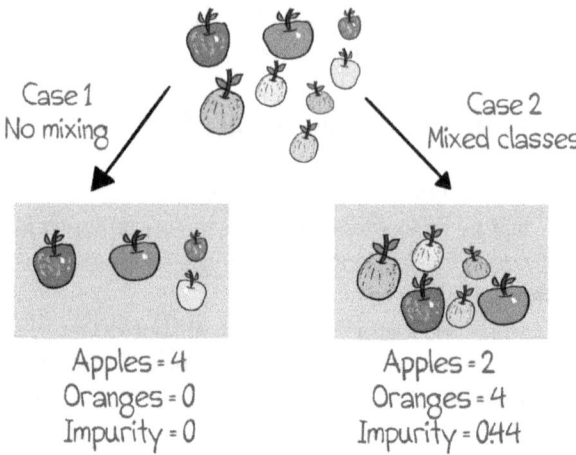

Figure 3.7. Impurity measures help decision trees make the right splits.

on their loan. To mitigate this risk, the institution needs to evaluate the creditworthiness of each applicant.

Here's where decision trees come in.

The financial institution could create a decision tree model where the features include the applicant's income, employment status, credit score, existing debts, and the loan amount requested. Each feature helps assess the potential risk of lending to the applicant.

For instance, a significant decision node might be "Is the applicant's credit score above 700?" If the answer is yes, we traverse the tree, leading to other questions like "Does the applicant have a stable job?" Each answer continues to narrow down the risk category the applicant falls into, leading to a leaf node that could classify them as a "low," "medium," or "high" risk for loan default.

This process of credit risk assessment, which can be complex and tedious if done manually, becomes simplified and automated with decision trees. And the best part? The decisions made by the tree are transparent and easy to interpret, making it a go-to method for such applications.[8]

Tuning Decision Trees

One crucial aspect we haven't discussed is how deep our trees should grow. A tree that's too shallow might miss important patterns in our data, while one that's too deep might memorize the training data (remember overfitting?). Thankfully, we have a few knobs we can tweak to make sure our decision tree is robust.

- *Maximum depth*: How many questions we allow the tree to ask.
- *Minimum samples per leaf*: How many data points must end up in each final group.
- *Maximum features*: How many different types of questions we allow the tree to consider.

These parameters help us control the balance between underfitting and overfitting.

Decision Trees and Regression

So far, we've been talking about decision trees in the context of classification problems. But these trees can also tackle regression problems.

We know that each leaf node represents a class label in a classification tree. However, each leaf node represents a real number or a continuous value in a regression tree. Remember our house price prediction problem? A regression tree might ask questions like "Is the house larger than 2000 square feet?", "Is it less than five years old?", "Is it in a good school district?", and so on.

Each leaf node then represents the average price of houses that match all the conditions along that path. It's like breaking the housing market into increasingly specific segments, each with its own typical price range. Once we have such a tree ready, we can predict the housing price of a new house based on these questions.

Advantages and Limitations

Like every algorithm, decision trees come with their own set of advantages and limitations.

Let's look at the positives. Decision trees are easy to understand and visualize, which makes them perfect for explanatory purposes. They can handle both numerical and categorical data. They can also deal with missing values and outliers, making them quite robust. Importantly, they implicitly perform feature selection, identifying the most critical variables, which can be a massive bonus in high-dimensional datasets.

However, decision trees also have their limitations. They can easily overfit the data if not tuned properly, leading to poor generalization. They are also quite sensitive to small changes in the data, causing drastic changes in the tree structure.

However, despite these limitations, decision trees serve as a building block for more advanced algorithms like Random Forests and Gradient-Boosted Trees, cementing their place as a fundamental tool in any machine learning practitioner's toolkit.

Random Forests

When you have to make a crucial decision, you often seek the opinions of various experts, weigh their advice, and make your final decision based on collective wisdom. This concept of utilizing multiple views to make an informed decision is known as ensemble learning in machine learning.

Random forests are an example of ensemble learning. The "forest" is a collection of decision trees, each contributing its opinion or prediction to the final decision. All trees vote on the final prediction, with the majority ruling in classification or the average being taken in regression. This way, even if some trees make poor predictions, their errors can be averaged out by the other trees.

But why are these forests random? Randomness arises from two key factors. First, each decision tree in the forest is trained on a different subset of the training data. Secondly, trees can only consider a random subset of features, forcing them to make decisions based on different aspects of the data. The idea behind introducing this randomness is to make each tree in the forest unique. When combined, these diverse perspectives often lead to better decisions than any single tree could make alone (Figure 3.8).

A Few Good Algorithms

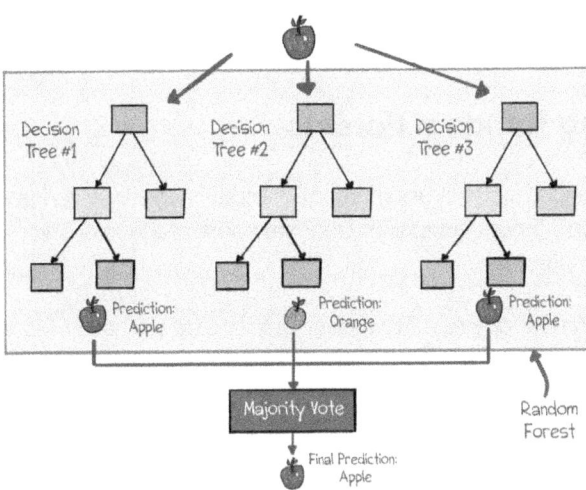

Figure 3.8. A random forest aggregates multiple decision trees.

Let's bring this concept to life with a real-world application. Consider a patient walking into a hospital with chest pain, shortness of breath, and fatigue. A single decision tree might focus too heavily on the chest pain and rush to diagnose a heart condition. But medical diagnosis is rarely this straightforward.

Random forests handle this complexity naturally. While a single decision tree follows one path, a forest examines the evidence from multiple angles. Some trees might focus on the patient's symptoms, others on their medical history, and still others on their test results. It's like having a team of specialists look at the same case, each bringing their expertise to the table.

The power lies in how these different perspectives come together. If 90 percent of the trees predict a particular condition, doctors can be more confident in that diagnosis. If the trees are split between different conditions, it might signal that more tests are needed. This ability to measure uncertainty, combined with the model's skill at finding subtle patterns in patient data, makes random forests particularly valuable in healthcare. They can spot complex relationships between symptoms that might escape both simpler algorithms and human observation.

Like decision trees, random forests can also be adapted for regression problems. When used for regression, the random forest takes the average of the predictions made by each decision tree to arrive at a final prediction.

Tuning Random Forests

While random forests are more robust than single decision trees, they still require thoughtful tuning. Here are some of the knobs you need to carefully consider:

- *Number of Trees*: How many opinions do we need? More trees generally give better results but take longer to train.
- *Sample Size*: How much data should each tree see? This affects how different each tree's perspective will be.
- *Feature Selection*: How many features should we consider at each split? This balances diversity against individual tree accuracy.
- *Tree Depth*: Should we allow each tree to make very detailed decisions, or keep them more general?

These choices help us balance the forest's complexity against its performance and training time.

Advantages and Limitations

Like any tool, random forests have strengths and weaknesses. On the plus side, they can handle large datasets with many features and perform well even with missing or unbalanced data. They also provide feature importance, which can be very insightful in understanding which features are most influential in making predictions.

However, random forests can be computationally intensive and slow to train, especially with massive datasets. They can also overfit if not correctly tuned.

Despite these limitations, random forests represent a powerful evolution of decision trees, addressing many of their predecessor's limitations while introducing new capabilities. Random forests often serve as a robust baseline. Any complex model you use should justify its additional complexity by meaningfully outperforming a well-tuned random forest. So, the next time you face a complex prediction task, consult a forest.

We've journeyed from simple decision trees to powerful random forests, seeing how combining multiple models can overcome individual limitations.

Next, we'll explore K-means clustering, which takes a fundamentally different approach to learning from data. While trees and forests help us make predictions based on past examples, clustering will show us how to find natural patterns and groupings in data without any predefined categories. This shift from supervised to unsupervised learning opens up new possibilities for discovering hidden structures in our data.

K-Means Clustering

Dividing and conquering, grouping and segregating, and clustering are some of the most common tactics we apply in daily life. Imagine sorting clothes into different piles—summer wear, winter wear, party wear, and so on. The K-means algorithm works similarly but further partitions an entire dataset into k distinct, non-overlapping subgroups or clusters.

K-means clustering is a type of unsupervised learning that does not need labeled data to make sense of things. It discovers hidden structures within data on its own. The goal is simple: group similar data points together and find underlying patterns. To accomplish this, K-means needs an input of K, the number of clusters to be created.

This algorithm groups data into "K" clusters. Hence the name. We choose the value of K, and the algorithm faithfully partitions the data into K groups.

How does it do that? Let's find out! (Figure 3.9)

Understanding the K-Means Algorithm

Let's use the example of customer segmentation for targeted marketing to illustrate the steps involved in the K-means algorithm.

Initialization

Imagine you're a marketing manager at a large retail store trying to understand your customers better. You have data about how much

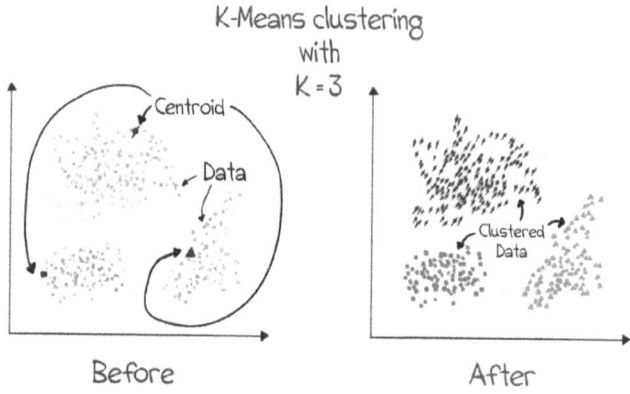

Figure 3.9. We tell K-means how many groups we'd like, and it does the rest.

each customer spends, what times they shop, and what types of products they buy. Looking at individual customers is overwhelming. There are thousands of them. Instead, you want to find natural groups of similar customers to create targeted promotions.

Suppose each customer becomes a point on a graph, with money spent on one axis and shopping frequency on the other. Our goal is to find K centers (called centroids) that best represent different customer groups. Think of these centroids as the "typical customer" for each group. But how do we find these centers?

Your boss has given you a budget to run at most three promotions. So all you know is that you want to segregate customers into three groups. Thus, K equals three in this example. The K-means algorithm begins by randomly choosing three customers as centroids.

Cluster Assignment

Next, the K-means algorithm goes through each data point and assigns it to the nearest cluster centroid. Imagine placing three pins randomly on our customer graph. Each customer is then assigned to their closest pin, creating initial groups. But these initial groups are based on random placement. Thus, they're unlikely to be the best grouping possible.

Centroid Calculation

Now that the customers have been initially assigned to groups, the algorithm recalculates the centroids for each cluster. This is where the "means" part of K-means comes in. For each group, we calculate the average position of all customers in that group. These averages become our new centroids. Think of this like calculating the average customer profile for each cluster and moving our pin to their location. Now we reassign each customer to the new centroids again, as some might be closer to a different center than before.

Iteration

Just like a good marketer would, the algorithm then repeats the process of assigning customers to groups and recalculating the average customer profile until the composition of the groups does not change. This is the point at which the algorithm has converged, and the customer groups are finally formed.

Before we move on, there's one salient point we missed. We didn't discuss what makes a customer "close" to a centroid. This is where distance metrics come in. The most commonly used one is the Euclidean distance.[9] Intuitively, it's the same method you'd use to measure distance with a ruler. In our example, it helps us determine how similar two customers are based on their spending and shopping patterns. A customer who spends $100 weekly is likely "closer" to another who spends $110 weekly than to someone who spends $5000 monthly.

Once we have our final groups, what can we do with them? We might discover three distinct customer types: weekend shoppers who make large purchases, daily visitors who buy few items regularly, and monthly bulk buyers who stock up.

Each group might respond differently to promotions. Weekend shoppers might appreciate early-bird specials, while daily visitors might prefer loyalty rewards. Armed with the clustering results, we can create meaningful promotions for each segment.

Evaluating the Clusters

How do we evaluate our clustering model? In other words, how do we know that the groups we identified are meaningful? That's where clustering metrics come in. Good clusters have two key properties: customers within each group should be similar to each other (cohesion), and different groups should be distinct from one another (separation). For example, the weekend shoppers should be bunched together but separate from the monthly bulk buyers. Formally, K-means uses Within-cluster Sum of Squares (WSS) and the silhouette score to measure these qualities.

In practice, K-means has many applications beyond retail. Streaming services use it to group viewers with similar tastes, social networks use it to suggest friends, and image processing systems use it to reduce color palettes. But, we need to understand its strengths and weaknesses to use it effectively.

Advantages and Limitations

K-means is a simple and efficient algorithm but has a few limitations. For starters, you are required to specify the number of clusters (K) beforehand. In many real-world applications, the ideal number of clusters is not known in advance. The initial placement of the centroids can significantly influence the final results. Poor initial choices can lead us away from the best possible clustering. K-means is also sensitive to outliers. Since it uses the mean value for the centroid calculation, an outlier can pull the centroid toward it, resulting in suboptimal clusters.

Despite these limitations, the K-means clustering algorithm is extremely handy. There are other more sophisticated clustering methods like hierarchical clustering and DBSCAN. However, K-means is a great place to start when you are looking to garner insights and extract patterns from your data.

So far, the algorithms we've seen represent just a sampling of the rich toolkit that machine learning offers. Each one serves a specific purpose. Some predict values, others classify data, and still others, like K-means, find hidden structures. While we've covered some of the most fundamental and widely used algorithms, there are many more specialized tools available for specific problems. Covering the gamut would require a separate book altogether.

In the next chapter, we'll dive into neural networks and deep learning. Instead of using carefully crafted algorithms for specific tasks, we'll discover how artificial neural networks can learn to handle a wide variety of challenges, from understanding human language to recognizing objects in images.

Chapter Summary

In this chapter, we explored traditional machine learning algorithms and their real-world applications. Through practical examples, we saw how these algorithms help us make sense of data in different ways.

Our journey began with linear regression, where we learned to predict house prices based on features like square footage and location. We saw how finding the best-fit line helps us understand relationships between variables and make predictions about unseen data.

We then explored classification with logistic regression, turning numerical predictions into categories. Using examples like spam detection, we discovered how this algorithm helps make binary choices by calculating probabilities.

Decision trees introduced a more intuitive approach to machine learning. Like a flowchart of questions, these models break down complex decisions into simple, sequential steps. This made it easier to understand how machines can learn to make decisions similar to humans.

Building on decision trees, we discovered random forests. By combining multiple trees, each looking at different aspects of our data, we learned how ensemble methods create more robust and accurate predictions.

Finally, K-means clustering showed us how machines can discover hidden patterns without prior guidance. Through a customer segmentation example, we saw how this algorithm automatically groups similar data points together, revealing natural structures hidden within our data.

These algorithms represent different approaches to learning from data. While we've covered fundamental techniques that form the backbone of many applications, they're just a drop in the ocean.

In the next chapter, we'll explore deep learning, where we'll discover how machines can learn to handle increasingly complex challenges, from understanding human language to recognizing objects in images.

Chapter 4
Neural Networks

The power of the human brain is unrivaled. Haven't you marveled at our ability to recognize faces, comprehend speech, or make decisions in the blink of an eye? This power springs from an intricate network of billions of neurons, buzzing and interconnecting, leading to conscious thought, memory, and learning.

Biological neurons have inspired an equally fascinating area of research in artificial intelligence—Artificial Neural Networks (ANN).

ANNs power many of the products and services we use today. They are a class of algorithms that identify patterns in data through a process *loosely* inspired by the human brain. They can adapt to various tasks and solve some of the most complex problems that challenge humankind today. Neural networks play a pivotal role in your favorite chatbot, medical diagnosis, drug discovery, apps that can create unique selfies for you, or even self-driving cars that keep you safe on the road.

So, what do these neural networks consist of?

Building Blocks

Just as biological neurons are the basic working units of the brain, artificial neurons are the fundamental building blocks of artificial neural networks. Each artificial neuron can take in multiple inputs, apply some processing, and produce an output. A neural network consists of many interconnected artificial neurons. As the data passes from one neuron to the next, it is transformed, allowing the network to learn complex relationships.

But what kind of processing does an artificial neuron do?

To understand this, we'll have to travel back in time to 1943. Researchers Warren McCulloch and Walter Pitts[1] created a model that tried to imitate a biological neuron. This artificial neuron could perform simple Boolean functions[2] like AND but couldn't handle non-Boolean inputs. Additionally, this model didn't treat different inputs in proportion to their importance.

Using this model as inspiration, Frank Rosenblatt developed the Perceptron[3] in 1957. The critical difference in the Perceptron was that it weighted each input to capture its relative importance. It could also handle numbers and not just Boolean variables. The Perceptron used these weights to compute a weighted sum of the inputs.[4] This result was then thresholded using a step function. So, if the sum were large enough, the Perceptron would produce the output 1. For all other cases, it would output 0. Why was this step important? There are three reasons. First, the Perceptron was designed to solve binary classification, that is, the output would belong to one of two classes. Second, the model drew inspiration from biological neurons. Our neurons "fire" and generate an output signal only when the input passes a certain threshold. The Perceptron mirrors this idea. Finally, it made the overall design simple. Thresholding with a step function produces a clear-cut decision on which of the two classes the output belongs to and naturally lends itself to the three reasons above (Figure 4.1).

However, the Perceptron wasn't perfect. It only worked when the input data was linearly separable. In other words, it would fail if the input data couldn't be separated by a straight line (or hyperplane in higher dimensions). For example, researchers showed that it couldn't model the XOR[5] logic function and claimed that the Perceptron wasn't the silver bullet that everyone thought it was. As a result, interest in artificial intelligence research cooled.

However, many limitations of a single Perceptron disappeared when multiple Perceptrons were stacked together as layers. This model was called the Multi-Layer Perceptron (MLP). Not only did it successfully model the XOR logic function, but it also became the design that pioneered modern neural networks.

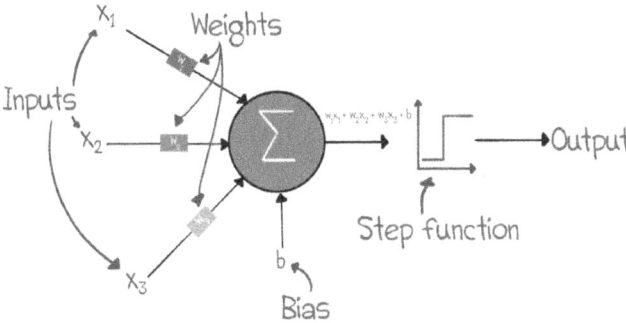

Figure 4.1. The humble Perceptron. The input values are multiplied by the weights, added to a bias term, and transformed through the step function.

The keen-eyed observer you are, you would have noticed that the Perceptron is eerily similar to logistic regression, which we saw earlier. You are partially correct. Logistic regression also computes a weighted sum of the inputs and adds a bias term. However, it applies a sigmoid function (a.k.a. logistic function) instead of a step function. Thus, a logistic regression model can output probability values, while the Perceptron can only output discrete values like 0 or 1. But, like the Perceptron, logistic regression also fails when the data is not linearly separable (Figure 4.2).

Artificial Neurons and Layers

So, we've seen that an MLP can overcome the limitations of a single Perceptron. But what does it look like? An MLP consists of three sections of layers. It has an input layer that receives the input data. The input layer has as many artificial neurons as inputs (plus a bias term).

Each neuron in the input layer processes the data (we saw the process above) and passes the results on to the next set of layers called hidden layers. The hidden layers are called so because they are sandwiched between input and output layers and thus are not visible

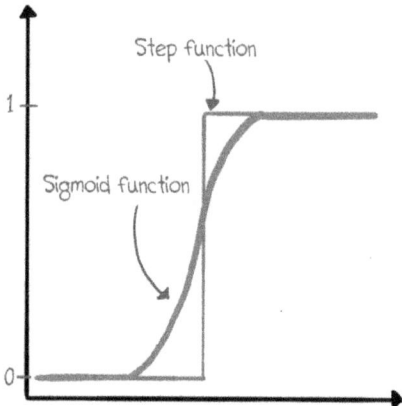

Figure 4.2. Comparing the step function against the sigmoid. Notice that the sigmoid has a continuous range of values while the step function abruptly jumps from 0 to 1 true to its name.

outside the neural network. Each neuron in a hidden layer is called a hidden unit. The number of hidden layers is arbitrary and is set by the user when defining the network.

This is where the term "deep" in deep learning comes from. Deep neural networks have several hidden layers between input and output and thus are called deep. There isn't a profound or deeper meaning behind the name. Modern networks have hundreds of hidden layers, allowing them to solve complex problems. Each hidden layer processes the data and passes it on to the next one.

Once processed, the output of the final hidden layer is passed on to the output layer. The output layer has as many artificial neurons as needed for the task. For example, if we need to classify whether a picture is of a dog or a cat, one neuron will suffice.[6] If we need to figure out which of a thousand categories a picture belongs to, we'll need a thousand neurons. The output layer is the decision-maker and makes the final predictions in the neural network.

Each layer in an MLP has a set of neurons. Each of these neurons is connected to every input. This type of layer is called a fully connected, linear, or dense layer. Note that these layers are called input, output, or hidden layers, depending on *where* they occur in the network positionally. However, they are called fully connected, linear, or dense layers because of their *type*.

This matters because layers in a neural network are like Lego blocks. We can use different types of blocks in different parts of the network. The dense layer is thus one type of Lego block. However, the position *where* these blocks are used determines whether they are input, output, or hidden. In the coming chapters, we'll see other types of Lego blocks used to construct neural networks, like convolution layers, recurrent layers, and others.

The big idea is that we combine these layers together just like we would with Lego blocks and separate the layers with activation functions.

This is a lot of information, so let's consider a simple analogy to understand it better.

Think of each layer as a miniature decision factory. It takes in raw materials (inputs), runs them through the machinery (processing done by neurons in the layer), and outputs the finished product (output). The kind of processing each factory does depends on the type of factory. There are special types of factories for different tasks (Figure 4.3).

Now imagine a bunch of these factories scattered around. Let's connect them via roads. The outputs from some factories serve as raw materials (inputs) for others. Together, they form a network of factories.

The first layer of factories in this network, the input layer, is like the import docks where raw materials (data) come in. Then come the hidden layers, the heart of the network, where all the processing happens. These factories consume the output of the input layer factories. Consider car manufacturing. The input factories would give us rubber, steel, and glass. The hidden layer factories would convert these raw materials into windows, tires, and chassis. Each hidden layer continues the processing, leading one step closer to the finished product. Lastly, the output layer is like the showroom where the finished product (final output) is ready for purchase.

This analogy gives us a picture of its structure. But we still need to answer a few questions. How are these networks trained? How do they work? Why are they so effective?

Let's look at that next.

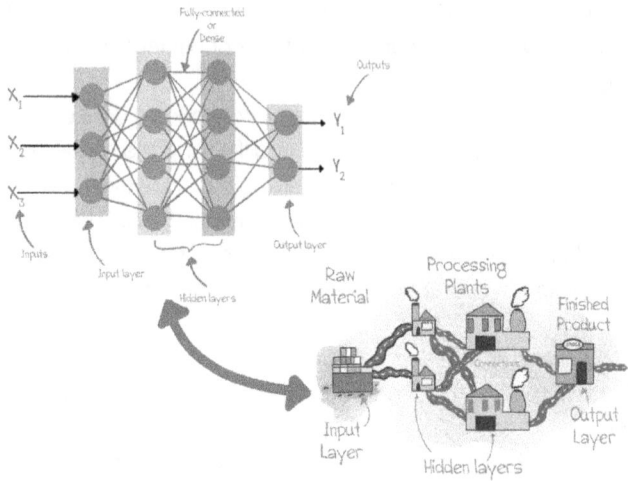

Figure 4.3. The neural network factory taking raw material and transforming it into actionable insights.

Nonlinearities and Activation Functions

We saw that the Perceptron takes a weighted sum of the input and passes it through a step function. The step function is one example of something we call an activation function. Every artificial neuron has one of these functions, which applies a non-linear transformation to its input.

This is the secret sauce of neural networks.

Let's face it. Most of the data we encounter in real life is complex and hardly ever linear. This capability to handle non-linearity allows neural networks to solve complex tasks ranging from image and speech recognition to language translation and even crush video games! In essence, activation functions are what make neural networks so powerful and versatile.

To see why, let's consider that we have linear layers where neurons just compute a weighted sum of the inputs. Let's assume that there's no activation function at all. When we connect such linear layers with each other, we end up with a giant linear transformation. At the end of the day, the output we calculate is still a linear combination of the original inputs. Thus, such a network can't model complex real-world data.

However, when we add activation functions, they introduce nonlinearities into the mix. Once nonlinearities come in, the output can no longer be produced just by linearly combining the inputs. This enables networks to model complex data. Now, imagine what happens when we stack several linear layers together with activation functions separating them. Such a network becomes incredibly good at solving complex problems.

To drive the point home, imagine having a car that can only move in a straight line. Driving such a car through the windy, curving roads of a mountainside would only end badly. Now, imagine a car that can turn and adapt to twists and turns in the road. Such a car would easily navigate the same route. A neural network without activation functions is like the former. Which car would you prefer? (Figure 4.4)

There are several types of activation functions used in neural networks. The most commonly used ones are the Rectified Linear Unit (ReLU), the Hyperbolic Tangent (Tanh), the Sigmoid, and the Softmax activation function. Typically, the ReLU activation is used in hidden

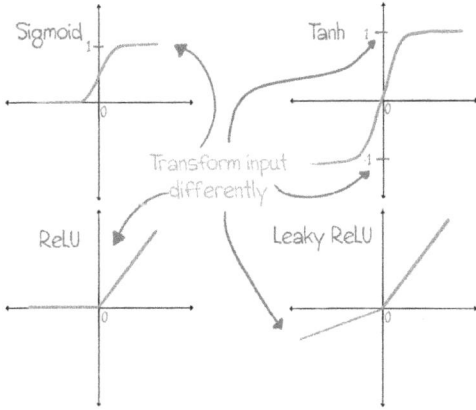

Figure 4.4. Commonly used activation functions. Notice how each function treats positive and negative values differently.

layers, while the softmax[7] is preferred for output layers since it produces values between 0 and 1, like a probability score.

Activation functions are the reason why neural networks are called universal function approximators—meaning that, given enough layers and neurons and activations, these networks can learn to mimic almost any process or pattern we see in real life.

Cool! So, we've unearthed the secret sauce that makes neural nets powerful. That brings us to the question: how are the values of these weights and biases for each neuron set?

Learning from Mistakes

If you've operated a radio or a music mixer, you'll find it easy to visualize the myriad knobs it has. Each knob controls a particular setting, and the correct combination of these knobs produces pleasing results. Weights and biases in a neural network are like these knobs. They need to be tweaked so that the network produces the desired results. But given how large some of these networks are, you're talking about a lot of knobs to tweak manually. Instead, we let the network learn the correct settings for all these knobs on its own.

To understand how a neural network finds the correct weights and biases for each of its neurons, we need to examine two processes: forward propagation and backward propagation.

Forward Propagation

We've already covered forward propagation (a.k.a. the forward pass) in the previous section. It's how data flows from the input layer to the output layer. At each layer, the neurons calculate a weighted sum, add the bias, and then apply an activation function before passing the processed information further. Think of this like a busy restaurant's kitchen where each cook handles one part of the meal before it goes out to the customer. Each cook receives the dish from the previous cook and transforms it before passing it on to the next cook.

At the end of forward propagation, the neural network is ready with a prediction for the input it was provided. Now comes the fun part!

Backward Propagation

A neural network is rarely correct from the get-go. It makes a ton of mistakes and has to learn from them. So, how does a neural network learn from its mistakes?

After the forward pass, we have the network's predictions. But what happens when these predictions are wrong? That's where backpropagation (backprop for short) and gradient descent come in. Together, they help the network adjust its weights and biases to improve the predictions.

To understand backpropagation, let's revisit our restaurant analogy. Before the dish goes out to the diner, the head chef takes a final taste to ensure the flavors are balanced. When a new dish is designed, the cooks usually don't get it right on the first go. The head chef tastes the dish and identifies what is missing and what went wrong. He then traces the mistakes back to the cooks who made them. Similarly, backprop helps the neural network trace back its predictions to see where the mistakes happened (Figure 4.5).

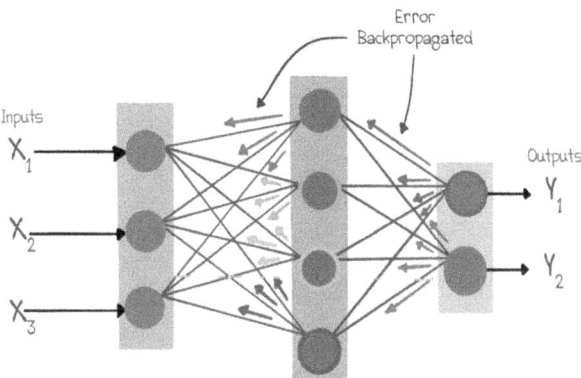

Figure 4.5. Teaching a network to learn from its mistakes. The error backpropagates through the network, allowing it to adjust the weights accordingly.

The first step in backpropagation is to determine how wrong the network's predictions are. This is done by comparing the predicted and actual values using a loss function. The loss function is like a measuring stick and gives a numerical value representing the error of the predictions. The higher the loss, the more inaccurate the predictions.

Once we know the loss value, we can use backprop to distribute this error back through the network. Each weight and bias in the network contributed to the final prediction and, consequently, the error. Backprop helps us understand how much each weight and bias contributed to the overall error. This is done using a method in calculus called the chain rule.[8]

Next, we need to update the network's weights and biases so that the overall error is minimized. That's where gradient descent comes into play.

Gradient Descent

The end goal of training the neural net is to have it make the fewest mistakes possible, meaning a very low error in its predictions. During training, we measure errors using a loss function. This function computes the difference between the network's predictions and the actual answers. Gradient descent is an algorithm used to minimize this loss function. It's like a navigation system guiding a ship toward a destination by modifying its direction. Gradient descent iteratively adjusts the weights and biases of the network in the direction that reduces the loss. To find the direction, it computes the gradients of the loss function with respect to every weight in the network.

Confused? Here's an example that will help you understand better.

Consider a hiker figuring out their way back to base camp after a day in the wilderness. It's gotten dark, and the hiker's headlamp and cell phone have run out of juice. In other words, our hiker friend is blind and in bear country. He needs to get back pronto.

Given that our hiker needs to go downhill as fast as possible, it makes sense to go along the path that has the steepest slope. Unable to see anything, he decides to use his feet as a guide to gauge the steepness of the terrain. Feeling the slope around him with his feet, he figures out where to descend the valley.

In a neural network, gradients are like the slope of this terrain. They indicate both the direction and magnitude of the steepest increase in the loss function because they are the partial derivatives[9] of the loss function with respect to each of the network's parameters (weights and biases of the network).

To minimize the loss function, we must move in the *opposite* direction of the gradients. Doing so reduces the gap between the network's predictions and the actual answers. This is done iteratively by updating the network parameters based on the gradient. There are different flavors of gradient descent, which we will cover in the next section (Figure 4.6).

After this step, we know the respective contributions of each weight and bias and how they should be updated to minimize the error. So, we make corrections to the weights and biases proportional to their contributions to minimize the overall error.

Quickly recapping what we've seen so far: Backpropagation computes the gradients, and gradient descent minimizes the loss based on this.

Thus, the neural network can learn from its mistakes through backpropagation and gradient descent. Over time, this iterative process of making predictions, calculating the loss, backpropagating the error,

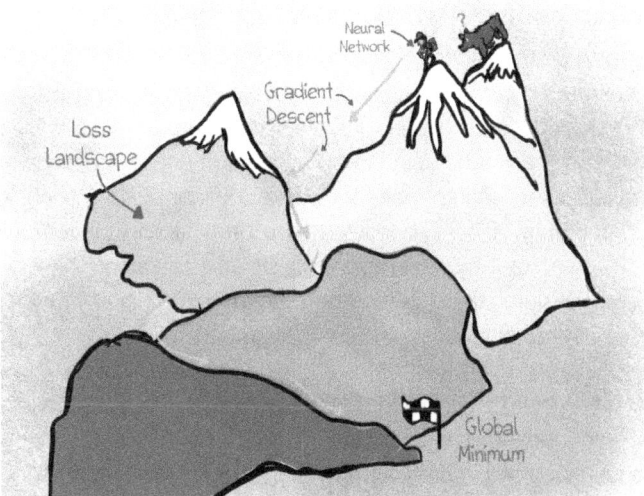

Figure 4.6. Gradient descent imagined as a hiking problem.

and adjusting weights and biases using gradient descent leads to a properly trained neural network. This network can make accurate predictions on new, unseen data, which is the ultimate goal of any machine learning model.

Let's take a real-world problem and walk through it to clarify this process.

Training a Network End-to-End

Imagine you've been hired to set up a defect detection algorithm in a factory that produces screws. Good screws have a specific range of diameter, hardness index, and length values (recall these are called features). The factory wants to automate the removal of defective screws from the assembly line. You decide to use a neural network to identify defective screws.

Designing the Network

Your input data has numerical values for each of these features. We need to feed these three values to our network. Thus, the input layer will have three neurons plus a bias term. Let's assume that we have two hidden layers. Let's further assume that the first hidden layer has eight neurons, while the second has sixteen.

These are arbitrary numbers that we set when defining the model. Such values are called hyperparameters. A hyperparameter is a setting that we can tweak when setting up an experiment. It is not the actual parameters of the neural network but a configuration. The choice of hyperparameters affects the outcome of the training process. There are a few important hyperparameters that we'll see along the way. For example, the number of hidden layers and the number of hidden units within each hidden layer are hyperparameters.

Simply put, hyperparameters are configurations set by the user. Model parameters are learned during training.

Let's get back to our network.

We just need one neuron in the output layer. It gives us the probability of whether a particular screw is good or defective. The higher the probability score, the more likely that the screw is good.

Finally, all the weights and biases in the network are assigned random values. We don't know what they should be yet, but they must be set to some non-zero value. After this step, our network is ready to be trained.

Setting Up the Dataset

Let's say the factory has 100,000 screws, for which they have the values for diameter, hardness index, and length. For the sake of simplicity, let's assume that these are evenly split between good screws and defective screws.[10]

To train the network, we can randomly choose one screw at a time and have the network make predictions on it. We can then use backpropagation and gradient descent to update the weights before feeding in the next screw.

This process is called *Stochastic Gradient Descent (SGD)*. The advantage is that the weight updates are done after each example in the dataset, so it's faster. However, this method results in the weights oscillating a lot during training since the updates will dramatically differ from example to example. Thus, it might not find the best set of weights at the end of the process.

On the other hand, we could feed the entire dataset to the model. Yes, all 100,000 examples at once. This is called *Batch Gradient Descent*. The update takes longer in this case since the model needs to work through the entire training set. However, this approach oscillates less and usually is more stable. But this approach is a memory hog, and if you don't have enough memory space in your computer, you're out of luck. Also, the noisy updates in SGD can help the model learn better and reduce the chance of getting stuck in a false dawn (technically called local minima).

By now, you would have guessed that there's a third approach. This feeds small chunks of data, called mini-batches, at a time to the model. This results in reduced oscillations and reasonably quick updates. This Goldilocks approach is called *Mini-batch Gradient Descent*.

Most, if not all, training setups use this approach when training networks.

Ok, so we'll chunk up our data randomly into small sets. The size of each of these sets is called the *mini-batch size*. This is another hyperparameter.

Now that we have the data ready, let's train the network.

Training the Model

This is the easy part. We take a mini-batch and feed it to the model. The model makes predictions for each example in the mini-batch. We then use a loss function to compare the model's predictions with the actual answer. Using the accumulated error, we can update the weights using gradient descent and backpropagation.

But there's one more thing. We're a cautious bunch. Just because gradients tell us to go in one way doesn't mean we have to. We want to take baby steps. Trust but verify. We use a hyperparameter called the *learning rate* to adjust the size of the step we take. A large learning rate means we take big steps, while a smaller one means we take smaller steps. A large learning rate can make us jump over the minimum and miss the destination. A small learning rate will take us forever to get to the minimum. Thus, setting the learning rate appropriately plays a significant role in getting the network to reach its best setting (Figure 4.7).

To summarize, we use the learning rate to control how big of a step we take toward minimizing the loss. But are we done training once we feed the network all the mini-batches? Nope! A network needs to see the data several times before it learns to make good predictions. One pass through the entire dataset is called an *epoch*. A network needs to be trained for several epochs to make accurate predictions. As you might have guessed, the number of epochs is also a hyperparameter (Figure 4.8).

So, to recap:

1. We define and initialize the neural network.
2. Then, we split the data into small chunks called mini-batches.
3. We feed the mini-batches to the network randomly.
4. The network makes predictions on each example in the mini-batch.

5. We use a loss function to evaluate these predictions and compute an error value.
6. We use this error value to update the weights and biases of the network using gradient descent and backpropagation.
7. We repeat steps 3 to 6 for several epochs until the network has learned to make good predictions.

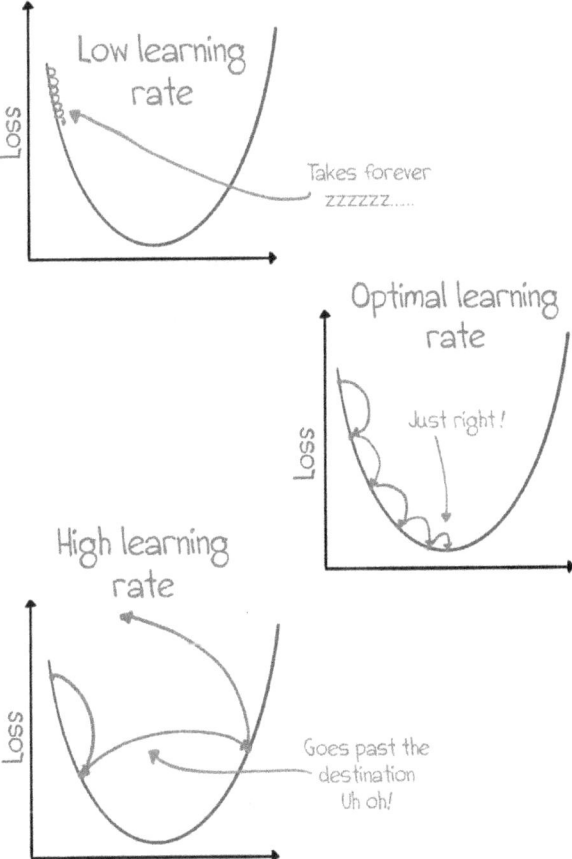

Figure 4.7. The Goldilocks problem revisited. Choosing the correct learning rate helps the network reach the bottom of the loss curve.

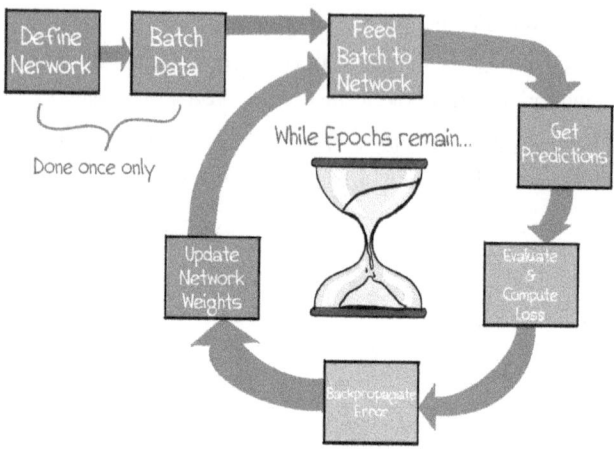

Figure 4.8. The neural network training cycle.

How do we know that the network makes good predictions? We monitor the loss value. Over the course of training, the loss has to decrease, and the accuracy (or desired metric) has to improve. In practice, we monitor the model's performance on the validation set in addition to the training set. This is crucial to ensure that the model generalizes well and doesn't blindly memorize the training data.

There are many more intricacies and nuances when it comes to neural networks, but we've covered the basics. Next up, we'll look at how deep learning has been applied to a variety of tasks. For now, though, I'd suggest another epoch of training on this chapter's material. What do you think?

Chapter Summary

Let's break down our exploration of neural networks—algorithms that take inspiration from our own brains. At their core, neural networks are intricate webs of artificial neurons working together to make sense of data. We started with the humble Perceptron, the ancestor of modern networks, before graduating to more sophisticated MLPs.

We saw that activation functions are the secret sauce behind neural networks' success. These mathematical operations transform neural networks from simple linear systems into powerful problem solvers capable of capturing complex, non-linear patterns.

We dove into how these networks learn: first through forward propagation, where information flows through the network's layers, and then through backpropagation, where the network refines its understanding. Using gradient descent, the network methodically adjusts its internal parameters, learning from each mistake until it makes accurate predictions.

Training these networks requires patience, precision, and intuition. We explored various approaches—from processing small batches of data to analyzing entire datasets at once—and examined how crucial parameters like learning rates and training duration shape a model's development.

With these fundamentals under our belt, we're ready to explore how neural networks are transforming various applications.

Chapter 5
AI That Reads and Writes

Every time you translate a web page, get autocomplete suggestions while typing, or use a search engine, you're interacting with AI that can read and write. While machine learning powers many applications, language understanding represents one of its most fascinating frontiers. Human language is complex. It's packed with ambiguity, idioms, metaphors, and cultural nuances. From professional documents to emoji-filled texts, from academic papers to meme-speak, computers must navigate this rich tapestry of human expression, sometimes containing internet slang,[1] lingo, and regional dialects. Thankfully, researchers started working on this fascinating problem decades ago.

Welcome to Natural Language Processing (NLP), the field of AI that focuses on bridging the gap between human communication and computer understanding. NLP enables computers to read, decipher, and understand human language so that it can be used in valuable ways. While we often take it for granted, NLP powers everything from your spam filters to virtual assistants, from automated customer service to real-time translation services.

As much as we marvel at computers for completing ridiculously huge calculations in record time, they still face many challenges. For starters, if we showed a computer some words, it wouldn't know what they were. Computers speak in the language of numbers. Specifically, they talk in binary—ones and zeros. This creates our first challenge:

how do we transform the richness of human language into something a computer can process?

Imagine trying to teach a child about language. First, you'd start with the basics—the alphabet. From there, you'd build words and then sentences. Over time, the child learns on top of this foundation and understands dialects, slang, and more. Now imagine doing the same with a machine. We need to follow the same steps with computers, but somehow using numbers. This journey begins with text preprocessing—transforming raw text into a format that computers can digest and learn from.

Text Preprocessing

How do we convert mountains of text data into a format the computer likes? Glad you asked. There are many text preprocessing steps, each of which serves a specific purpose. Let's take a look at them one by one.

First, a large body of text needs to be broken into individual words. Just as you'd never stuff an entire bowl of food into a toddler's mouth,[2] you can't stuff an entire document, or worse, an entire corpus, into a computer. *Tokenization* breaks text into individual words or subwords—the basic units our computer will learn to understand. Each of these units is called a token. While this might sound straightforward, language throws us plenty of curveballs. Should "isn't" be one token or two ("is" and "n't")? What about compound words like "dataset" versus "data set"? Or emoji sequences that convey meaning?

Modern tokenization systems handle these challenges differently depending on the task at hand. Some might break words into even smaller pieces, called subwords. These allow the system to better handle new or uncommon words by recognizing familiar parts within them. Think about how you might understand a word you've never seen before by recognizing parts of it. If you encountered "ungooglable" for the first time, you'd probably understand it by breaking it down into "un-," "google," and "-able"—each part contributing to its meaning. This is similar to how subword tokenization works.

Tokenization also needs to be smart about context. The period in "Dr." is different from the period in "The end." Numbers introduce their own complexity—should "2,000" be one token or three? What about dates, web addresses, or hashtags? The choices we make in tokenization can significantly impact how well our AI system understands the nuances of language.

Now that we have our text broken down into manageable pieces, we face another challenge. The same word might appear in different forms throughout a text—"HELLO," "Hello," and "hello" are identical to us but look completely different to a computer. This leads us to our next crucial step.

Converting everything to lowercase removes these surface-level variations, helping our computer focus on meaning rather than format. However, this seemingly straightforward step requires careful consideration about what types of words the corpus contains. For example, "Polish" refers to something or someone from Poland. Without capitalization, the same word, "polish," refers to making something smooth or shiny.

A document usually has many frequently occurring words with very little meaning. These are called stop words. You know, words like—at, the, of, and so on. These words occur so often that the computer can think they're hugely important when the reverse is true. Thus, we remove these words from the data.

It's important to be careful to retain some words like wouldn't, shouldn't, and so on. These words are beneficial for tasks like sentiment analysis, where the goal is to understand the sentiment of the text. For example, if someone says, "I wouldn't watch that movie again," we want to retain "wouldn't" since it conveys much of the meaning.

After removing stop words, we remove punctuation marks since they, too, don't add much value like most stop words.

Like reducing a sauce to its essence, we can distill words to their core meaning through either *Stemming or Lemmatization*. Stemming just truncates the words down to their base form. For example, words like "running," "runner," and "runs" could all be stemmed down to the root word "run." Doing this lets the computer understand that these seemingly different words are just variations of the same idea.

Lemmatization is a more sophisticated approach when compared to stemming. Here, the words are reduced to their root form, called a lemma. This process is usually done according to the word's dictionary definition. Thus, it considers the word's context, part of speech, and the grammatical relations within the sentence. So, unlike stemming, which just chops off inflections, lemmatization takes a more sensible approach. For our example above, the word "ran" would just be stemmed to "ran," but would be lemmatized to "run." Lemmatization is computationally more complex than stemming but is more accurate. So, it's usually better for systems that require high precision (Figure 5.1).

The art of preprocessing lies in choosing the right combination of steps for your specific needs. In other words, not all of these preprocessing steps are necessary for every problem. As always with anything in

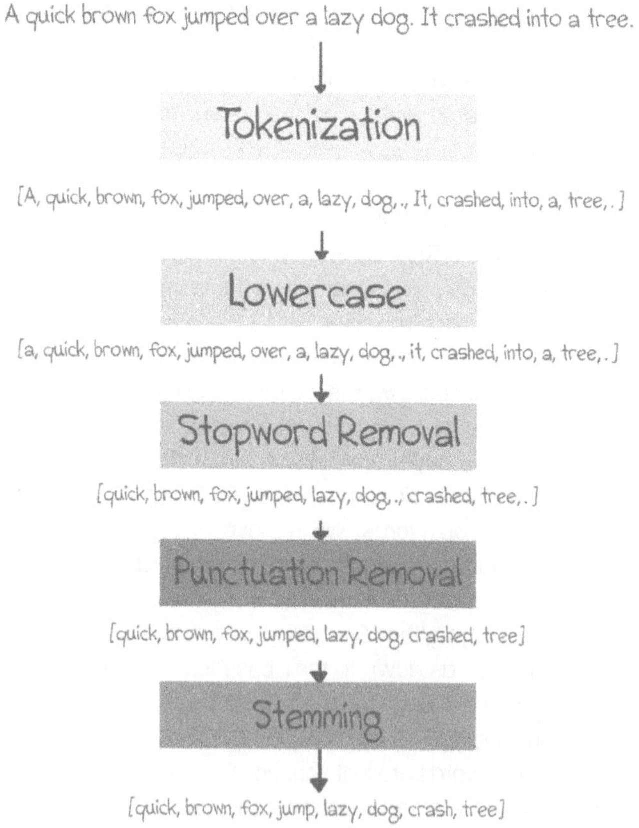

A quick brown fox jumped over a lazy dog. It crashed into a tree.

↓

Tokenization

[A, quick, brown, fox, jumped, over, a, lazy, dog, ., It, crashed, into, a, tree, .]

↓

Lowercase

[a, quick, brown, fox, jumped, over, a, lazy, dog, ., it, crashed, into, a, tree, .]

↓

Stopword Removal

[quick, brown, fox, jumped, lazy, dog, ., crashed, tree, .]

↓

Punctuation Removal

[quick, brown, fox, jumped, lazy, dog, crashed, tree]

↓

Stemming

↓

[quick, brown, fox, jump, lazy, dog, crash, tree]

Figure 5.1. An overview of text preprocessing. Note that not all steps are needed.

machine learning, the correct answer is, "It depends." When in doubt about whether to use a particular preprocessing step, give it a go and see if it helps the model learn better. There are also other preprocessing steps I've left out, like handling n-grams, which I encourage you to explore. In the next section, we'll explore how computers learn patterns from this carefully prepared text, leading us toward more sophisticated language understanding.

Words as Numbers: The Evolution of Language Representation

Early researchers tackling machine language understanding faced a fundamental challenge: how do you capture the meaning of words using just numbers? Their journey to solve this problem reveals how our understanding of language representation has evolved over time. Let's explore some key approaches.

Random Assignment

The most straightforward approach to converting words into numbers is to just assign a number to each word in the dictionary and be done with it. We could, but the results suck. The simple reason is that you don't get any context if you randomly assign numbers to words. It's an arbitrary assignment. For example, look at the two sentences below. They use similar words, but the ordering of the words changes the meaning. Computers can't get that context or capture the relationship between words from random numbers. They also can't appreciate how the order of the words in a sentence affects the meaning (Figure 5.2).

Bag of Words

As the name implies, this approach is relatively straightforward. It treats the document as a bag containing a bunch of words. This approach doesn't care for grammar or word order but keeps track of how frequently each word occurs in the document. The more frequently a word appears, the more important it is. Remember when we removed

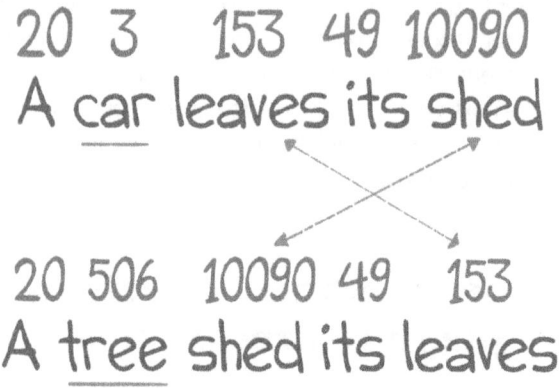

Figure 5.2. Randomly assigned numbers don't carry context information which the model can use.

stop words from the document? This is why. Stop words would be considered supremely important in the bag of words approach. For instance, in analyzing restaurant reviews, words like delicious, terrible, or expensive might appear frequently, giving us a rough idea of sentiment. However, we lose crucial nuance as both "not terrible" and "terrible" would be treated similarly. Why? Word order is ignored. This approach is like taking the attendance of words sitting in a classroom—you care about how often they show up. However, like random assignment, this approach also fails to capture context and ignores word order.

Term Frequency-Inverse Document Frequency

Term Frequency-Inverse Document Frequency or TF-IDF builds on the concept of the Bag of Words technique. The term frequency (TF) represents how frequently a word occurs, just like the approach used in the bag of words. The inverse document frequency (IDF) diminishes the weight of words that occur very frequently across documents and increases the weight of rare words. Imagine analyzing news articles where words like "said" appear frequently but carry little unique meaning, while terms like "cryptocurrency" or "pandemic" might appear less often but are more informative. TF-IDF helps highlight these distinctive terms. However, TF-IDF also suffers from limitations similar to those of the bag of words method. Further, some infrequent words that are actually noise might be given higher importance.

One-Hot Encoding

Imagine creating a massive grid where each word gets its own column. For any given word, we place a 1 in its column and 0s everywhere else. This gives each word a unique digital fingerprint, called a one-hot encoding. To one-hot encode a word, we simply create a vector of all zeros as long as the number of words in our vocabulary. The vector for a word has zeros everywhere except at the index corresponding to that word (Figure 5.3).

In the example above, we have four words in our input sentence and five in the vocabulary. Thus, the length of each vector is five. The encoding for each word has a "1" at the index corresponding to that word. To encode a sentence, we can concatenate the one-hot representations of each word.

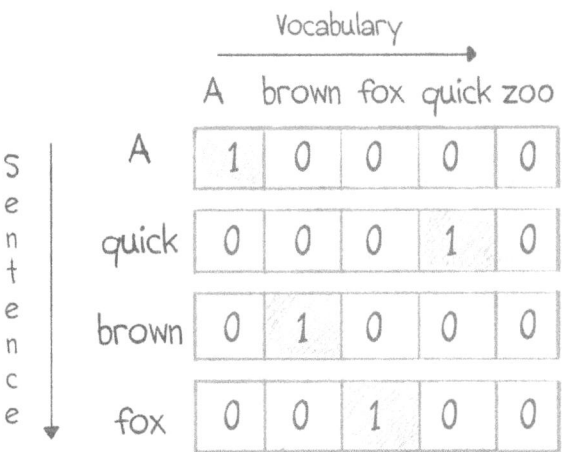

Figure 5.3. How one-hot encoding works for the sentence "A quick brown fox."

However, this approach has two significant limitations. First, each time we add a new word to the vocabulary, we need to increase the length of the vectors and redo the encoding process. This is tedious and wastes a lot of memory since the one-hot representation is sparse (99.9 percent of the values in a one-hot vector are zero!). Imagine that your vocabulary has 100,000 words. Each word would need a vector with 99,999 zeros and a single one! Now, what if you need to add a new word to the vocabulary? You'd have to redo the encoding all over again, which is tedious. Second, one-hot encoding doesn't place similar words closer together. "King" and "queen" are represented as differently as "king" and "bicycle." Therefore, we are deprived of context!

So what's the solution?

Embeddings: Teaching Computers to Understand Context

Unlike one-hot encoding that treats "king" and "bicycle" as mathematically equal, what if we could represent words in a way that captures their meaning, relationships, and context? This is exactly what embeddings achieve.

Embeddings are vectors too, but unlike one-hot vectors, they are dense and packed with information. In fact, these vectors contain floating point numbers that are learned, not assigned!

This approach solves three critical problems we encountered earlier. Since embeddings are learned, we don't need to design them by hand. This reduces tedium significantly. Also, we don't need to change the length of the vectors each time we ingest a new set of words into the vocabulary. So, the vectors can be of a fixed length, which is far more scalable than the one-hot approach. Finally, these vectors are learned by feeding machine learning models tons and tons of data. They see where a given word appears in various sentences and with which other words. Thus, these models see words in context.

Let's dive into this a bit more.

What's in a Word?

To learn embeddings, we take a large corpus of text and train a model to predict something based on that text. Imagine teaching a computer to read millions of books, articles, and websites, paying attention to which words appear together and how they're used. We could ask it to guess the most likely words that can surround a given word in a sentence or guess a word given its surrounding words. This is exactly how Google trained their famous Word2Vec (Word to Vector) model[3] way back in 2013. While we trick the model into thinking it's learning to solve a prediction task, the real gold is in the model's weights (trainable parameters).

During training, something remarkable happens. The model discovers patterns in how words relate to each other, automatically organizing them in a mathematical space. Words with similar meanings or usage patterns naturally cluster together, while unrelated words drift apart. Amazing, right?

What Do Embeddings Look Like?

Recall that embeddings are just vectors of floating point numbers. Imagine a vast multidimensional space where each word is represented by a point. We can pull out some graph paper and visualize these points on the graph. During training, the model tweaks the individual numbers in each vector so that points corresponding to two contextually dissimilar words are pulled far away from each other. Similarly, points that correspond to contextually similar words are pushed together. That's literally it!

But what is the connection between the numbers in each vector and the similarity or context between words? These numbers are measures of various attributes. For example, if we looked at the word ball, it would score high on the roundness attribute but low on the height attribute. Likewise, a cake would score high on sweetness but low on strength. Each number (attribute) in a vector is tweaked so that collective values in the vector represent the word. This allows the model to push and pull words based on their similarity. The critical thing to note here is that we don't tell the model what these attributes are. Instead, it learns the best attributes from the data we provide (Figure 5.4).

This might sound really complicated. So let's take a simple example to understand this better. Let's say that we trained a model on all the fictional work that exists in the world. Consider the world's most famous detective, Sherlock Holmes. He would appear close to Dr. John Watson

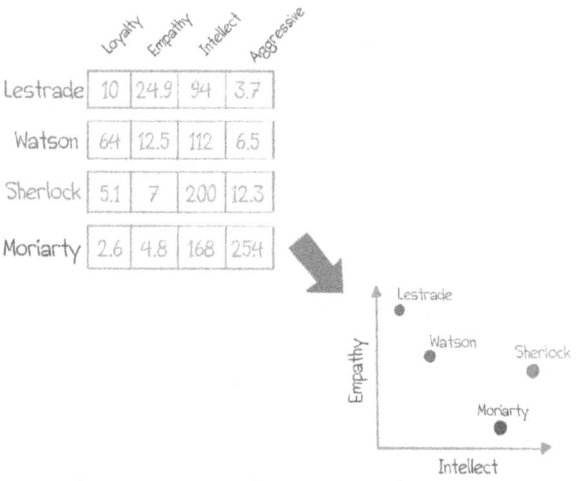

Figure 5.4. We can plot embeddings like points on a graph.

in embedding space since they frequently appear together in the series, share similar attributes, and so on. However, Sherlock would be far, far away from the embedding of a sponge that lives under the sea and wears pants.

But embeddings don't stop at just putting frequently co-occurring words closer together. They can also learn characteristics (provided the corpus is large enough). The embeddings for words representing qualities and traits like clever, power, kind, evil, and so on, also appear in context. That's the real magic of embeddings.

This rich representation enables fascinating applications. You can use embeddings to spot oddballs from a list of items. For example, if you had a list of words including "good," "bad," "red," and "amazing," embeddings can help identify "red" as the odd one out in the list because it represents a color rather than a quality judgment.

Word Similarity and Arithmetic

The next question we need to answer is how exactly do we measure how "close" or "similar" two words are in this embedding space? To understand how we measure similarity between words, we need to think about these points in a slightly different way. Each word-point can be connected to the origin (0,0) in the graph by drawing a line. These lines are actually our word vectors. Picture them as arrows pointing in different directions. The direction of these arrows is crucial. Words with similar meanings will have arrows pointing in similar directions, while unrelated words will point in different directions.

Like in a compass, if two arrows are pointing in nearly the same direction (like North and North-Northeast), the words are similar. If they're pointing in very different directions (like North and West), the words are dissimilar. The angle between these arrows gives us a mathematical way to measure this similarity.

Dust off your high school math textbook and turn to the chapter on trigonometry. The cosine of an angle is the ratio of the adjacent side of a right-angled triangle to its hypotenuse. The cosine of 0 degrees is 1. The cosine of 90 degrees is 0.

I agree. On face value, this definition is absolutely useless to you. But, it turns out that the cosine can be used to measure the similarity between two vectors. Here's how. The keen-eyed observer that you are, you would have immediately noticed that the cosine of an angle decreases as the angle increases.

Thus, for similar word vectors pointing in the same direction, the cosine value of this angle will be high. Conversely, if two word vectors are dissimilar, the angle between them will be larger, and the cosine value will be smaller. This measure is called the cosine similarity metric. Look at this example in Figure 5.5:

Sherlock and Watson both share similar characteristics and thus will have a smaller angle between them. This would lead to a higher cosine value. However, if we compare the words Sherlock and sea sponge, they'll have a larger angle between them and, thus, a lower cosine value.

Perhaps the most fascinating aspect of word embeddings is their ability to perform "word arithmetic." For example, the words king, man, queen, and woman will appear clustered together in the embedding space. Thus the arithmetic operation "king − man + woman" yields the result "queen." This isn't just a mathematical trick but reveals how embeddings have captured meaningful relationships between concepts. The same logic would also yield "Paris − France + Italy = Rome," "warm − cold + dark = bright," or "uncle − man + woman = aunt."

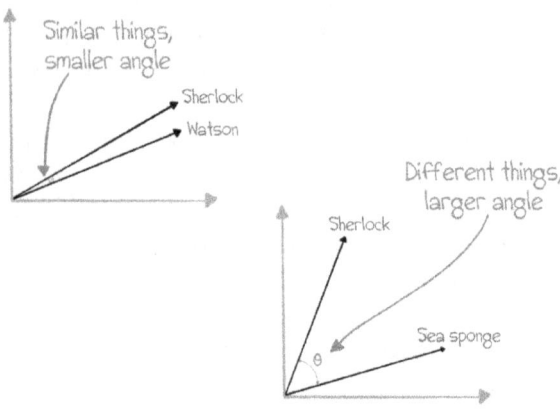

Figure 5.5. Similar minds think alike. Similar embeddings point alike.

Where Are Embeddings Used?

While understanding how embeddings work is fascinating, their true power becomes apparent in real-world applications. Embeddings power countless technologies we use daily. While we've discussed how text gets converted to embeddings above, you can create embeddings for just about anything—music, images, categories, and much more. Let's explore some key applications:

- *Modern Search Engines and AI Assistants*: You'll be hard-pressed to find any language model that doesn't use embeddings in some way. These models power search whether you are searching for things, searching within documents, searching for your favorite song, image-based search, and so on. They also power chatbots like ChatGPT.
- *Creative AI Systems*: These models take prompts from people and produce sophisticated imagery. So how do they know what to do from cryptic prompts? They understand our queries using a bunch of embeddings (both text and image) under the hood to make it possible.

- *E-commerce and Music Streaming*: Recommendation systems that power Amazon's online store or Spotify also use embeddings. Let's say you love to listen to Eurodance. You'd probably also listen to Pop and Techno music. How does your favorite streaming service find this out? Every user has an embedding associated with them. That means you have one too! This embedding is updated based on the songs you listen to. The service might use this to put you next to other users who listen to similar music. It also has another embedding table with embeddings for each song, and similar songs are closer together. Using these pieces of information, it can recommend new songs for you.

There are many other uses of embeddings that I've not listed above. They are like Swiss army knives, versatile and powerful.

We now have a way to feed text to computers. But while embeddings give us a powerful way to represent individual words, human language is more than just a collection of isolated words. We communicate in sequences: sentences, paragraphs, and documents. How do we help computers understand not just words, but their order and relationships? This brings us to our next topic, namely sequence models, where we'll explore how computers learn to process and understand text as it flows naturally.

Sequence Models

Imagine reading a book backward, sentence by sentence. Even with perfect understanding of each individual sentence, the story would make little sense. This is because language derives meaning not just from words, but from their sequence—their order and relationships. Whether it's understanding a story, following instructions, or engaging in conversation, sequence is crucial.

Let's explore this with a practical example. Suppose we want to build a topic identifier. Such a system can read text and classify it as fiction, news, sports, and so on. While our word embeddings help the computer understand individual words like "touchdown," "quarterback," or "field goal," it needs to process these words in sequence to confidently identify the topic as sports.

So how do we build models that can handle sequences? Let's explore our options, starting with the simplest approach.

The most straightforward approach might seem to be feeding our word embeddings into a standard dense neural network.[4] Ok, that's great. After all, these networks have proven powerful for many tasks. But there's a fundamental problem.

Take the very first linear layer of our dense model. It, and every linear layer, for that matter, expect fixed-sized inputs. That means that the length of the sentences it receives has to be of a fixed size! This creates an immediate challenge. In real-world text, sentences naturally vary in length. An article might start with "Breaking news!" followed by "The unprecedented development in quantum computing this afternoon has scientists worldwide reconsidering their approach to cryptography." So, how do you feed sentences of varying lengths to a dense model?

We're forced to either pad shorter sentences with meaningless filler words to reach the required length or cut off longer sentences, potentially losing crucial information.

Neither approach is great and leads to poor performance. It's like trying to fit every book into the same number of pages. You'd either have blank pages at the end of short stories or incomplete endings in longer novels.

Why don't we feed the network input one word at a time if that is an issue? That way, we can avoid padding or truncation. Your head's in the right place, but this won't work either. The model will treat each word independently, devoid of context from other words. In fact, we can switch up the order of the words, and it wouldn't notice. In short, it has no way to connect one word with another.

This fundamental limitation leads us to an important realization: we need models specifically designed to handle sequences. We need models that can process words in order while maintaining their relationships.

Recurrent Neural Networks

Recurrent Neural Networks (RNNs) were specifically designed to handle sequential data—whether it's text, stock prices, weather patterns, or any information where order matters. What makes them special?

RNNs take inputs one by one in order. This has two benefits. First, the issue with fixed input sizes goes out the window—words go in one at a time. Second, the words go into the RNN as they appear in the sentence. Thus the context that comes from relative word order is preserved. But their real power comes from their memory mechanism—a feedback loop that connects one step to the next. This allows them to use previously computed results to help process current inputs.

Think of an RNN like someone reading a book: they process one word at a time, and their understanding of each new word is influenced by what they've read before. The RNN first processes each word it receives and produces two things: an output and a hidden state. The hidden state captures what the RNN has seen so far. When the following word needs to be processed, the RNN combines the hidden state with this input to produce the next output (and updated hidden state). The hidden state acts like a note-taker, keeping track of important information as the network reads through the text (Figure 5.6).

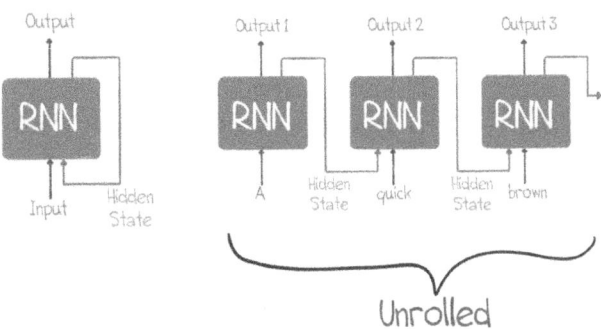

Figure 5.6. An RNN unrolled. Note that it isn't multiple copies of the same network. It's the same network processing each word of the sentence one at a time.

In the diagram above, we can see what the RNN looks like. However, the feedback loop might be a bit confusing. That's why we show an RNN unrolled over time to illustrate how the hidden state is passed on to help understand the next input better. While it looks like multiple networks, it's actually the same RNN being used repeatedly. The RNN uses the same set of weights for all the words in the text. The unrolling merely shows how the process works over different time steps.

If RNNs are really good, why don't we see them used for a lot of NLP applications? One of the crucial limitations of RNNs is that they're very forgetful. If we have a really long sentence, the RNN forgets what was said at the start of the sentence by the time it ends. Imagine reading "The small dog that my sister, who lives in Paris with her husband and three kids in a beautiful apartment near the Eiffel Tower, adopted last summer . . . is actually a cat." By the time an RNN reaches "is actually a cat," it has forgotten that we started talking about a dog!

Another critical limitation of RNNs is that they suffer from twin issues called the Vanishing/Exploding Gradient problem. Remember how neural networks learn by adjusting their weights based on error gradients? The gradients that work their way back during backpropagation from a particularly long sequence would either diminish (and thereby vanish) or compound significantly and be extremely large.

The former is called vanishing gradients. Over a long sequence of updates, the gradient values diminish further until they are insignificant. This results in no updates to the weights of the network. In essence, it doesn't learn anything. It's like trying to whisper a message through a hundred people. By the time it reaches the last person, the message is lost.

The latter is called exploding gradients, where the updates are so huge that they destabilize the network altogether. Exploding gradients can occur when one or more weights or inputs are large. During backpropagation, the gradients accumulate rapidly and make the weight updates oscillate significantly. It's like a game of telephone where each person shouts the message louder than the last. By the end, it's just noise.

Both these issues are bad news. How do we fix them?

Improving Memory

Researchers developed two new architectures to overcome these limitations: Long Short-Term Memory (LSTM) units and Gated Recurrent Units (GRU). LSTM units revolutionized sequence processing by solving the core problem: selective memory. Unlike RNNs that struggle to remember, LSTMs can actively choose what to remember and what to forget.

Let's envision the LSTM as having two parallel conveyor belts: one for long-term memory and one for short-term memory.

The long-term memory belt holds onto the critical details from earlier parts of the text, acting like a quality control unit that keeps only the most relevant information. As the words in the sentence progress, this conveyor belt decides whether to keep or discard information based on its relevance.

The short-term memory belt, on the other hand, deals with the most recently seen words. It constantly updates as new words arrive and old ones are processed, similar to how we listen and process conversations in real-time.

This dual-memory system is controlled by a sophisticated gating mechanism. The LSTM uses three types of gates: the input gate, the forget gate, and the output gate. Like security checkpoints, they control the flow of information from one step in the sequence to the next.

Here's how each gate functions:

- *Input Gate*: This gate determines which new information should be stored in the cell state (long-term memory).
- *Forget Gate*: This gate decides which memories should be discarded from the cell state.
- *Output Gate*: This gate controls how much of the stored information is used to influence the current hidden state (short-term memory).

Thus, LSTMs can decide what to remember and what to forget, making them more efficient at understanding the context in long sequences (Figure 5.7).

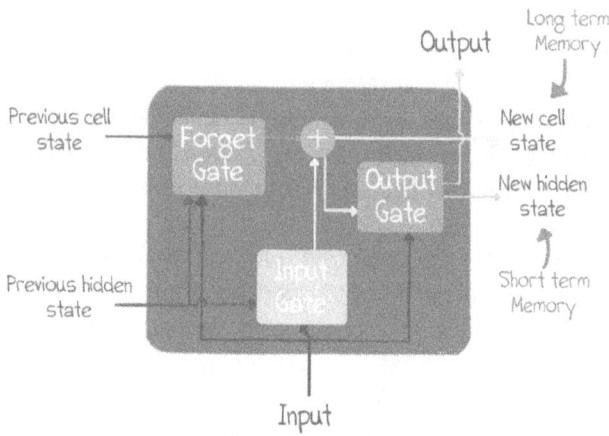

Figure 5.7. One does not simply enter the gates of an LSTM.

GRUs are a simplified version of LSTMs that are comparable in most tasks. They merge the input and forget gates into a single "update gate" and operate without a separate cell state, making them less complex but equally capable in many tasks.

These enhancements enable LSTMs and GRUs to overcome the memory issue that plagues RNNs, significantly mitigating the vanishing gradient problem. However, they aren't without limitations themselves.

Limitations

These improved networks still suffer from exploding gradients. Also, since they process information sequentially, one word at a time, computation within these units cannot be parallelized. Thus, they are slow to train and use.

This would be a very small chapter if there weren't a solution to these issues. So where do we go from here? Are there models that can process text faster, remember longer sequences, and overcome other limitations of RNNs, LSTMs, and GRUs?

Well, that's where we're headed next. The answer lies in a revolutionary architecture that would transform not just language processing, but the entire field of artificial intelligence: Transformers.

Chapter Summary

How do we teach machines to understand language like humans do? We explored this fascinating challenge in this chapter, revealing how modern AI processes everything from simple sentences to complex documents.

We started with the basics: preparing text for computers. Just as a chef preps ingredients before cooking, we process text through essential steps: breaking it into meaningful pieces (tokenization), standardizing its format, and removing unnecessary elements. This careful preparation ensures our AI models can focus on what truly matters in the text.

Understanding language isn't just about recognizing words. It's about grasping their meaning and relationships. This led us to embeddings, a breakthrough that allows computers to see words not as arbitrary symbols, but as rich, interconnected concepts. Through embeddings, computers can understand that king and queen are more closely related than king and bicycle, capturing subtle relationships that make language meaningful.

Yet real language flows in sequences, and just understanding individual words isn't enough. Traditional neural networks proved inadequate here. They either needed all sentences to be the same length (imagine forcing every book to have the same number of pages!) or lost the connections between words. RNNs offered a solution by processing text more naturally, word by word, maintaining context as they go.

When basic RNNs proved forgetful over longer sequences, we turned our attention to their more sophisticated cousins, LSTMs and GRUs. These architectures brought human-like selective memory to the table. They could remember important details while forgetting irrelevant ones, much like how we remember the plot of a movie but not every single scene.

These advances revolutionized how machines process language, but they weren't perfect. The sequential nature of these models made them slow, and they still struggled with very long texts. These limitations set the stage for our next exploration: the rise of the Transformers—models that would fundamentally change how AI understands language.

Chapter 6
Transformers and Large Language Models

Before 2017, if someone mentioned Transformers, you'd probably think of shape-shifting robots or electrical equipment. Today, these AI models power everything from ChatGPT's responses to scientific discoveries in drug development. But what makes them so special?

Picture yourself in a conversation where someone says, "I love it!" Your brain instantly searches for what "it" refers to. Was it a movie just mentioned? A restaurant? A book? You don't process the conversation word by word from the beginning. Instead, you naturally connect "it" to the relevant subject being discussed. This ability to make immediate connections between words and their meanings, regardless of how far apart they are in a conversation, is what makes human language understanding so powerful.

AI models like RNNs that we saw in the previous chapter worked more like someone reading a scroll in ancient times. They had to process information strictly in order, word after word, maintaining a mental chain of what came before. This approach had two major problems: memory and speed.

For example, consider these sentences—"The animal didn't cross the road because it was too tired" and "The animal didn't cross the road because it was too wide."

In these simple sentences lies a complex challenge. One word changes, and the meaning shifts dramatically. When you read them, your brain instantly knows whether "it" refers to the animal or the road.

You make this connection effortlessly because you can consider all the words simultaneously and understand their relationships. RNNs, however, would struggle. By the time they reach "it," they've already processed the earlier words in sequence, making it harder to maintain and interpret these relationships.

This limitation became even more apparent with longer texts. Imagine listening to a very long story over a phone call with poor reception. You might catch every word, but if the story is too long, you'll start forgetting important details from the beginning. The longer the story continues, the harder it becomes to maintain those crucial early details that might be essential for understanding later parts. This is the problem that RNNs struggle with.

The Power of Paying More Attention

To address these limitations, researchers developed the concept of "attention," a mechanism that would fundamentally change how AI processes language. Imagine having a perfect transcript of that phone call, where you can instantly check any part of the conversation whenever needed. That's what attention mechanisms provided—the ability to reference and connect any part of the text, regardless of how far apart they might be.

But while attention helped RNNs better understand context, these models had a second problem. They were slow. RNNs processed text like an assembly line. They processed words one by one waiting to understand each word before moving to the next. In an era where AI needs to process billions of words across hundreds of languages in seconds, this sequential approach created a massive bottleneck.

The Transformer architecture solved this by introducing parallel processing. Instead of one worker on the assembly line, imagine having hundreds working simultaneously, each focusing on different parts of the text but able to instantly share insights with each other. What started as a solution to process text more efficiently soon sparked a revolution in artificial intelligence.

Looking Inside Transformers

In 2017, researchers from Google published a paper titled "Attention Is All You Need,"[1] and the Transformer architecture was born. True to the paper's name, this architecture showed that focusing on the right parts of a sentence was the key to understanding language.

The original Transformer excelled at tasks where it needed to convert one sequence of information into another. Such a model is known as a sequence-to-sequence model. One type of sequence goes in, another comes out. For example, translating English to French, or understanding a question to generate an answer. What makes them special is their ability to handle inputs and outputs of different lengths naturally. Think about translating "I am hungry" to "J'ai faim." Different lengths, same meaning, and yet the Transformer can handle this effortlessly.

At its core, a Transformer has two main components: an encoder that understands the input and a decoder that generates the output. The encoder is like an expert reader who analyzes and understands a text deeply, while the decoder is like a skilled writer who takes that understanding and crafts the appropriate response. Both components rely heavily on attention mechanisms, which empowers them to focus on relevant parts of the text while processing it (Figure 6.1).

But what do the encoder and decoder look like? How do they work together? How does text flow through the Transformer? Let's look at the answers to each of these questions one by one.

The Encoder

The encoder isn't a single giant monolith. It consists of several smaller encoder blocks. Each encoder block is identical in design but helps extract rich context from the input. In the original Transformer, both the encoder and decoder had six blocks each. This number is arbitrary, and modern Transformer models have significantly more of these blocks (Figure 6.2).

In each encoder block, the input flows through several layers. But, before these blocks begin their work, the input text needs to be prepared. This happens through two crucial layers:

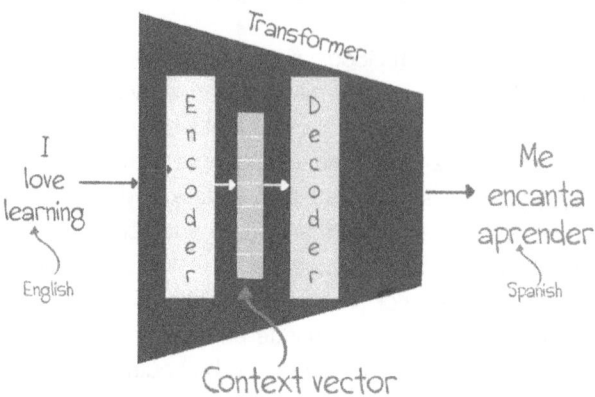

Figure 6.1. Looking inside the Transformer black box.

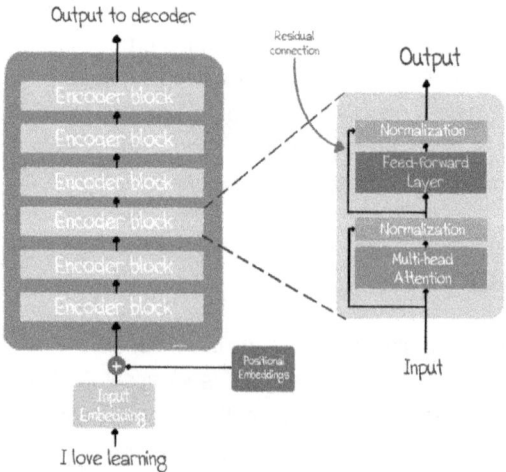

Figure 6.2. A closer look at the encoder.

Input Embeddings

We've already covered embeddings in detail, so I'll keep this brief. Given a word, we preprocess it as before (remember tokenization?) and feed it to the embedding layer. This layer converts it into a vector of numbers that capture the meaning of the word. The embeddings themselves are learned and refined during the training process.

Positional Encoding

Unlike RNNs that process words one after another, Transformers look at all words simultaneously. Therefore, they don't know the order of the words in the sentence. This creates a challenge. How does the model know that "The dog bit the man" means something very different from "The man bit the dog"? The positional encoding layer "encodes" this information, allowing the Transformer to learn the position of each word and where it lies relative to other words in the sentence. There are different types of positional encodings in the literature, but it's sufficient to know this layer adds special markers to each word's numerical representation, telling the Transformer exactly where that word appears in the sentence.

These preparation steps happen only once at the start. So, both input and positional embedding layers are present only before the very first encoder block. Every subsequent encoder block receives the output of the previous encoder block directly.

Self-Attention: The Heart of the Transformer

So far, we've seen how the Transformer converts words to numbers and maps their positions in a sentence. With our words represented as numbers and their positions encoded, we now come to the most crucial part of the Transformer. Attention layers allow the Transformer to map each word in the input to every other word to learn relationships. Don't be intimidated by all the fancy terms in the diagram. Let's break each one down piece by piece.

Self-attention measures how much focus a word should put on other words in the sentence. To motivate this, let's return to the sentences we saw earlier. This mechanism teaches the Transformer to focus on the word "animal" in the sentence, "The animal didn't cross the road because it was too tired" and on "road" in the sentence, "The animal didn't cross the road because it was too wide."

So, how is self-attention computed? There are a bunch of steps involved, so hold on to your seats. We'll first look at the steps themselves and then at the intuition behind them.

Ready? Let's begin.

Every time a word enters the self-attention mechanism, three things happen. First, the word's numerical representation is transformed into three different versions: a query (Q), a key (K), and a value (V). Think of these as three different perspectives of the same word, each serving a specific purpose. These transformations happen through three sets of learnable weights, called the query, key, and value weights, respectively. This is like having three different lenses to look at the same word.

Ok, so we have these three new representations. Now what?

The query version of each word interacts with the key version of every word (including itself) to produce attention scores.[2] This score determines how much focus to place on other words in the sentence for a given word. That is, it helps determine which other words in the sentence are most contextually relevant for the current word being processed.

Good. We now scale the score by a constant so that its value is under check. This is more to stabilize the training process.

After this, we normalize the score using a softmax function so that each score is positive and the sum of the scores of all the words in the sentence adds up to 1 (like in probability). Recall the softmax layer from Chapter 4. The one that we used to output probability scores from our neural network? This is the very same one.

Finally, these percentages determine how much of each word's value version contributes to the final representation. Thus, words which are "more relevant" will contribute more to the final representation (Figure 6.3).

Intuitively, this keeps the words we want to focus on and diminishes the importance of all the irrelevant ones. The higher the attention value, the more the importance.

To drive this point home even further, here's an analogy. Imagine you have a file cabinet containing dossiers of different animals. Let's say these animals are the elephant, lion, rhinoceros, hippo, chipmunk,

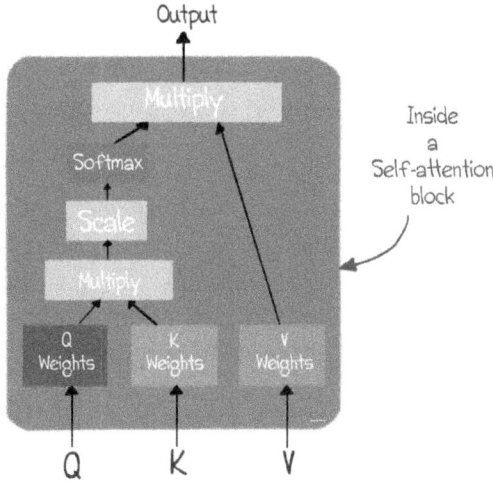

Figure 6.3. How is self-attention calculated?

platypus, and whale. If I ask you to find information on African mammals, you'll retrieve the elephant, lion, rhino, and hippo and keep the rest where they are. Here, the query is "African mammal." The keys are the animals. The values are the contents of the dossier. The attention score measures how much the contents of each dossier contribute to the final result, which in this case primarily consists of African mammal photographs (yay!).

Multi-head Attention

A single self-attention layer is powerful by itself. But imagine many self-attention layers working together to understand the text. How powerful would that be? This many-headed layer is called multi-headed attention and is what the Transformer uses.

Why is this useful?

Think about how you understand language. When you read a sentence, you simultaneously process multiple aspects like grammar, context, tone, relationships between words, and so on. Multi-head attention works similarly. Each attention head can focus on different aspects of the text.

How does this work? Remember our three transformations—query, key, and value? In multi-head attention, each head has its own set of weights to create these transformations. During training, these weights evolve differently for each head, allowing them to specialize in capturing different patterns.

For example, one head might learn to focus on adjacent words, helping with phrases like "New York." Another might learn to connect related words even when they're far apart, like matching pronouns ("she," "her") with the person they refer to. Yet another might focus on punctuation and sentence structure. When combined, these different perspectives give the Transformer a rich understanding of the text (Figure 6.4).

Let's quickly look at the remaining parts of the Transformer encoder.

Residual Connections and Normalization Layers

Residual or skip connections (borrowed from computer vision) and the layer normalization layers ("normalization" in the encoder diagram) improve training stability and prevent the vanishing gradient issue we

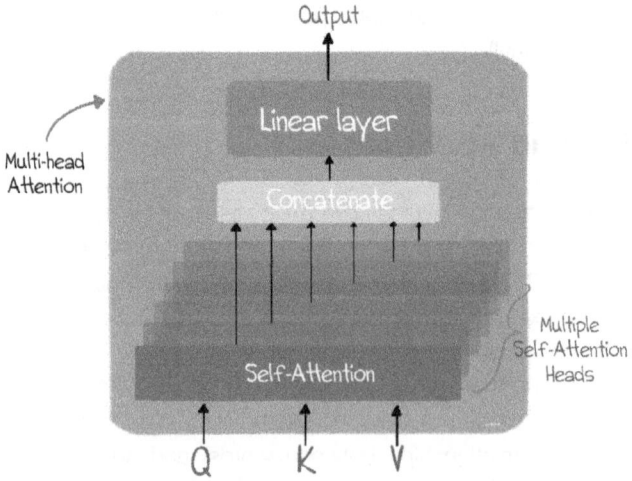

Figure 6.4. Many heads are better than one.

saw earlier. Layer normalization also speeds up training. These layers ensure that no important information is lost.

Feed-Forward Layers

Recall the linear layers we saw in Chapter 4. Yep. Same idea. These are the final processing stages in each encoder block. They take the combined output from all attention heads and transform it further, helping the model build a complex understanding from the attention patterns.

The Decoder

Like its counterpart, the decoder consists of several identical blocks, each containing self-attention and feed-forward layers. The decoder takes the previous outputs as inputs and an additional input from the encoder. Like in the encoder, these inputs initially go through the input embedding and positional embedding layers. While similar to the encoder in many ways, the decoder has a unique responsibility: it must take the encoder's understanding of the input sentence and generate meaningful output, one word at a time.

Before diving into how it works, let's understand what makes the decoder special. Imagine that our Transformer is translating a sentence from English to French. The encoder has already understood the English sentence. Now the decoder needs to (a) keep track of what it has already generated in French, (b) use the encoder's understanding of the English sentence, and (c) figure out what French word should come next. To help it in this arduous task, it has two special features.

First, the decoder has a new type of layer called the "encoder-decoder" or "cross" attention. This layer allows the decoder to focus on relevant parts of the original input while generating each output word. Specifically, the encoder's output provides the key and value vectors for this attention mechanism, while the query vectors come from the decoder's self-attention layer. This way, at each step, the decoder can reference back to the original input while considering what it has generated so far.

Second, the decoder's self-attention layers are masked. That is, its self-attention layers can only look at words it has already generated in the output. Think about it. When you're writing a sentence, you can refer to words you've already written, but you can't peek at words you haven't thought of yet! This is why this layer is called "masked" self-attention. They mask out words that come after the current word, preventing the decoder from looking at them. Besides, looking into the future would be cheating and, more importantly, would defeat the purpose of these models (Figure 6.5).

One More Linear Layer

The decoder's output is still in the form of numbers. We need to convert these back into words. For this, the decoder is connected to a linear layer followed by a softmax layer. The linear layer maps the decoder's output to a vector where each entry is the size of our vocabulary.[3]

The softmax layer generates a probability score for each one of these entries. In other words, it calculates the probability of how likely each word is to be the next word in the output. The word in the vocabulary corresponding to the entry with the highest probability score is selected as the result.[4] This process repeats until the decoder generates a special "end" token or the output reaches a maximum length.

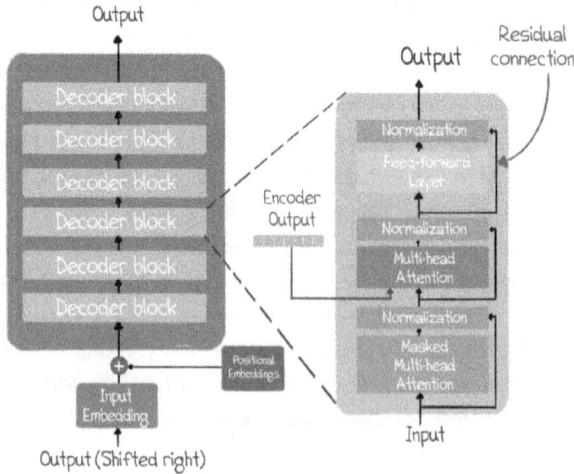

Figure 6.5. A closer look at the decoder.

For example, when translating "The cat sat" to French, the decoder might do the following. First, it might generate "Le." Then, looking at "Le" and the encoder's understanding of "The cat sat," it generates "chat." Finally, looking at "Le chat" and the encoder's understanding, it generates "s'assit."

Training the Transformer

So that's what the Transformer looks like under the hood. How is it trained? We've seen how the input in one language goes through the encoder. The encoder digests the input and converts it to a form the decoder understands. The decoder then uses this to predict the output in another language. To train the Transformer, we need to simply compare what the decoder predicts with the actual translation during training! That's it.

The loss function compares the decoder's predicted word to the actual word (from the ground truth translation). It computes the difference between the two, and this difference is used to update the weights of the model using backpropagation. Now, you might be wondering how you compute the difference between two words.

Great question! The output of the softmax layer is a probability distribution, right? Each word is assigned a probability score that tells us how likely that word is the result. We also have a probability distribution for the actual translation. The probability of the correct next word is one, while the probability score for all other words is 0.[5]

By comparing these two probability distributions, we can measure exactly how far off the model's predictions were. Through this process, the Transformer gradually improves its predictions. The weights in both the encoder and decoder are updated to minimize the difference between predicted and actual translations.

Speed Boost

Unlike RNNs, Transformers can process all the words in a sentence at the same time. The self-attention mechanism just computes a weighted sum of all the input tokens (words). The computation for each token can be done independently and in parallel. Since they primarily consist of attention layers, Transformers are incredibly parallelizable. Thus, they run blazing fast compared to traditional sequence-to-sequence models while delivering top-notch performance.

We've now grasped how the Transformer works and its advantages. But this isn't the end of the story. Once the Transformer was introduced, researchers quickly realized that these models became dramatically more capable as they grew larger. This discovery led to an explosion of increasingly powerful Transformer models, each bigger than the last.

These humongous models are what we now know as large language models. But what makes these models large? What made them so effective for various tasks within NLP and beyond? Do they work differently? Let's find out!

Large Language Models

Large language models, or LLMs, are called so because they have billions of parameters.[6] Remember, parameters are the model's knowledge-storing connections. Just as your brain forms new neural connections when learning, these parameters capture patterns during training, from simple word associations to complex logical relationships. The fascinating part isn't just the amount of information these models can store, but how this massive scale leads to emergent abilities.

Emergence refers to capabilities that weren't explicitly trained for but arise naturally as models grow larger. For instance, while a model with 100 million parameters might struggle with basic arithmetic, models with billions of parameters can solve complex math problems, understand analogies, and even demonstrate basic logical reasoning. Generally, doubling the model's size doesn't just double its capabilities—it can lead to entirely new ones.

But why is size so important? Imagine exploring a vast library. Think of a small model having access to a single shelf, allowing you to look up specific facts. A medium-sized model might have access to several sections, enabling you to make connections between different topics. But a large model is like having a master librarian who not only knows every book but understands the relationships between all the information they contain. In the case of these language models, size does seem to matter.

Perhaps the most remarkable capability of large language models is their ability to learn new tasks from just a few examples. We call this few-shot learning. Where smaller models might need thousands of examples to learn a new task, LLMs can often understand and perform new tasks after seeing just a handful of examples. Thus, as these models grow in size, so do their abilities and the way they can use stored information.

The Types of LLMs

We've seen why LLMs are large. But do all LLMs have the same underlying architecture? Is it only their size that has changed? Nope. As researchers experimented with these large models, they discovered that different architectural choices led to different strengths. Today's LLMs come in three main flavors.

Encoder Based

These types of models use only the encoder from the original Transformer. They are also called auto-encoding Transformer models. Think of them as expert readers and analysts. BERT[7] (Bidirectional Encoder Representations for Transformers) is an example of this category. The self-attention layers within these models can look at all parts of the input, just like the encoder from the original Transformer. As these models are trained in a way that helps them understand entire bodies of text, they are particularly good at analyzing sentiment in product reviews, classifying documents by topic or category, finding answers within text passages, and understanding the relationships between different pieces of text.

Decoder Based

As the name implies, these models only use the decoder from the original Transformer. They are also called auto-regressive Transformer models. The GPT (Generative Pretrained Transformer) family of models belongs to this category. They're like skilled writers who excel at generating coherent text. Their unique ability to build text one word at a time makes them exceptional at writing creative stories and articles, completing partial code snippets, generating natural dialogue, crafting emails and business documents.

Encoder-Decoder Based

These models have both the encoder and decoder and are also called sequence-to-sequence Transformer models. T5 (Text-To-Text Transfer Transformer)[8] and BART (Bidirectional and Auto-Regressive Transformer) are examples of this class. They're like expert translators, not just between languages, but between different forms of text. They shine at tasks like converting complex text into simple explanations, summarizing long documents, translating between languages, and answering questions with detailed explanations.

This specialization has led to an ecosystem of LLMs, each optimized for different purposes. Some focus on coding, others on scientific research, and still others on creative writing. Yet they all share one common trait—the ability to process and work with language in ways that continue to surprise and impress.

Training an LLM

All of this is well and good. But these models are enormous. Naturally, the training process must be complicated, right? Despite their vast capabilities, these models learn through a surprisingly simple process. Predicting what's missing in a sentence.

But if these training methods sound straightforward, why operate at such a humongous scale? These models require billions of parameters and enormous datasets for a reason. Human language is incredibly nuanced and complex. To capture the full depth of meaning, context, and knowledge in language, we need systems of matching complexity.

Let's look at the training process in depth, which happens in two distinct stages.[9]

Pretraining

In the pretraining stage, the goal is to teach the model the semantics, structure, and grammar of language by showing it millions of examples.

Think of all the text on Wikipedia, books, articles, and websites—that's the scale we're talking about. Pretraining is the longest and most computationally expensive part of the learning process. It requires petabyte-scale datasets and loads of computation power. To put this in perspective, if you printed out a petabyte of text, it would fill roughly 20 million filing cabinets.

During pretraining, which can take months even on powerful computers, models process this massive amount of text using different learning strategies. Each strategy offers a unique way to help the model grasp language. Let's look at three common approaches. A model is repeatedly shown examples from these datasets and eventually learns the rules. So, how does it learn? (Figure 6.6)

Depending on the type of model, pretraining can be done in a number of different ways. Here are a few common ones.

Auto-regressive Language Modeling

Look at these sentences. What comes instead of blank? (a) The chef carefully chopped the fresh "blank." (b) After the storm, a rainbow appeared in the "blank." (c) The pianist performed "blank."

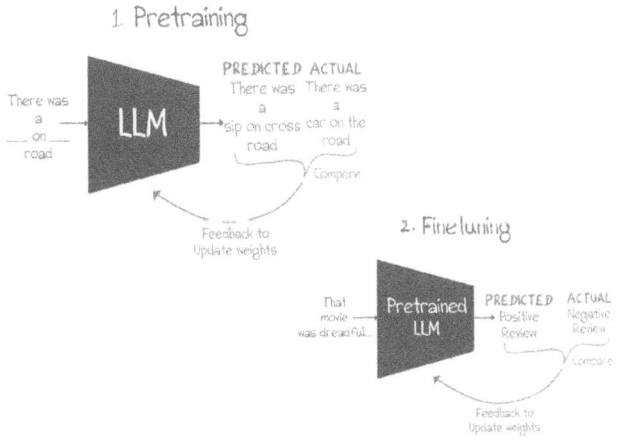

Figure 6.6. The two stages of training an LLM: pretraining and fine-tuning.

This is one way decoder-based models like GPT are pretrained. Given a partial sentence, they predict the next word, then the next, and so on. Even though complete sentences exist in the training data, we only show the model text up to the word it needs to predict. This prevents the model from "peeking ahead" at the answer.

Masked Language Modeling

Let's try that exercise again with a twist. Can you complete the sentences here? (a) The cat "blank" on the "blank" mat. (b) The "blank" building "blank" tall windows. (c) Scientists "blank" a new "blank" in the rainforest.

This is called masked language modeling. Here, we randomly blank out words in a sentence and have the model guess what they might be. Unlike the previous approach, the model can see the full sentence with blanks, allowing it to use context from both directions. Models like BERT are pretrained this way.

Next Sentence Prediction

Does the second sentence in these examples follow the first sentence? (a) I love baking cookies. The sweet smell fills the kitchen. (b) The car won't start. Penguins live in Antarctica. (c) She opened the book. The pages were yellowed with age.

In this exercise, the model learns to recognize if two sentences logically connect or are randomly paired. This helps the model understand broader context and relationships between ideas.

These three approaches represent just a few ways models learn to understand language during pretraining. What makes this process remarkable is that the models learn entirely from the text itself, without any human-provided labels or answers. When a model predicts a missing word or decides if sentences are connected, it already knows the correct answer because it's right there in the original text. This ability to learn from the data itself makes the training process incredibly efficient at scale.

After pretraining, we end up with what researchers call a "foundation model." These models are like a highly educated undergraduate student who has read extensively but hasn't yet specialized in any particular field. However, having developed a broad understanding of language and knowledge, they can be adapted to many different tasks. Let's look at that next.

Fine-Tuning and Instruction Tuning

There are two main approaches to transform these foundation models into practical tools, each with its own strengths.

In fine-tuning, we take our foundation model and teach it to perform specific tasks by showing it targeted examples. For instance, to create a model that can detect the emotional tone of text, we might show it thousands of examples of tweets or reviews paired with their sentiment—positive, negative, or neutral. For question-answering, we would present it with many examples of questions and their correct answers. Through fine-tuning, models learn to apply their broad knowledge to specific tasks.

However, researchers discovered that fine-tuned models, while skilled at specific tasks, often struggled to understand what users wanted them to do in everyday interactions. This led to the development of instruction tuning, a crucial advancement in making language models more practical and user-friendly.

Instead of training for specific tasks, here, models learn to understand and follow natural instructions. They train on diverse examples of instructions and their appropriate responses. When someone asks "Explain this concept simply" or "Write this as a formal email," instruction-tuned models understand not just the words but the intent behind these requests. This approach maintains the model's broad capabilities while making it more practical and user-friendly.

Fine-tuning and instruction tuning transform a foundation model into one that can not only perform specific tasks but also understand and respond to a wide range of user needs. These approaches are particularly attractive because they require much less data than pretraining. But this raises a crucial question: Where does all this training data for pretraining come from?

Datasets for Pretraining an LLM

Modern language models are trained on an unprecedented scale of human knowledge. In the pretraining phase, these models are trained on billions of books, articles, websites, research papers, and code repositories. In other words, much of humanity's documented knowledge. That's another reason why they are large by design. A model needs massive capacity to capture and store the patterns, relationships, and knowledge contained in such vast datasets. Smaller models simply don't have enough parameters to effectively learn from this scale of information.

In the fine-tuning and instruction tuning phase, smaller in-house datasets relevant to your application are used. So, if you wanted to train a model to review customer feedback, you'd have a small dataset of reviews to fine-tune the model. Similarly, instruction tuning uses carefully crafted instruction-response pairs. The critical point here is that these fine-tuning datasets are several orders of magnitude smaller than the pretraining datasets. While pretraining might use hundreds of billions of tokens, fine-tuning might only need thousands of examples.

Limitations

LLMs have some limitations, though. First, only a few well-funded organizations can train these models since they require substantial computational resources (with costs often running into millions of dollars). Second, they have significant environmental impacts since the energy it takes to train these models amounts to several years of electricity consumption for an average household.

Even though these models can perform many tasks, they do not "understand" the tasks or the text in the same way a human does. Their responses are based on patterns they've learned during training not on actual understanding. This can lead to responses that appear confident but contain subtle inaccuracies or contradictions.

Moreover, as LLMs are trained on data from the internet, they can unknowingly absorb and perpetuate biases present in that data. They might also inadvertently learn and propagate toxic or harmful content. This is particularly challenging because these biases can be subtle and deeply embedded in the training data.

These models can struggle when faced with scenarios or information that differs significantly from their training examples. For instance, they might confidently make up answers rather than admitting uncertainty.

Ensuring that these models consistently generate appropriate and safe content remains a significant challenge.

Lastly, given how proficient these models are at generating human-like text, they could be exploited to spread disinformation, a significant concern that needs addressing. Researchers worldwide are currently working on finding solutions to these issues.

Despite these challenges, LLMs represent a significant advancement in NLP, opening new possibilities while also demonstrating the complex power of AI. But as we scale and enhance these systems, it's crucial to tackle their ethical, computational, and environmental challenges.

Such advances will bring us closer to AI systems that not only excel in performance but also align with human values and societal needs.

Next, with all this context on LLMs, let's look at a particularly interesting breakthrough in training LLMs with human feedback and how this has led to a new wave of intelligent assistants.

Learning from Human Feedback

While pretraining and fine-tuning give language models impressive capabilities, researchers noticed a crucial gap: these models didn't consistently generate helpful, truthful, or safe responses. A model might be technically correct but rude, or friendly but prone to making things up.

Traditional training approaches couldn't reliably prevent these issues. This led researchers to ask if we could teach models to better align with human preferences. The solution emerged through a combination of careful supervision and a novel feedback mechanism.

Using a combination of supervised fine-tuning and a technique called Reinforcement Learning with Human Feedback (RLHF), researchers could train models that showed remarkable improvements at being more truthful, more helpful, and better at understanding what users actually wanted. While supervised fine-tuning teaches models basic conversational abilities, RLHF helps them understand and align with human preferences.

This training process represented a fundamental shift in how we teach AI systems. Rather than simply showing examples and hoping the model learns desired behaviors, we actively guide its learning through human feedback. During RLHF, human evaluators regularly review the model's outputs, rating responses based on their quality, truthfulness, and helpfulness. These ratings help the model understand what makes a response truly valuable to humans.

To understand how this works, we need to examine three distinct stages: supervised fine-tuning, which establishes basic capabilities, followed by the two components of RLHF—reward modeling and reinforcement learning. Let's look at each of these steps in detail.

Supervised Fine-Tuning

The first stage in making language models more aligned with human preferences begins with supervised fine-tuning. Starting with a pretrained model, we teach it the basics of helpful interaction through carefully crafted examples.

Unlike traditional fine-tuning that focuses on specific tasks, this stage uses examples of complete conversations that demonstrate ideal model behavior. These conversations cover a wide range of scenarios—from answering questions and explaining concepts to handling complex requests.

Skilled AI trainers generate these examples by creating both sides of each conversation. They carefully craft user requests and model responses that demonstrate key qualities like helpfulness, accuracy, safety, and clarity. Using thousands of two-sided prompt response combinations, they fine-tune the model to respond as if they were responding to questions themselves. This encourages the model to emulate these desired behaviors. Once this process has completed, we have a foundation for the next stages of training.

Reward Modeling

Having human evaluators review every response isn't practical at scale. This is where reward modeling comes in.

In this stage, we first generate multiple responses to various prompts using our fine-tuned model. Human evaluators then compare these responses, ranking them from most to least preferred based on criteria like accuracy, helpfulness, and safety. For example, given a complex question, evaluators might prefer responses that are both accurate and easy to understand over those that are technically correct but confusing.

These rankings create a specialized dataset that captures human preferences about what makes responses good or bad. This dataset is used to train a new model called the reward model. It learns to predict how humans would rate any given response, that is, it learns to evaluate responses much like a human would.

This model serves a crucial function. It provides immediate, automated feedback about the quality of responses. While it's not perfect, it can reliably estimate how helpful or appropriate a response might be to humans. This automated evaluation becomes essential for the final stage of training.

Reinforcement Learning

The final stage uses reinforcement learning to systematically improve the base language model's responses. Using a technique called Proximal Policy Optimization (PPO),[10] the language model learns to generate responses that would receive high ratings from the separate reward model we created earlier.

Here's how it works: When given a prompt, our language model generates multiple possible responses. The reward model then evaluates each response, providing higher scores for those that align with human preferences. Based on these scores, the language model learns to adjust its behavior to generate better responses. This creates a feedback loop. With each iteration, the language model gets better at generating responses that the reward model (and by extension, humans) would rate highly. Since the reward model was trained on actual human evaluations, this process helps align the language model's outputs with human preferences.

However, this process needs careful tuning. If pushed too hard to maximize rewards, language models might learn to game the system by finding responses that get high scores from the reward model without actually being helpful. This is why researchers carefully balance the pursuit of high rewards with other training objectives. Additionally, over-optimization and feedback loops make this system finicky and challenging to train (Figure 6.7).

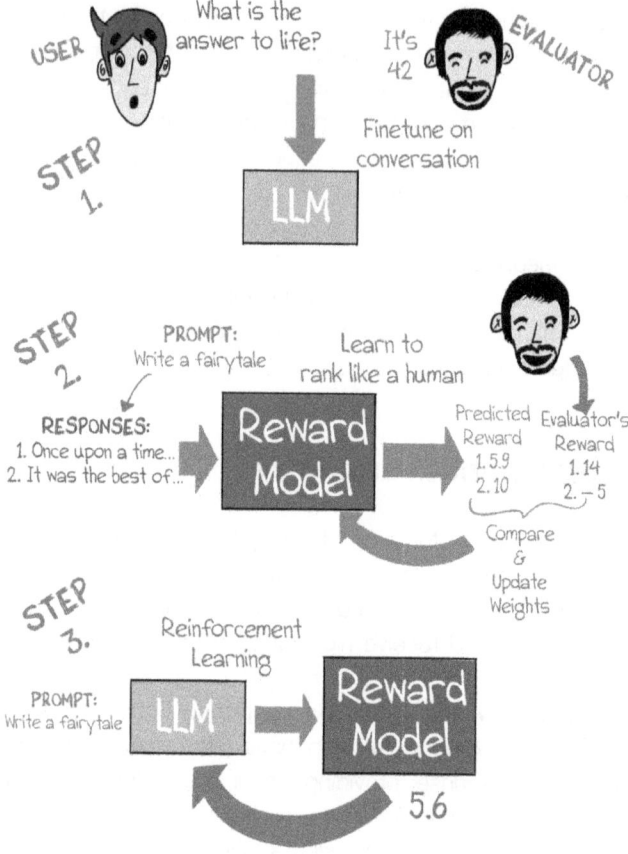

Figure 6.7. An overview of RLHF. Who knew humans in the loop would do a world of good?

Despite these challenges, RLHF-based training has dramatically improved LLMs' capabilities, leading to systems like ChatGPT. While RLHF was groundbreaking, researchers have since developed other approaches to align language models with human preferences. Methods like Direct Preference Optimization (DPO) and Reinforcement Learning with AI Feedback (RLAIF) have shown promising results. However, exploring these techniques in depth is beyond the scope of our discussion.

As these models learn and improve from human feedback, they are evolving AI into an even more powerful tool and enriching human-computer interaction.

A Timeline of LLMs

The field of large language models continues to grow, with new models emerging regularly. While we can't cover every model,[11] we can trace the key milestones that have shaped this technology.

Since the Transformer's introduction in 2017, we've seen steady innovation. The first generation emerged in 2018, when BERT and GPT-1 demonstrated the architecture's potential with 340M and 117M parameters respectively. GPT-2 followed in 2019, advancing text generation capabilities with 1.5B parameters.

GPT-3 marked a turning point in 2020, using 175B parameters to enable few-shot learning. That same year, Google's T5 (11B parameters) showed strong performance across multiple tasks. The year 2021 brought Google's PaLM (540B parameters) and AI21's Jurassic-1 (178B parameters), along with Codex, a GPT-3 variant for code generation.

ChatGPT's release in 2022 demonstrated how RLHF could make these models more useful, followed by Meta's open-source OPT (175B parameters) and Google's PaLM 2. Innovation continued in 2023 with GPT-4's multimodal capabilities, Anthropic's Claude, Meta's Llama 2 (7B-70B parameters), and Mistral's efficient 7B model. In 2024, Google's Gemini series, Anthropic's Claude 3 variants, and GPT-4 Turbo pushed boundaries further in reasoning and efficiency.

So, where is the field headed?

Recent trends point to several directions. Models are becoming more efficient. For example, Mistral showed that better architecture can achieve strong results with fewer parameters, making AI more accessible and sustainable. Specialized models are becoming important. Rather than building general-purpose models, we're seeing more focus on specific domains like scientific research, coding, and creative writing, leading to better performance in these areas.

The focus on safety and reliability continues to grow. Techniques like constitutional AI and improved alignment methods are creating models that are more trustworthy and consistent, shaping how future models are designed.

We're also seeing signs of more sophisticated reasoning capabilities. Future developments might help bridge the gap between pattern recognition and problem-solving, advancing areas like mathematical proofs and scientific discovery. These trends suggest a future where AI systems are not just more capable, but also more efficient, specialized, and reliable—qualities needed for meaningful impact in real-world applications.

We've explored how AI processes language. Next, we'll examine how AI learns to see and understand the visual world.

Chapter Summary

In this chapter, we explored how the Transformer architecture revolutionized language processing in AI. The Transformer's attention mechanism enables efficient processing of long sequences by allowing each word to directly interact with every other word. We examined its key components: the encoder-decoder structure, self-attention mechanism, and supporting elements like residual connections and normalization layers, seeing how they work together in tasks like machine translation.

We then investigated LLMs, which built upon the Transformer to achieve unprecedented capabilities in understanding and generating text. These models learn through pretraining on vast amounts of text, followed by either fine-tuning for specific tasks or instruction tuning for better alignment with human needs. While larger models have shown impressive abilities in few-shot learning and complex reasoning, they also raise concerns about computational costs, environmental impact, and accessibility.

We also covered how these models are made more helpful and reliable through careful training. We explored traditional fine-tuning approaches and the breakthrough technique of RLHF. RLHF uses human preferences to guide model behavior, though it comes with challenges like reward gaming. Recent developments show a shift toward more efficient architectures and specialized models, suggesting a future where AI systems balance capability with responsibility.

Looking at the field's evolution from the first Transformer models to current systems like GPT-4, Claude, and Gemini, we saw how rapid innovation has made these models more capable, efficient, and aligned with human values. However, significant challenges remain in ensuring these systems are truthful, safe, and beneficial to society.

Chapter 7
Machine Vision

In 2012, a neural network called AlexNet achieved remarkable accuracy in identifying objects in images, sparking a revolution in visual understanding. Today, AI systems can spot tumors in medical scans, guide self-driving cars through busy streets, and even help restore old family photos. But teaching machines to see was far from straightforward.

At first glance, you might think computers would be naturals at processing visual information. After all, they can create stunningly realistic images in modern video games and movies. This field, known as computer graphics, works because we give computers precise instructions: the shape of a coffee cup, the texture of its surface, and the direction of light falling on it. Using this information, computers render these descriptions into realistic images.

But what about the reverse problem: given only an image, can a computer understand everything in the scene? Can it identify objects, their relationships, lighting conditions, and depth? This turns out to be surprisingly challenging. When you look at a photograph of a beach, you instantly grasp the whole scene. You see the waves rolling onto the sand, seabirds wheeling overhead, and people walking along the shore. Your brain effortlessly separates foreground from background, understands depth and perspective, and recognizes objects even when they're partially hidden or in unusual positions. For computers, however, an image is just a grid of numbers, with no inherent understanding that certain patterns represent waves, birds, or people.

This challenge of teaching machines to understand visual information by working backward from images to meaning is called computer vision.

Computer vision is the study of how computers see and understand the world. This problem is particularly challenging because images are flattened representations of the world. We see in 3D. When we take pictures, we lose depth and scale in the process. For example, when you take a selfie in front of a mountain, it suddenly looks smaller and closer than it feels in real life. Imagine being a computer and making sense of it based on this diluted 2D representation.

Over the past few decades, researchers have made tremendous progress in developing algorithms to help computers perceive the world from visual information.

While traditional hand-crafted computer vision algorithms have been used for most use cases in the past, deep learning has pushed the boundaries of what is possible.

Before we look at these modern algorithms, let's get a sense of how a computer receives visual information.

Images

When we look at images, we see blobs of color, lines, and textures that we can synthesize into objects and scenes. On the other hand, computers just see a stream of numbers without any context.

Yes, images are just two-dimensional grids of numbers.

To understand images, computers must learn to extract meaningful information (called features) from these numbers. Then, using this information, they must build representations of the world.

Thus, numbers are used to represent visual information, and computers manipulate these numbers to understand the world.

Pixels

So, if an image is just a grid of numbers, what do these numbers represent? Every point on an image grid is called a pixel. A pixel is the abbreviated form of the two words "picture element." Every pixel has a number associated with it. This number represents the color of that pixel.

Grayscale Images

Let's start simple. Think of a black-and-white image (a.k.a. grayscale images). You know, the pictures from movies like *Citizen Kane* or *Casablanca*? Each pixel in such an image is associated with a single number that ranges from 0, representing black, to 255, representing white. All values in between these two represent various shades of gray (Figure 7.1).

Brighter regions in the image have a higher pixel value and vice-versa. So a pixel with the value 200 is brighter than a pixel with the value 20 (Figure 7.2).

Grayscale images have a single channel or component. Why? Each pixel in a grayscale image only needs one value to describe its color (intensity or brightness, to be more specific).

So, naturally, the next question is, how do you represent other colors?

Figure 7.1. The range of grayscale intensities. Black is 0, while white is 255. Everything in between are shades of gray.

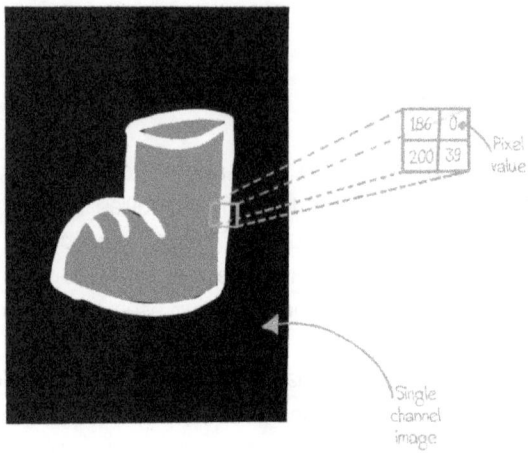

Figure 7.2. An image is just a collection of numbers.

Color Images

Unlike grayscale images, color images typically have three components—red, green, and blue. Colors are represented as a combination of red, green, and blue values. Any color can be produced by combining a specific amount of red, green, and blue. Each of these components is called a color channel.

Each channel in a color image is like a grayscale image when viewed alone, so the same rules apply. Each of these channels has pixels whose values range from 0 to 255.

Thus, a color image is simply three grayscale channels stacked on top of each other (Figure 7.3).

Thus, instead of having a single value representing a colored pixel, a set of three values (R, G, B) is used. So, a black pixel is represented as (0, 0, 0), and a white pixel is represented as (255, 255, 255).

From a computational perspective, mapping colors to grids of numbers makes it easy to process and manipulate images.

Thus, manipulating and extracting features from images boils down to mathematical computations on these numbers.

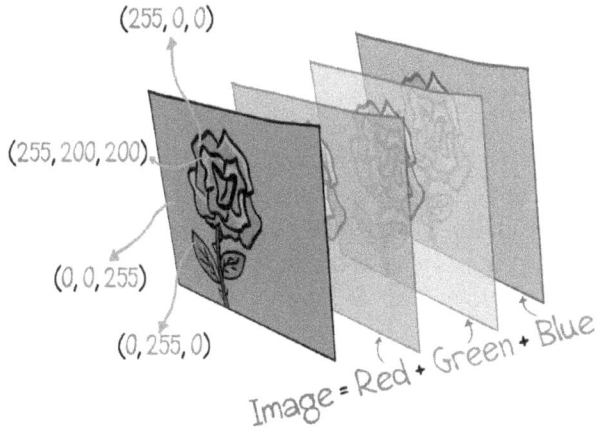

Figure 7.3. Every color image usually has three channels: red, green, and blue.

The Fundamental Problems of Vision

As humans, we're constantly scanning our surroundings for survival and safety. For the vast majority of this endeavor, we use three fundamental skills. First, we recognize both familiar and unfamiliar objects. Then, we locate these objects. Where are they? How far are they from us? For example, if we see a juicy red apple on the table, excellent. Time for a quick snack. If the same apple levitates in the air, we try to make sense of why that delicious fruit is flying. Sometimes, objects of interest might be hidden in plain sight. Think of a TV remote that is nestled between couch cushions or a leopard camouflaged in the bushes. Identifying the exact boundaries of the object becomes critical, doesn't it? You'll need to identify the boundaries and shape of the remote so that you can pick it up. For that matter, you'll need to identify where the bush ends and where the leopard's shape begins instantly. In order to help computers perceive images, we need to teach them these three skills which are called Image Classification, Object Detection, and Image Segmentation.

- *Image classification*: Guessing what objects are in an image.
- *Object detection*: Where are objects in an image?
- *Image segmentation*: Identifying and labeling objects in an image in minute detail to understand their shapes.

In real life, machines already use a combination of these skills for a variety of use cases. Think of self-driving cars or how your phone unlocks itself by looking at your face. While there are other skills machines can learn, these are the most essential ones. So let's jump right into how we can teach computers to accurately guess which objects are present in an image.

Image Classification

As the name suggests, image classification is the task where a model is trained to recognize the dominant object in an image. It's the process of teaching a computer to look at a picture and say, "That's a dog" or "That's a car."

In image classification, the model simply focuses on whether a particular object exists in an image or not. It doesn't care where it is in the image, how many occurrences of the object exist in the image, and so on. Here are the common types of image classification problems:

- *Binary Classification*: This is the simplest type of image classification. There are only two possible answers for a given image. Either the object exists in the image or it doesn't. For example, if we want our model to recognize images of dogs, we could have two categories: "Dog" and "Not Dog." Think of it like a light switch: it can be ON (Dog) or OFF (Not Dog).
- *Multiclass Classification*: This extends the previous problem to multiple categories. Here, each image can belong to one of many categories. For example, an image could be classified as a "Dog," "Orc," or "Car." This is like a multiple-choice question on a quiz. Each question has several options, but only one is the correct answer. It's up to the model to guess the correct class.[1]

- *Multilabel Classification*: Sometimes, an image can have more than one type of object. For example, an image might have a dog, a cat, and a cow.[2] We might want our model to identify all three animals in that situation. A nice way to visualize this is thinking of labels as hashtags on a social media post. A single post can be tagged with several relevant topics.

We've seen the definition of image classification. But we need more than definitions to get us far. We need to understand how an image classifier works. So let's pick a real-world application where these models are used. How about photo tagging?

Photo Tagging

Most modern smartphones and social media platforms have this feature built-in. Whenever we take a picture using our phone's camera or upload one as a post to social media, we get asked if we'd like to tag the picture. What's impressive is that sometimes, these applications ask us if the picture is of a specific person or pet. How do these applications know who is in these pictures without us telling them? How do they "tag" images? Let's find out!

What Does the Photo Tagger Do?

Let's assume for a second that the photo tagging application is a black box. Tell me, what goes into this black box? Images. What comes out? A tag or identification of who is in that image. So, you'd give this application a picture of your great uncle Algie, and it would return "Algie" as the result. Provided it's seen him before. If not, it will look puzzled and ask you who this is.

So far, so good.

What does this black box need to do to achieve this result? For starters, it needs to be able to ingest the numbers (pixels) from the image. Then, it needs to recognize colors, shapes, edges, and textures from the pixels and use these to build more abstract patterns like "bald head" or "walrus mustache." Finally, it needs to guess which person or pet has patterns like this.

Sounds straightforward enough. So, how do we teach it to recognize features from the image? We train it with labeled data.

Training Our Photo Tagger

First, we'll need to collect a dataset. The dataset should consist of pairs of images and labels for these images. The images will belong to all those friends, family, and furry companions whom we need the model to recognize. These labels will be the category or class of the object in the image. In the case of photo tagging, this would be the name of the person or pet that the photo is of.

You might have already guessed it, but this is an example of supervised learning. We give the image to the model. We ask it to guess who is in the image. We then compare this guess to the actual label (the name) of the person or pet in the image. We give feedback to the model based on whether it got it right or not. Then, we rinse and repeat this a bunch of times for all the images we have until the model learns to recognize all the people and pets. Standard gradient descent and backpropagation.

Simple right? Not quite.

You need a very large number of labeled images to train the model from scratch. Imagine having to manually label every picture you have as "Uncle Algie," "Evelyn," or "Mocha." But why don't we use transfer learning,[3] you ask? Won't we need fewer labeled images, then? Excellent idea!

After this step, you have a model trained to recognize all the faces you've shown during training. But what if you show this model a picture of someone it hasn't seen before? What happens, then?

Therefore, naively using supervised learning alone won't work.

In practice, these systems are much more complicated. Whenever you show a model a new photo, it does one of two things. It checks to see if it's seen the person or pet before. If so, it asks you if the picture is of that person or pet. You can then let it know if it's guessed correctly or if it's made a mistake. The model will then update itself accordingly and tag the picture properly.

If it's never seen the person or pet in the picture before, it will tell you that too. Once you let it know who the picture is of, it updates its information.

Does this sound familiar? It's semi-supervised learning! Initially, we tell the model who the picture is of a few times. It then uses this information to label new pictures without us having to explicitly tell it. When it can't find a match, it asks us for the label.

So we have an idea of what the tagger does at a high level and how to train it to tag images successfully. Let's now look inside the black box.

Building the Photo Tagger

Most, if not all, modern photo taggers use neural networks under the hood. We've already seen the different building blocks used to build neural networks in Chapter 4. Recall that a neural network is a combination of linear layers and activation layers.

To build our photo tagger, why don't we use the same strategy here?[4] One problem. The linear layer is one-dimensional. Our image, however, is two-dimensional. What do we do? We could unravel the image from a 2D grid to a long sequence of pixels. That would make it one-dimensional and ready for a linear layer to consume (Figure 7.4).

But here's the problem. We lose valuable information if we do this! Why?

Look at any picture, and you'll notice that pixels that are close together are often similar. Let's imagine you're looking at an image of a beautiful landscape on a clear sunny day. If a pixel is blue and is part of the sky in this picture, chances are that the neighboring pixels are

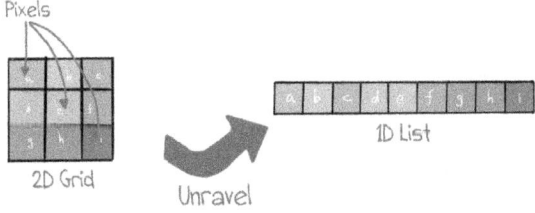

Figure 7.4. Flattening a 2D image grid into a 1D list.

also blue and part of the sky. If a neighboring pixel is different, that's a valuable piece of information. It could indicate a transition point, for example, from the sky to the ground, or it could be an object in the sky like a cloud or a bird. Similarly, neighboring pixels help define the shape of objects in the picture. In fact, we scan pictures from left to right and top to bottom. This allows us to put neighboring regions in context and make sense of the picture.

When we stretch an image out into a long one-dimensional string of pixels, we lose this context.

But that isn't the only problem.

Let's go back to the neural network we're building. For the very first layer of our photo tagging network, we'll need a linear layer that is as long as this string of pixels we just created. So, consider an image that is 100 pixels wide and 100 pixels tall. When we stretch this out to a one-dimensional sequence, it has a length of 10,000 (image width times height). Our first linear layer will need 10,000 input units to process the image and extract features from it.

Doesn't seem too bad. That is until you realize how big images are in real life. The average phone camera these days has a 20-megapixel sensor. The images that it produces have 20 million pixels.[5] Can you imagine stuffing that into a linear layer with 20 million weights? That's for only just the first layer of the network! We'd need to combine several linear layers for our tagger. Each neuron in a linear layer would be connected to every neuron in the next one. Computationally, that would blow up—you'd be waiting for days to get results.

Thus, we need a better way of processing images—a way that preserves 2D spatial information and isn't computationally prohibitive.

Enter convolutions.

Convolutions

Like linear layers, a convolutional layer is another building block used to construct neural networks. This layer consists of a set of 2D grids.[6] Each of these grids, called kernels or filters, is much smaller than the image they operate on. Each value inside a kernel is a weight, just like in the linear layer. These weights are learned by the network during training and help it extract features from an image.

But if the kernels of a convolutional layer are much smaller than the image itself, how do they process the image entirely? Great question! These layers "slide" over the image, starting from the top left of the image all the way over to the bottom right. At every step of this adventure, they extract features from the part of the image that they are superimposed on.

This method is called the sliding window technique.

Imagine you're in a completely dark room. All you have is a flashlight. When you turn on the flashlight and point it at something in the room, a part of the room comes into view. You can only make sense of what you see in this light. Once you have an idea of what you're seeing, you then slide the light across the room to figure out what's there. Each time you do this, you uncover new information about the room. But at no point are you seeing the whole room at once.

How does a convolutional kernel extract features? The part of the image that the kernel is currently superimposed on is called the *window*. The kernel multiplies its weights with the corresponding pixels inside this window. Then, it adds up all these resulting values to compute a final result. Thus, it simply computes the weighted average of the pixels it is currently superimposing. It repeats this process over the entire image (Figure 7.5).

We've seen how a single convolutional filter extracts features from an image with a single channel. In practice, though, images have more than one channel. We also want our convolution layers to extract as much useful information as possible from the image. Thus, a convolutional layer with just one filter won't do much.

Typically, convolutional layers have several filters. There are a few knobs we can tweak to make convolutional layers just the way we'd like them. We can specify the number of filters in a layer, the size of the filters (called kernel size), and also how much the filters slide between computations (called stride).[7]

Each of these filters learns to extract something different from the image. Some of these filters might be sensitive to a certain color, like orange. Others focus on edges or lines at certain angles. Some others might only want to find dots.

Here's the best part. We don't ask these filters[8] to identify these features. We don't even tell them what features to find. They learn to do it themselves over the course of the training process!

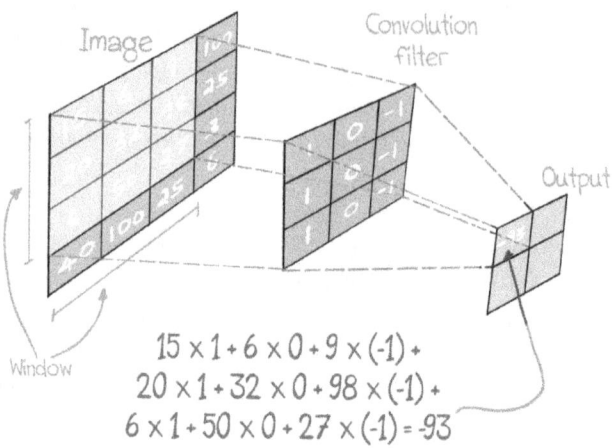

Figure 7.5. A convolution example. Note that the lighter gray window on the image matrix slides to the right after making this calculation to compute the next value.

As we stack more and more convolutional layers together, the latter layers use the features extracted by the earlier layers to identify parts of the object. For example, our photo tagging model might use the edge information from earlier layers to recognize mouths. It might use corners to identify eyes and so on. Eventually, these deeper layers have enough information to make a prediction about who is in the picture. All from just a few additions and multiplications. Mindboggling, isn't it?

So, convolutional layers preserve the 2D structure of images and leverage that information. Awesome. But are they efficient at computing these features? Yes! Convolutional layers only see a part of an image at a time. Regardless of which part of the image they see, they use the same set of filters (and, therefore, weights) to extract features.

This has some awesome advantages. First, we need to store much fewer weights in memory compared to a large linear layer earlier. Yay! This is called weight-sharing and makes convolutions very efficient. Secondly, since they use the same weights everywhere in the image, they can identify a particular type of object regardless of where it appears in the image. A cat is a cat, whether it is up in the sky or on the ground.

As a rule of thumb, we typically increase the number of filters in convolution layers as we go deeper into the network and reduce the size of the image as it progresses through the network. This allows the network to extract more useful information (via more filters) and keep computation costs (smaller image size) in check.

Neural networks that are built up using convolutional layers are called, yep, ding ding ding, Convolutional Neural Networks (CNNs). They are much better for complicated image tasks than just stacking a bunch of linear layers together.

To quickly recap, CNNs preserve the 2D structure of images, reduce the overall computation by significantly reducing the number of weights needed for modeling images, and can identify objects regardless of where they appear in an image.

Before we go back to our photo tagger, there's one more neural network building block that you need to know about.

Pooling Layers

Pooling layers are like trusty sidekicks to convolutional layers. You can almost always find one beside a convolutional layer. Pooling layers serve one simple function. They reduce the size of the image passing through them. This results in reduced computation, fewer overall parameters (reducing overfitting), and better efficiency.

Like convolutional layers, pooling layers also work in a sliding window fashion. They shrink the part of the image that they currently see and then move on to the next part. Pooling layers are categorized by how they shrink the image. There are a few types of pooling layers, but we'll look at two of the most popular types: max pooling and average pooling.

As the name suggests, max pooling retains only the largest value in a window and discards the rest. Average or mean pooling takes the average of all the values in the window and returns that as the result. Most neural networks typically use max pooling (Figure 7.6).

Like convolutional layers, we can specify the size of pooling layers and how much they slide between operations. As we increase the value of both of these, the size of the image reduces proportionally. Unlike convolutions, though, pooling layers don't "learn" anything. They simply take the image and reduce it (either through the max or averaging strategy).

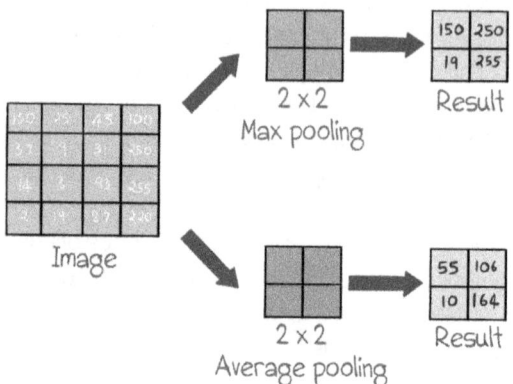

Figure 7.6. The two popular varieties of pooling layers.

Back to the Tagger

With these two new building blocks, we can now build our photo tagging neural network. Now, our images pass through a series of convolutional layers and pooling layers. We still need to use activation layers since they help to learn the complex patterns in the data. As the image moves through our network, the layers extract increasingly complex features. Once we have sufficiently complex features, we can then ask the network to make guesses on who it thinks this image is of.

Our network returns a list of probability scores, one score for each person or pet it has seen so far. We usually pick the one with the highest score as the network's guess. Since we have been working with images so far, we need a way to map the image to a list. This is where we flatten or unravel the image. Since the network already has a great understanding of what it's seen, we can flatten the image into a list without worrying about losing information. Once we flatten the image, we can connect it to a linear layer, which will give us our list of probability scores (Figure 7.7).

Thus, to recap, our network takes an image and extracts features from it. It preserves the 2D structure of the image thanks to the

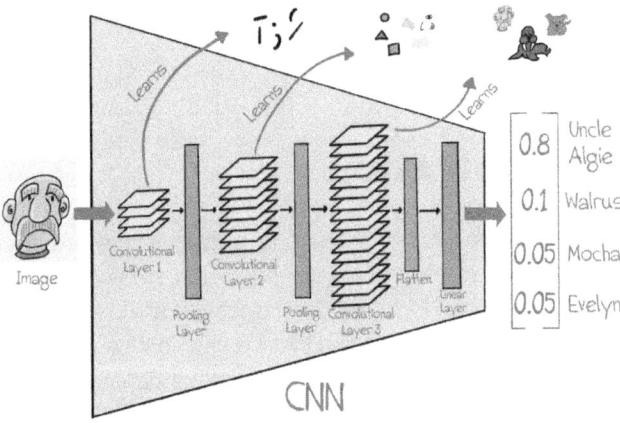

Figure 7.7. Looking inside a convolutional neural network.

convolution and pooling layers. Eventually, it flattens the result into 1D so that it can connect this to a linear layer to give us probability scores. We take the highest probability score as the model's guess.

To evaluate our model, we can use accuracy as a metric. However, that isn't always the best choice, as we've seen in Chapter 2. In the next section, we'll look at some better metrics we can use.

Hopefully, our model recognizes Uncle Algie. I mean, nobody has a walrus mustache like him.

Choosing the Right Architecture

But how do we know how many convolutional layers to use? What should their sizes be? What about the pooling layers? Activation functions? As you can imagine, there are an exponentially large number of options to choose from.

Thankfully, you don't need to be a hero and do this all by yourself.

Researchers have spent years tinkering and tweaking the combinations to find the best image classifiers. Some of the more popular ones include ResNet, SqueezeNet, EfficientNet, and ConvNext.[9] When in doubt, use one of these. In fact, just start with a ResNet (Residual Neural Network). It's ridiculously effective.

Now that we know how models can guess which objects are present in an image, let's explore how they can learn to find where they are in the image.

Object Detection

Have you ever encountered those visual puzzles where you are asked to find an object cleverly camouflaged in the background? Almost everything in the image looks like the object you are searching for. You think you see the object only to find that it is yet more background noise. Animals do this in real life. Whether it's an octopus stalking its prey on the ocean floor or a chameleon on a tree—they make it hard to find them.

To find an object, we scan everything in front of us, carefully trying to match how we remember the object to look—its shape, colors, patterns, and size with what is in front of us.

That's what computers need to do, too. Except, they need a lot more help. For starters, we have a very large bank of "imagery" in our heads which we can use as a reference. This is something each of us has built from our infancy. Unfortunately, a computer doesn't have this context, as all it gets are just streams of numbers. A red and white star to a computer is just the same as a candy cane, a beach towel, or something else that has similar colors. Thus, we need to repeatedly show examples of what a particular object looks like and identify *where* it is in pictures by drawing rectangles around it. These rectangles are meaningfully named bounding boxes—they *contain* the object within them.

Detection Is Challenging

Image classification deals with recognizing "what" an object is. In other words, a classifier doesn't care where the object is. It just cares if it is in the image or not. Object detection, however, deals with both "what" an object is and "where" it is in an image. Not just "where" but "where all" it is (Figure 7.8).

To understand this better, think about an image of flowers (or perhaps choose your favorite animal from the African savanna). Flowers usually

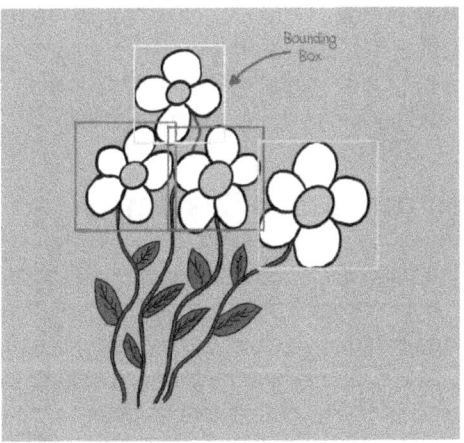

Figure 7.8. What is a bounding box?

occur in bunches, and you'd be hard-pressed to find a single flower waving merrily in the wind.

Let's say you have a detector whose sole purpose of existence is to detect flowers in images. To be good at this gig, it would have to not just detect one flower but all of them. This opens up a can of worms.

What if a flower is partially hidden behind a few others? What if there are flowers of different sizes, some in the foreground and some in the distance? Should it return a single box encapsulating all the flowers or one box per flower? What if it partially detects a flower and returns an incorrect box? What if it returns duplicate boxes for the same flower?

These are just some of the many problems that object detectors face. To successfully train a detector, you'll need labeled data that identifies each object's type and provides a tight bounding box to demarcate its position. Here's the kicker.

Neural networks need a ton of training data, and in the case of object detection, it becomes tough to collect this data. Imagine sitting in a room, drawing rectangles around miscellaneous objects all day and labeling them. Thankfully, some existing datasets, like MS-COCO,[10] can help us.

Object detection has several applications. Surveillance cameras, autofocus in your camera, medical imaging, counting objects in a factory or assembly line, and self-driving cars, to name just a few. So, it's a problem with a lot of commercial value. Let's look at how we might design an object detector for the autofocus application.

Building an Autofocus System

You're out in the park. It's a beautiful summer afternoon. Your dog is running around trying to catch stray frisbees. Without thinking, you pull out your phone to capture a picture of the pooch suspended in midair. Your camera preview feed alternates between being blurry and clear. You touch the screen to tell your camera to focus on the dog. It almost instantly obliges.

Regardless of how far or close the dog is, the camera preview always has it in sharp focus. After a few botched attempts, you get a perfect picture of your dog with a frisbee in its mouth flying in the air.

Think about it. You probably use this feature without even thinking each time you take a picture or a video with your phone. In fact, sometimes, you don't even need to press the screen to tell the camera where to focus. It automatically focuses on commonly photographed objects, like faces, for example.

This system has a lot of moving parts to it, but one of the core elements driving the system is an object detector.

The detector identifies objects of interest either based on the user's input (touching the screen) or based on commonly photographed objects (like faces). It then provides the location of the object to the autofocus system. The autofocus system adjusts the focus so that the selected object appears sharp and crisp in the image.

With neural networks, these systems have become more powerful. Let's go behind the scenes and understand these detectors.

Anatomy of a Detector

Like our image classifier, we can use a CNN to build a detector, but there is one big difference. Unlike our classifier, the detector should return two things, not one. It should return both the category of the object (like the classifier) and a box that locates where the object is in the picture.

Here's the interesting bit—identifying the category of the object is still a classification task. Returning the box containing it is a regression task. Thus, the detector needs to perform both classification and regression for each object. Cool right?

Neural networks can return as many outputs as we like. All we need to do is design the last layer of the network accordingly.

The advantage here is that we can reuse a lot of the architecture from our classifier network from before. After all, we still want the detector to identify interesting features in the image and build an understanding of what it contains. So, most of the early layers of our detector can mirror our classifier. However, the last few layers have to account for both the class of the object and its location in the image.

Crucially, we need to consider a few things. There might be more than one occurrence of an object in the image. There could be multiple types of objects, each occurring a different number of times in the image. There could be some categories that the detector is trained on that don't occur in the image at all. So we'd need to ensure that the output layer of the detector has provisions for all these situations.[11]

Training the Detector

We've designed a detector. Now, we need to train it to detect objects. For this, we'll turn our attention to the training dataset. First, we'll need to decide which objects our detector can identify. Then, we'll have to collect a dataset containing images of these objects for the model to learn from. Note that we'll have to prepare our training data properly so that the network learns what is expected. In this case, our training data will be pairs of images and a list of objects in the image. Each item in this list will contain not just the category of the object but where it is located in the image. If there are multiple occurrences of the same object in the image (e.g., flowers), the list must contain all occurrences of the object (Figure 7.9).

Armed with this data, we can train our detector using the standard gradient descent and backpropagation loop. Our loss function will have to account for both how accurate the model is in identifying what the object is and where it occurs in an image. For the classification part of

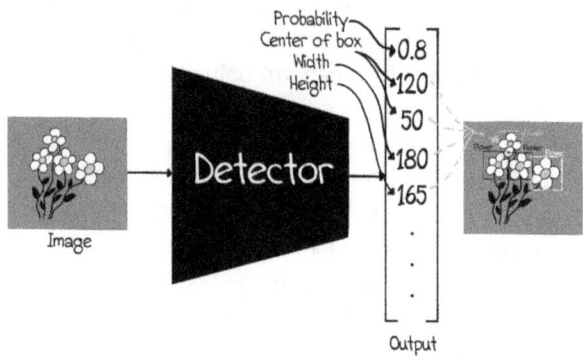

Figure 7.9. How the object detection network predicts bounding boxes.

things, we can use the same loss function as our image classifier (such as cross-entropy loss). For the detection part, we can use something like a mean squared error that compares the predicted bounding box with the true bounding box. Let me stop you before you start worrying about how to design a detector. In the next section, I've shared a few popular object detectors that have been meticulously designed by researchers.

But before that, we need to discuss how we can figure out if a detector is good at its job.

Analyzing a Detector's Performance

A good detector does two things right: it draws a tight bounding box around an object and correctly identifies the type of object. What we need is a metric that can evaluate both of these criteria.

Intersection over Union

IOU, or Intersection over Union, is a metric that measures how good the detector's predicted bounding boxes are. The idea is straightforward. To evaluate the quality of a predicted box, we compare it with the actual ground truth. In the image below, the lighter colored box is the ground truth box, while the darker colored box is the prediction. To calculate the IOU score, we simply calculate the intersection area between the two boxes and divide it by the area of the union of the two boxes. The higher the IOU, the better the detector predicts bounding boxes. Simply put, a good prediction intersects significantly with the ground truth.

Since the detector is unlikely to get the exact ground truth box, we need to design a way to identify if a predicted box is good and can be used. To do this, we can set an IOU threshold to identify good boxes versus bad ones. For example, we could say that if the IOU score for a prediction is greater than 0.5, we'll use that box for further processing (Figure 7.10).

Mean Average Precision

mAP, or mean Average Precision, is the metric commonly used to evaluate object detectors. To understand it, we need to understand a couple of related metrics called precision and recall. These can sound scary, but they're really just common sense measurements (Figure 7.11).

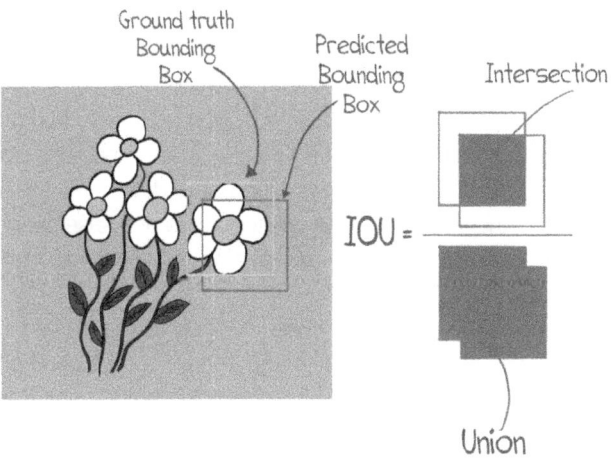

Figure 7.10. The IOU score helps us evaluate how good our predicted bounding boxes are.

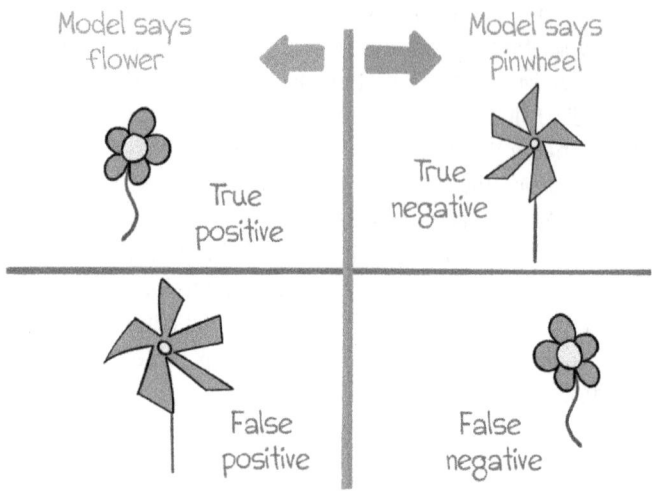

Figure 7.11. The four kinds of guesses a model can make. Only two are good.

Precision is the portion of positive predictions that the detector got right. What do I mean by positive here? Let's go back to our detector from earlier, which enjoys detecting flowers. If our detector truly finds a flower in the image, that is a positive prediction for this detector. Now, say we show it an image of a pinwheel and some flowers hanging out. It does its thing and returns bounding boxes for each flower and the pinwheel. But, it labels the pinwheel as a flower too. You now have two types of predictions—true positives (calling a flower a flower) and false positives (calling a pinwheel a flower). The precision of our detector is the ratio of true positives to the total number of positives (true and false positives).

In other words, precision measures how accurate the detector's predictions are.

Recall measures how well the detector finds all the positives. Let's say that in our pinwheel and flower image, there are six flowers and just one pinwheel. Our detector found five flowers correctly, but it missed one of them. This missed flower is called a false negative. The five flowers it detected are true positives. The recall is the ratio of the true positives to all positives (true positives + false negatives).

Our IOU threshold from earlier has a bearing on precision and recall. If we set the IOU threshold higher, we get high-quality boxes. This correlates with higher precision scores, but we'll get fewer detected boxes since we only return the very best. Thus, our recall will be lower as there's a chance we will miss some true positives because the bounding box associated with that object had a low IOU score. As you can see, it's a tradeoff.

How do we capture how well the model does if the IOU threshold we choose determines the precision and recall values? Simple. We can average the precision over multiple IOU thresholds to get a holistic picture.

That's precisely what mean average precision is! A good detector has a high value of mAP.

Which Detector Do I Choose?

We now have enough context to look at the approaches researchers have used to build robust object detectors.[12] Before Transformers, CNNs were the predominant architecture choice for any vision problem. Object detectors evolved from two-stage detectors to single-stage detectors. Both styles of detectors used CNNs as the backbone architecture.

In two-stage detectors, a set of candidate objects is first proposed, and then the second stage refines these proposals down to the final predictions. Typically, one model extracts these candidate regions, and a second model classifies and refines the bounding boxes for each object. Why not use just the first model, then? Well, the first-stage model is fast but inaccurate. It can ensure higher recall but not high precision. The second-stage model is more accurate. It can ensure higher precision, but it is compute-heavy and slow. Thus, it is used only after candidate proposals are generated by the first model. Some popular two-stage models include RCNN, Fast RCNN, Faster RCNN, and Feature Pyramid Networks (FPN).

Single-stage detectors overcame these limitations and consolidated the entire process into one stage (hence the name). These are also fast and lightweight. Popular single-stage detectors include YOLO (I kid you not. It's actually called that), SSD, and RetinaNet.

If you're interested in building a detection-based application, consider something like YOLO as a starting point. It's a really fast and effective model to use.

We've now seen how to identify which objects are in an image and where they are located. But how do we teach machines to learn to separate them from the rest of the image? For that, we'll look at a class of algorithms which can identify every single pixel that belongs to that object.

Image Segmentation

I've belabored the point that images are just a stream of numbers to a computer. So, if a picture is worth a thousand words, then we want the computer to understand every single one of these words, right? That's what image segmentation is about.

In object detection, the model returns what objects are in the image as well as where they are. Segmentation takes this a step further. It gives you a label for every single pixel in the image. Imagine a jigsaw puzzle where each piece is a unique object from the image. Segmentation doesn't just return a box and a category. It returns the exact shape! (Figure 7.12)

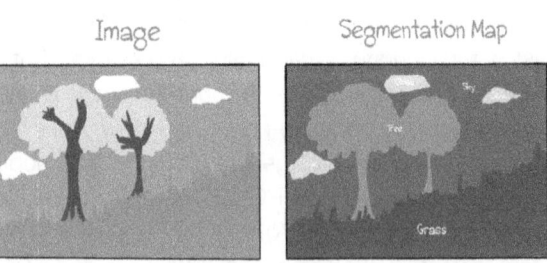

Figure 7.12. Segmentation is like assigning each pixel a specific color depending on what that pixel represents.

If we already have object detectors, why do we need segmentation models? These models allow self-driving cars to understand the world around them, help doctors identify tumors in scans, and power mixed-reality applications. But why go that far? They also allow you to edit out that random middle-aged gentleman unwittingly photobombing your selfie at the beach.

Building a Photobomb Remover

The goal of this application is to remove objects from an image that the user doesn't want. There are two ways to do this—either physically walk up to the intruding object and remove it from the shot or edit it out using some post-processing magic. Since this is a book about AI, I'll show you how you can do the latter. The former is best reserved for a book on working out.

The user captures an image. Upon looking at the image, said user frowns since there's an intruding signpost in the background. The user then paints on the screen to highlight the intruding object. Our model magically removes the intrusion. The user beams with happiness.

This application combines a technique called image inpainting along with segmentation. We'll focus on the segmentation aspect alone. The segmentation model uses the hand scribble or paint cue from the user to identify a region of interest. It then identifies what objects are present within that region. Finally, it returns every pixel that belongs to that object to the image inpainting algorithm. The inpainting algorithm replaces (fills in, to be precise) every pixel with a neighboring pixel. The intruding object is removed!

Let's look at segmentation models behind the scenes.

Anatomy of a Segmentation Model

Unlike classification or detection models, segmentation models return an image as the result. An image goes in. An image comes out. Technically, the image that comes out is called a segmentation map. However, the image that comes out is like the labeled jigsaw puzzle I mentioned earlier. Every piece is an object in the image.

We can use a CNN just as before. The earlier layers focus on understanding the image, extracting features, and recognizing patterns.

However, the magic begins in the latter half of the model. Rather than just identifying or classifying objects, these layers start to build up a segmentation map (Figure 7.13).

They reconstruct the original size of the image from the compact feature representation created by the earlier layers. Every pixel in the segmentation map corresponds to a pixel in the input image and carries a label. This label could be anything from sky, ground, train, to person or dog, based on the classes the model has been trained on.

But, wait. So far, we've seen convolutions take an image, extract features, and make it smaller in the process. How do we make a smaller image bigger? We use a new kind of layer called transposed convolutional layers. Transposed convolutions do the opposite of regular convolutions by taking a small image and making it bigger by spreading out each pixel's information. When the network is trained with several examples, these layers master the process of upsampling.

Training a Segmentation Model

As before, we'll need to prepare our data in a certain way. This time, we'll need an image and its segmentation map. Using several (a lot, to be honest)

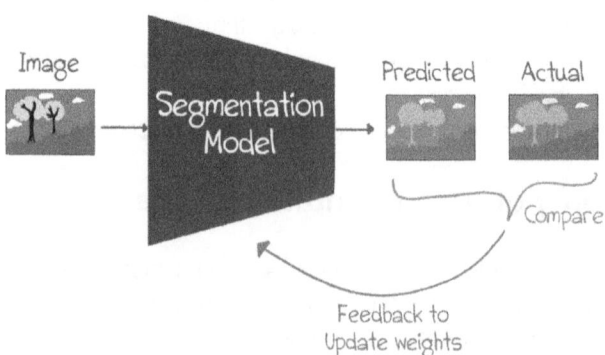

Figure 7.13. To train segmentation models, we compare two images. One of these is the actual segmentation map. The other is predicted by the model.

pairs of these, we can teach the model to label images. The loss function we'll have to use needs to compare pixels. The loss function measures the disagreements between the model's predicted segmentation map and the ground truth map for each pixel. The goal of the model is to minimize this disagreement as much as possible. The weight updates, as before, happen through gradient descent and backpropagation. Finally, when evaluating these models, we use metrics such as Intersection over Union (IOU) or pixel accuracy. These metrics help us understand how well our model is performing by measuring how closely the predicted segmentation maps align with the ground truth labels.

As you can see, with a few small changes to the data, the architecture, and the loss function, we can make neural networks do various things.

Types of Segmentation Tasks

There are different flavors of segmentation tasks depending on the granularity of the labeling.

- **Semantic Segmentation:** In this, every pixel is labeled with the class it belongs to. Take the example of a park with a tree, a dog, and a blue sky. Here, the pixels that make up the trees are labeled as "tree," the pixels that make up the grass as labeled as "grass," and so on. However, it doesn't distinguish between different objects of the same class. Say there are two trees in the image. The model would just label them as "tree." Not as "tree 1" and "tree 2." Semantic segmentation is typically used to study objects that have an amorphous shape, like grass or roads.

- **Instance Segmentation:** Here, we not only assign every pixel to a class but also distinguish between different objects of the same class. So if there are two trees in the image, they would be labeled as "tree 1" and "tree 2." Instance segmentation is typically used to study objects that have a well-defined shape, like people, cars, and so on.

- **Panoptic Segmentation:** This combines both semantic segmentation and instance segmentation. This means each pixel is labeled with a class, and objects that belong to the same class are differentiated. It also handles classes that don't have a well-defined shape, like sky, road, or grass (Figure 7.14).

Popular Segmentation Models

Mask R-CNN, DeepLab, and U-Net are three popular segmentation models.[13] The U-Net model was designed to help in medical image segmentation and has recently found its way into generative models. To build your own segmentation model, consider starting with a U-Net.

Transformers for Vision?

In the previous chapter, we looked at how Transformers revolutionized the field of NLP. But they didn't stop there. Transformers have been conquering one field after another. In 2020, the Vision Transformer[14] (ViT) showed that a language-specific architecture could excel at image recognition.

But doesn't a Transformer expect a sequence of tokens like words in a sentence? Yes. If so, how can it work with images? Simple. Instead of treating an image as a grid of pixels, the ViT treats it as a sequence of patches. By simply cutting up an image into small squares, we can generate patches.

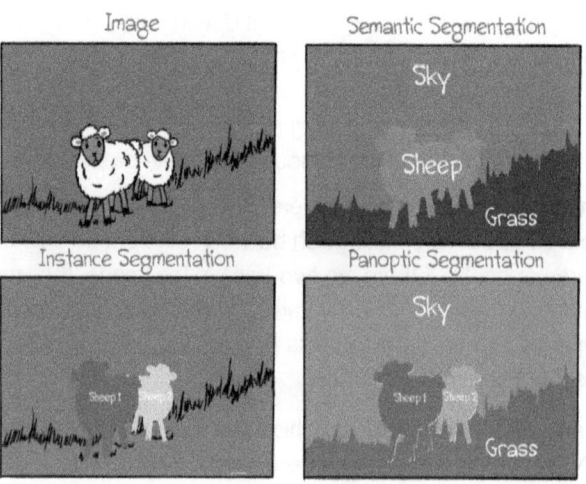

Figure 7.14. The different types of segmentation.

So, a ViT breaks an image into a grid of patches, much like a jigsaw puzzle. Each of these patches is then treated as a word in a sentence. By flattening and lining up the pixels within each patch, they are transformed into a sequence of "image words," and this is the sequence that the Vision Transformer works with (Figure 7.15).

Earlier in the chapter, we read about how flattening an image can remove positional information vital for understanding the image. In the case of ViT, it does what its language counterpart does. It adds positional embeddings into the mix. Here, each positional embedding indicates the position of a patch in the overall image.

Once these steps are done, the resulting image tokens can be processed through a regular Transformer. How cool is that?

In fact, this model beat many state-of-the-art CNNs in image classification. However, it requires a lot more training data than CNNs. Convolution layers in CNNs use the same set of weights for all parts of the image. Thus, they can use the same set of pattern matching to find the same object in different parts of the image. However, attention layers within Transformers are context-driven and thus don't make this assumption. Thus, it needs to learn this from data.

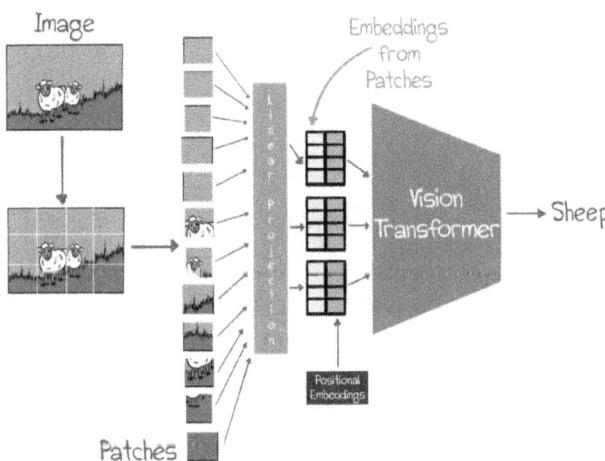

Figure 7.15. Transformers can work on images just as well as they do on text. All they need are a sequence of patches.

Borrowing from Language

Researchers found that when a Vision Transformer was pretrained like a regular Transformer, it could perform exceedingly well at various image tasks. For this, they borrowed a training technique from NLP called masked language modeling. Transformer models like BERT would be shown a sentence with some words missing, and it would have to guess what these "masked" words were.

Similarly, for images, researchers masked out some of the patches in the image with a MASK token. The Vision Transformer had to guess what the original patch was for each masked token. By forcing the Transformer to fill in the blanks, it learned the context of each patch in relation to the others. This process is called Masked Image Modeling (Figure 7.16).

Masked Image Modeling is an effective way to train Vision Transformers because it encourages them to understand not just the individual patches but also the image as a whole. It's like trying to solve a jigsaw puzzle where a few pieces are missing—you need to understand the overall picture to figure out what the missing pieces might look like.

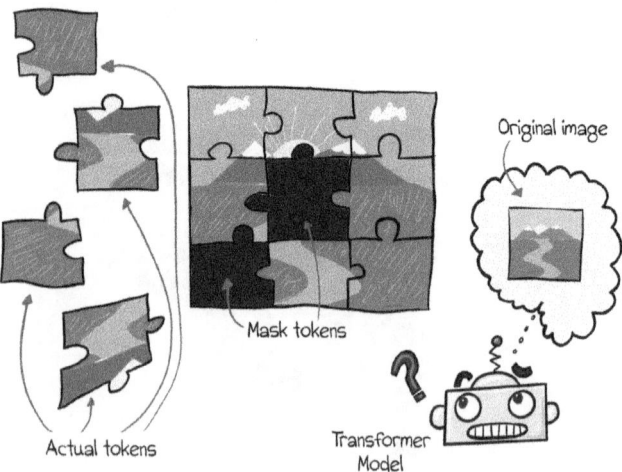

Figure 7.16. Masked image modeling is like completing a jigsaw puzzle. Which pieces make the image whole again?

Since the original Vision Transformer was introduced, these models have been able to solve other computer vision problems like detection, segmentation, and even image generation.

It's been fascinating to see the evolution of models in computer vision. Convolutional networks cracked the code on teaching machines to see, mastering everything from simple classification to complex segmentation. Then Transformers stepped in and flipped the script—turns out those language models had some serious vision skills too. But the real magic? These Transformers are breaking down walls, looking into multimodal problems—problems where more than one type of data is involved. It's starting to feel like we're watching the boundaries between different types of AI models just dissolve.

Now that we have a handle on the fundamental problems in computer vision, we're ready to explore how generative models are taking these capabilities in bold new directions.

Chapter Summary

Let's recap our dive into computer vision—the field that teaches machines to see. We started with the basics: how computers interpret digital images as data. It turns out that CNNs are the real workhorses here. These networks process images layer by layer, much like our own visual system, learning to recognize increasingly complex patterns until they can classify entire images.

We explored how machines can spot and locate specific objects in images, and then went even deeper with image segmentation. Whether it's broadly categorizing regions (semantic), picking out individual instances, or understanding entire scenes (panoptic), segmentation gives machines a pixel-perfect understanding of what they're seeing.

Finally, we looked at the Vision Transformer (ViT), which breaks images into patches and analyzes them like words in a sentence. Using clever techniques borrowed from language processing, like masked image modeling, these Transformers proved there's more than one way to teach a machine to see.

Now that we understand how machines interpret images, we're ready for something even more fascinating: teaching them to create images from scratch.

Chapter 8
Generative Models

Thanks to generative models like DALL-E, Midjourney, and Stable Diffusion, social media has exploded with images of astronauts lounging in coffee shops, renaissance paintings of robots playing chess, and photorealistic scenes that never existed. But how do machines learn to create imagery like this? So far, we've seen models that can recognize objects, locate them in an image, or even label every single pixel that belongs to them. Teaching a computer to understand images was challenging enough. Teaching it to create entirely new ones seemed like science fiction just a few years ago. After all, there's a world of difference between recognizing a cat in a photo and creating a convincing image of "a cyberpunk cat playing jazz piano in a neon-lit Tokyo alley." But before we look at all this, we need to understand some basic building blocks first.

That's why we'll be starting with the humble autoencoder.

Autoencoders

Have you ever watched a magic show live? Or, perhaps, have you watched an illusionist do seemingly impossible feats on TV? At the start of each trick, they show you something ordinary, like a coin or a bird. It's as ordinary as ordinary can be. There's nothing special about it, They do this to give you the impression that what you're about to witness next is out of this world. After having convinced you of the ordinariness of said object, they proceed to step two. Something extraordinary happens. You gasp. There's no way that bird disappeared between the magician's palms. But before you can recover, they bring back the bird or the missing object from a totally random location.

We have a magician in the machine learning world, too. Let's take a look at the humble autoencoder and how it performs an incredible trick—making data disappear! (Figure 8.1)

Anatomy of an Autoencoder

At first glance, the autoencoder looks deceptively simple. It consists of two components: an encoder and a decoder.

The autoencoder takes in images and makes them disappear. However, it can also bring the images back. How does it do so? It learns to represent data in an unsupervised manner.

The Encoder and Compression

Given an image, the encoder transforms it into a lower-dimensional representation called the latent space, where we represent complex

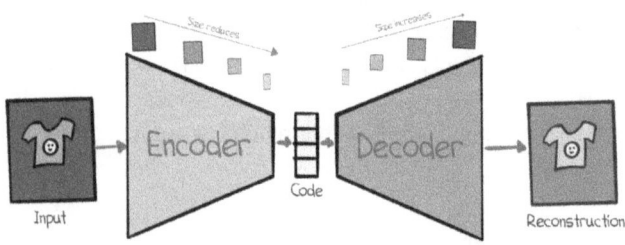

Figure 8.1. An overview of an autoencoder. The encoder compresses the input, which progressively shrinks as it passes through the encoder. The decoder reconstructs the original information. Thus, the input progressively increases in size as it passes through the decoder.

data, like images, in a simpler form. While an image might comprise thousands of pixel values, we can often describe its key features with far fewer numbers. The latent space is exactly that—a lower-dimensional space where each point represents an image's essential characteristics. Essentially, this is a form of compression. Since it has to compress the input, the encoder has to learn the most important features of the input data and can't simply copy over the input.

How does the compression happen? We've seen various layers that act as building blocks for neural networks. The encoder consists of a series of these layers with lower dimensionality than the input. With each successive layer, the network learns which features matter most—perhaps the shapes, colors, or patterns that define the image—while setting aside the less important details. Thus, as the image progresses through the encoder, it gets more and more compressed. The encoder's goal is to capture the essence of the input, making the actual input *disappear*.

Compressing input data is easy, right? After all, we are throwing away a bunch of information. Well, how do you recover the original data from this compressed representation?

The Decoder and Reconstruction

To complete the magic trick, our autoencoder brings back the original data from this compressed representation. The decoder, which is responsible for this, reconstructs the original data from the compressed latent representation. Architecturally, the decoder is typically a mirror image of the encoder and progressively increases the size of the data flowing through it.

Thus, as the latent representation flows through the decoder, it becomes larger and larger. Eventually, it becomes the exact size of our original image. Although the reconstruction may not be identical to the original, it will still be very close.

Training the Autoencoder

The real magic of the autoencoder is that it learns how to do this end-to-end without explicitly being told so. So, what are we hoping to achieve? Reconstructing the input image as seamlessly as possible, right?

For this to happen, the decoder and encoder must work harmoniously. That is, the input and output images must be near-perfect if not perfect clones.

That's where the reconstruction loss comes in. It gives us an idea of how close the reconstructed output is to the input. Typically, we can use something like the mean squared loss (MSE) to compute the difference between the input and the reconstruction. The MSE loss computes the pixel-wise difference between the reconstruction and the input and squares it. It then computes the average of all of these values.

Over the course of training, the autoencoder adjusts its weights so that this loss becomes smaller and smaller.

To train the autoencoder, we simply take an image and pass it through the network. The autoencoder produces a reconstruction that it thinks matches the input exactly. We then use the reconstruction loss to compare the reconstruction from the autoencoder with the original image. We can then use this error signal to provide feedback to the autoencoder. The autoencoder updates its weights based on this and tries again. When we repeat this exercise over a number of images a bunch of times, the autoencoder learns a robust latent space. Simple, right?

Applications

Autoencoders are pretty nifty and can be used for:

- *Dimensionality Reduction*: If you haven't already guessed, autoencoders learn compact representations of data, making them great for reducing the dimensionality of data.

- *Anomaly Detection*: Since autoencoders learn the important features from the input, they can spot abnormalities in data that deviate significantly from normal observations. These weird samples will have a higher reconstruction loss, and thus, we can spot them!

- *Denoising*: Autoencoders can be used to remove noise from input data. For example, if you add some noise to the images and pass them through the autoencoder, it will remove the noise reasonably well.

Standard autoencoders excel at compression—they learn to reconstruct their input data faithfully. But this strength is also their limitation. An autoencoder becomes really good at recreating images it has seen, essentially memorizing them, but it can't generate new ones. So, in that sense, they aren't really "generative" models. How do we solve that? By adding randomness into the mix. Let's look at our first generative model, the variational autoencoder—an autoencoder that doesn't purely memorize what it sees.

Variational Autoencoders

Once upon a time, a budding artist named Vincent lived in a quiet little town called Latentia. Latentia was renowned for its creativity. Many extraordinary artists had apprenticed here before moving to the big city to build stellar careers in art.

Vincent came from a long line of art forgers. His father, Arne Englebert, was a master at forgery. Arne was an autoencoder. He could replicate paintings flawlessly down to the tiniest detail. But that was all he could do. Arne trained his son in art from a young age, and soon, he, too, could recreate any painting blindfolded. But unlike his father, Vincent Arne Englebert wasn't happy with forging existing art. He wanted more.

Vincent diligently studied the works of artistic geniuses. Soon, he started understanding the essence of great works of art. He absorbed their techniques, their choice of colors, brush strokes, lines, and composition. Finally, he learned the underlying patterns and distribution of styles that made their art unique.

As Vincent honed his craft, he realized that just learning the great masters' styles would make him yet another accomplished forger. To truly master the essence of art, he needed to express his creative voice. A delicate balance between the two was vital. Whenever he painted, he would first follow the style of the great masters, using the fundamental principles he had learned through his studies. Then, he would add a touch of randomness—a subtle twist to the composition, an unexpected stroke of color, or a slight alteration in perspective—to make his creations truly unique. He became a true creator by infusing his creative expression with the framework of legends' past—an artist.

Vincent's relentless pursuit of artistic mastery eventually bore fruit. His newfound ability to create stunning, original pieces that captured the essence of the great masters left the art world in awe. His innovative style and technique became the talk of the town, and soon, Vincent's masterpieces were displayed in prestigious galleries and museums. Vincent had evolved from a simple autoencoder into a variational autoencoder.

Anatomy of a Variational Autoencoder

In case you haven't already made the connection, Vincent's apprenticeship is very similar to how a variational autoencoder (VAE) is trained. A VAE also consists of an encoder and decoder like a regular autoencoder. However, unlike traditional autoencoders (like Vincent's dad), which can only learn to recreate the input samples they see, VAEs can generate new, original samples. This is because VAEs are designed to model the underlying probability distribution (patterns and variations) of the data.

What does this mean? Traditional autoencoders learn exact one-to-one relationships—each input gets converted to a specific compressed representation. VAEs work differently: they learn a range of possible values and their relationships instead of exact mappings. When a VAE creates something, it can combine these learned patterns in different ways to generate fresh but realistic results.

A regular autoencoder maps the input data into a single fixed representation. In VAEs, however, the encoder learns two things for each feature: a typical value (the mean μ) and how much that value can reasonably vary (the standard deviation σ) while still looking natural. When creating something new, they can make inspired choices within these learned ranges.

This flexibility is what allows VAEs to generate new data points—they understand not just what something typically looks like but how it can naturally vary. This is the real magic of how VAEs work—they don't just memorize; they understand the space of possibilities. Under the hood, the decoder of a VAE and a regular autoencoder are very similar.

The secret sauce in a VAE is how the latent space distribution is learned. Let's look at that next (Figure 8.2).

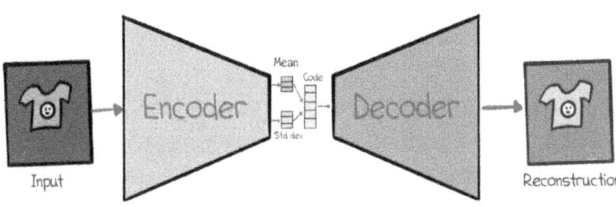

Figure 8.2. The VAE learns two codes, unlike the autoencoder. This enables it to produce new samples.

Learning a Latent Distribution

Traditional autoencoders aim to minimize only the reconstruction error, forcing them to replicate the input data faithfully. Thus, this single objective prevents them from generating new, diverse examples.

VAEs, however, have a two-part loss function and must find a balance between the two parts. The first part, the reconstruction loss, ensures that the generated samples resemble the original data. This is identical to the regular autoencoder we saw before. The second part, called the KL (Kullback-Leibler) divergence, ensures that the VAE can create new samples instead of just copying what it saw during the training process.

This dual nature of the VAE loss function is like Vincent's artistic compass. The reconstruction loss represents his ability to understand and reproduce the techniques of the great masters. In contrast, the KL divergence represents the creative freedom that allows him to generate entirely new and captivating pieces of art. Let's spend a little more time understanding the second part of this loss function.

KL Divergence?

The KL divergence loss helps organize how the VAE learns patterns by pushing them toward a standard Gaussian distribution. Imagine a bell curve where most values naturally cluster around the middle, with a balanced spread outward. This constraint serves three powerful purposes:

First, it creates order in the latent space. A VAE can only produce new samples that are as good as the latent representation it learns. The KL divergence ensures similar patterns sit close together, with smooth transitions between them. This organization means that when we sample from or move through this space, we get meaningful variations, which allows for a more effective generation of new samples.

Second, it helps solve the overfitting problem. Traditional autoencoders are prone to overfitting because they can learn to simply copy the input data to the output without extracting meaningful features. By introducing the KL loss in the VAE loss function, VAEs are encouraged to extract the most essential features from the input data, which helps prevent overfitting and leads to better generalization.

Third, the KL divergence acts as a constraint, ensuring that the latent space does not become overly complex and forcing the model to capture *only* the most important features of the input data.

When combined with reconstruction loss (which ensures accuracy), this creates a VAE that can both faithfully represent its training data and generate new, diverse examples in a controlled way.

Training a VAE

A VAE is trained in a very similar manner to a traditional autoencoder. We feed it images, and it tries to reconstruct them. However, as mentioned above, it receives feedback via a loss function with two parts, not one. We evaluate both how well it reconstructs the input (reconstruction loss) and how close the latent distribution it learns is to the target distribution (KL divergence).

The updates happen through backpropagation. But there's a problem here.

In Chapter 4, we discussed the chain rule and how gradients flow back through the network in backpropagation. Backpropagation

Generative Models

requires that the entire network be differentiable. This allows us to compute gradients at each step of the way to update weights. Here's where we hit a problem in the VAE.

Backpropagation works fine for the decoder part of the VAE, but then it encounters the sampling section. You can't differentiate a sampling process! Uh-oh. So, the backpropagation process stops there! What about the weights of the encoder? (Figure 8.3)

To clearly understand how big a problem this is, imagine a set of vertically connected pipes. We want the water to flow from the topmost pipe and reach the faucet at the bottom. But, the sampling process is like a stone stuck in the middle of the pipes, not allowing the water (the gradients) to flow further. What do we do?

Reparameterization

Thankfully, researchers devised an ingenious solution to this problem called the "reparameterization" trick. Instead of directly sampling from the latent distribution, we can first sample from a standard bell curve (Unit Gaussian Distribution). Then, we can shift and scale this by the latent mean and standard deviation that the autoencoder learns.

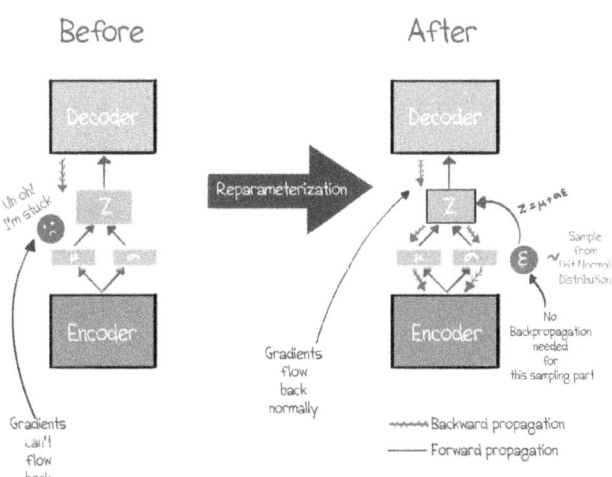

Figure 8.3. Fixing the plumbing so that our VAE can learn. This small change makes VAEs trainable like other neural networks.

The crucial detail here is that reparameterization separates the non-differentiable sampling operation from the rest of the network. Thus, backpropagation can continue without any issues.

Again, going back to our example of water and pipes, imagine that a plumber pushed the stone so that it moved out of the way. As a result, our water flows freely from top to bottom.

Generating Using the VAE

Once we've trained a VAE, we can use it to generate new images that are similar to the training data but not clones. We just need the decoder for the generation process. The process is surprisingly simple: we just use the decoder part of our network. We feed it a random point from our standard bell curve, and the decoder transforms this into a new image.

While VAEs opened new doors in AI-powered creation, they were just the beginning. Let's look at some even more powerful generative models that can create remarkably lifelike images.

Generative Adversarial Networks

We've all binge-watched TV shows and movies that pit a master thief against a shrewd detective. Each is an expert at their craft. Each tries to outthink and outdo the other, leading to several edge-of-the-seat moments and nail-biting finales. Who comes out on top? Interestingly, though, this same dynamic also plays out in machine learning. In this case, a master forger is pitted against a shrewd detective. So, grab your paintbrushes and magnifying glasses as we dive into the shadowy world of generative adversarial networks.

A Game of Cat and Mouse

Generative Adversarial Networks, or GANs for short, are a pair of neural networks pitted against each other. These networks are called the generator and the discriminator. As the names imply, the generator creates new images[1] while the discriminator detects whether they are real or fake. The generator's goal is to create samples that fool the discriminator, while the discriminator's goal is to remain vigilant and call out the generator's fakes.

The discriminator learns from both real and fake examples to catch the cunning generator. The generator, on the other hand, learns from its mistakes, each time producing samples that become increasingly indistinguishable from the real examples.

In a typical ending, the generator learns to outsmart the discriminator. The beautiful aspect of GANs is that both these networks are trained simultaneously. Each network gets better with feedback—the generator becomes a master forger, and the discriminator becomes an expert detective (Figure 8.4).

How do these networks learn? That's next.

The Players: The Forger and the Detective

Since GANs have typically been used to create images, let's run with that example. The generator starts with a blank canvas—random noise, to be specific. Initially, it has absolutely no clue. It tries to create what it thinks is a real image—an image that it thinks would fool the generator.

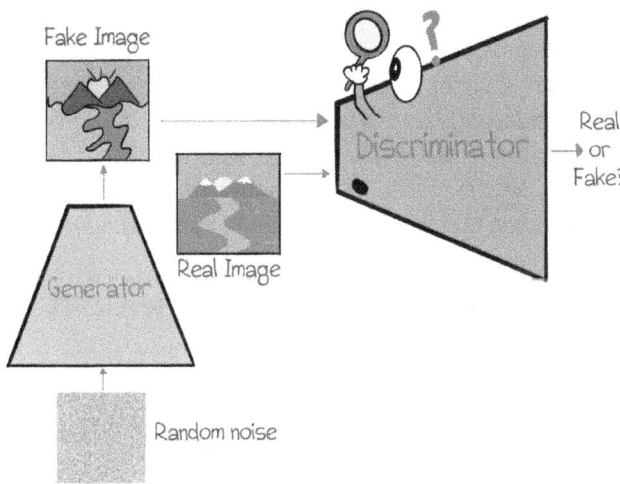

Figure 8.4. A tale of two networks: the discriminator is the detective, the generator a forger.

Recall how the decoder in the autoencoder works. It could generate new examples based on a distribution. The generator works in a very similar way. However, the generator doesn't have a well-defined latent space like the decoder. It has to generate examples from random noise, so its job is much harder.

At first, its results are terrible. In fact, they're no match for the discriminator who instantly tosses them aside as fakes.

But, after every attempt, the generator gets feedback via a loss function on how far off its creation was from a real image. It uses this feedback to update its weights. The next time it generates images, the results are better—a little closer to what a real image would look like but not quite there. The cycle repeats. Over time, the generator gets really good at producing realistic images.

Meanwhile, the discriminator is made to look at both real images and fakes that the generator produces. It makes a guess on which images are real and which are fake. It gets feedback on how well it did on this task. It uses the feedback to update its weights and get better at spotting fakes. Over time, the discriminator gets really good at spotting fakes.

But if both the generator and discriminator get really good at what they do, who wins the game?

That's the beauty of training GANs. Since both networks try to outdo each other, the training process ideally becomes a zero-sum game. In the best-case scenario, both networks reach a state of equilibrium. When this state is reached, the generator produces near-perfect realistic images. The discriminator, in this situation, has to toss a coin to guess whether the image is real or fake. It's too close to call.

Before we see the challenges with achieving this state, let's look at the unique training process used for training these networks.

The Training Process: Refining the Craft

Since both the generator and discriminator are trained simultaneously, the process happens in two steps.

Discriminator Training Phase

In the first step, the discriminator is shown a set of images. Half of these are real. Half are fake (created by the generator). The images are shuffled, so the discriminator can't cheat. We also provide the discriminator with labels for each image—perhaps the label "1" for real and "0" for fake. The discriminator looks at the images it's been given and guesses if they are real or fake. We then compare its predictions to the true labels for each image. This allows us to measure how well the discriminator did. Ideally, the discriminator was able to separate the wheat from the chaff. But, as is true in reality, it doesn't always do that. We backpropagate this error and update the weights of the discriminator. Do better next time, will ya? (Figure 8.5)

Importantly, in the first step, only the weights of the discriminator are updated.

Generator Training Phase

In the second step, the discriminator's weights are kept fixed. It's the generator's turn to learn. We ask it to produce a set of images which we then show to our discriminator. The discriminator looks at these images and guesses whether they are real or fake. We use the results from the discriminator to evaluate how well the generator did. We want the generator to be able to fool the discriminator. So, we measure how

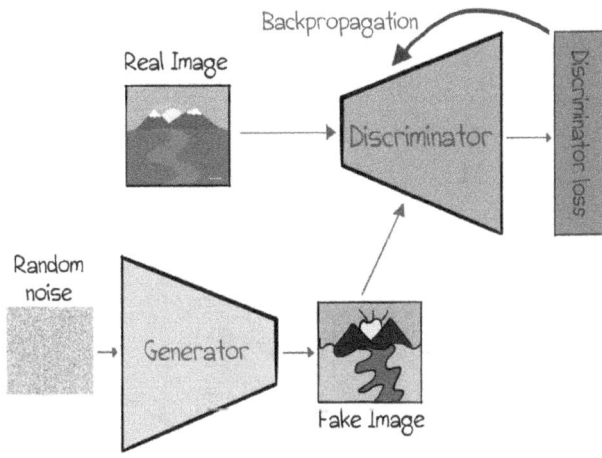

Figure 8.5. Training the discriminator network.

successful it was in fooling its keen-eyed competitor. The more it fools the discriminator, the better it does (Figure 8.6).

We backpropagate this feedback and update the weights of the generator. Remember, only the generator's weights are updated in this step. Those of the discriminator remain fixed.

This process[2] continues until we hopefully reach the state of equilibrium I talked about earlier. But stranger things have happened . . .

Challenges and Limitations

Training a GAN is hard. Training a single neural network is often challenging. Imagine training two of them at once. What could go wrong? A lot of things in this delicate dance, it turns out.

Mode Collapse

If we're honest with ourselves, we seldom step outside our comfort zone. If we can do something really well, we tend to only do that a lot and avoid things we aren't good at. This actually happens in GANs, too!

The generator can sometimes focus on producing only the specific images that successfully fool the discriminator. Technically, it's doing

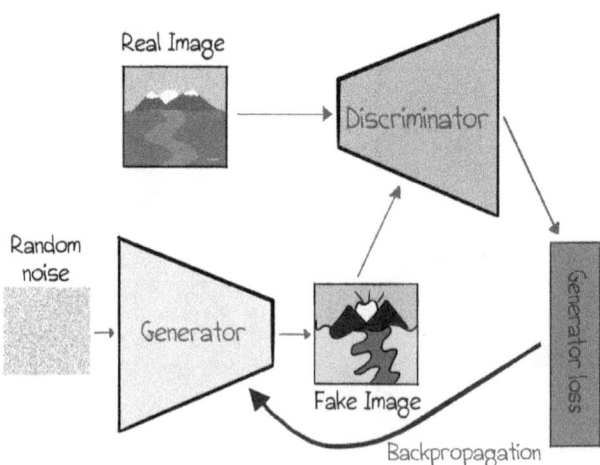

Figure 8.6. Training the generator network.

its job, right? But, this leads to a lack of diversity in the images that it produces. Let's say that the generator gets really good at producing realistic images of roses. It fools the discriminator every time it produces images of roses. But we want it to produce images of alpacas or platypuses. Unfortunately for us, the generator sucks at this. So, it plays safe and keeps producing roses. Gradually, it forgets how to produce anything else. This situation is called mode collapse.

Training Instability

Since both networks try to stay ahead of each other in this game, their weights end up oscillating a bunch during training. Thus, both networks are very susceptible to the choice of hyperparameters (knobs we can tweak in the training process). A lot of times, the training process diverges with neither network learning anything useful. A big chunk of research has focused on making these networks train stably without pulling each other's hair out.

Famous GANs

While covering every detail and development concerning GANs is beyond the scope of this chapter, the CycleGAN, BigGAN, and StyleGAN are worth checking out.[3]

However, like VAEs, GANs were the kings of the hill until another upstart came along. Let's look at that next.

Diffusion Models

It's 10 p.m., and your phone rings. The chief is on the other end. There's been a crime, and your expertise is needed ASAP. You throw on your jacket, grab your wallet, and rush into the chilly night. At the scene, the local beat cop explains what happened. It was a smash-and-grab. The scene? A local grocery store. The thief was smart enough to disable the surveillance camera before ransacking the store. Without the camera, there are no eyewitnesses.

As a seasoned profiler, your job is to figure out who might have committed this heinous crime. All you have are clues you can gather from the scene. You walk into the store, past glass shards and Swiss chard that have been strewn indiscriminately. Those would have been great in a warm soup. Not the shards, the chard. You look closely at the checkout counter and spot some smudgy fingerprints. The weird part is that these aren't human. Each finger is sharp, pointy, and tapers into a claw. The size of the hand is smaller than a human's. "Curious, curious," you mutter to yourself.

The register has been cleaned out. Walking past the produce aisles toward the dairy section, you notice that a shelf that once contained Twinkies is now empty. In fact, some of them lie open on the floor, half-eaten, with cream stains all around. A closer look reveals two distinct sets of prints. One that matches the hand from the cash register. Another that matches a human's. A picture begins to reveal itself. After scanning every square inch of the store, you further uncover traces of blue-colored fibers, size 12 shoe prints, and a can of black paint.

You meet the sketch artist outside to generate a profile of the suspect. "A man in a blue jacket and a raccoon, wearing a winter hat, size 12 shoes," you say to the artist. She worries for your sanity. But looking at your serious expression, she gets to work and draws tentative lines and patterns. At first, there's a bit of confusion because her version of the suspects differs from yours. Naturally, transferring over imagination is hard. So, you begin to give more details making it clearer and clearer for her. With each step, the sketch gets better and better. Finally, she gets a really nice illustration of the suspects ready for the detectives. Two weeks later, the detectives caught the suspects. The Twinkies were saved. Thank heavens!

In the machine learning world, diffusion models are like these sketch artists. You describe what you want in words, and they use their "imagination" to create an image that matches your description. As with any sketch artist, getting the image right takes a few tries.

More formally, these generative models create new data through a process called diffusion. During training, the model learns by watching images gradually turn into random noise. Then, to generate new images, it reverses this process—starting with pure noise and carefully removing it step by step, guided by patterns it learned during training. The result is a new image that matches your description. The strength of diffusion models lies in their ability to generate high-quality, realistic samples.

Let's look at how these models work from first principles. What would you do if you had to build something that took in a sentence and produced images? What would the parts of such a black box be? First, you'd need something that could understand what the words in the sentence meant. Then, you'd also need something that could use this meaning to put together all the elements in the image. Finally, you'd need something to "paint" this composition and bring it to life. That's exactly what diffusion models consist of.

I find it easier to think of diffusion models like a sculptor chiseling away at a block of stone. Every part of the stone the sculptor removes is noise. Eventually, what is left behind is the actual image.

Why Diffusion?

We've seen the intuition behind diffusion models. But why on earth are they called diffusion models in the first place? Imagine your favorite caffeinated beverage. Yes, coffee. Now imagine the precise moment when a drop of milk falls into a hot, freshly brewed cup of coffee. You can see that exact spot where it touched the coffee's surface for a fraction of a second. Before long, the milk has permeated the coffee, turning it into a beautiful amber color. You can no longer pinpoint where the drop of milk first hit the coffee. This process by which the milk randomly distributes itself within the coffee is called diffusion.[4] Our goal is to recover the original coffee and reverse the mixing of milk in it. This is the idea behind diffusion models too. They gradually try to unmix noise (milk) from the image (coffee). While this idea was introduced in 2015, it wasn't until 2022 that things really took off with the emergence of DALLE-2, Midjourney, and Stable Diffusion.[5]

Going Forward in Reverse

Everything about these models can be explained by two processes that go in opposite directions—the forward process and the reverse process. Yes, very creatively named.

The Forward Process

The forward process governs how these models are trained. We add noise to an image. It's the model's job to figure out the noise that we added. In other words, it has to figure out what must be removed to recover the original image. Neural networks are really good at these kinds of tasks.

Typically, U-Nets are used for this purpose. U-Nets are amazing for image segmentation tasks. Turns out, they're just as amazing for removing noise too! All we need is a small tweak to the network. In a segmentation problem, the model takes in an image as input and produces a segmentation map as output.

Here, it takes a noisy image as input and predicts the noise as output.

So, how do we train this model? We take a dataset of images of our choosing. These can be anything. If we have cat and dog images, the model will learn to create cat and dog images. If we have random cartoon images, it will learn to create random cartoon images. You get the drift.

Let's assume that the dataset has cat and dog images. From this dataset, we choose an image at random. We then add noise to this image. If we add a little bit of noise, we can still see the original image for the most part. If we add a ton of noise, the original image becomes unrecognizable—we no longer know what that cat or dog looked like or even whether it was a cat or dog in the first place.

Thus, for the same image, we can add different amounts of noise to create different training examples. So, for each image in our dataset, we can create several training examples for the model to learn from (Figure 8.7).

Great, we have a dataset to train the model on. Now what?

We show these noisy images to the model and ask it to guess the noise that was added to each image.

At first, the model doesn't have a clue how much noise has been added. It randomly guesses. Here's where our trusty backpropagation and gradient descent come in. We compare the model's predictions with the actual noise we added. We use this to point out where the model went wrong. The model updates its weights. Rinse and repeat (Figure 8.8).

At the end of this process, we have a superb noise-removal network. What does this have anything to do with generating new images?

Generative Models

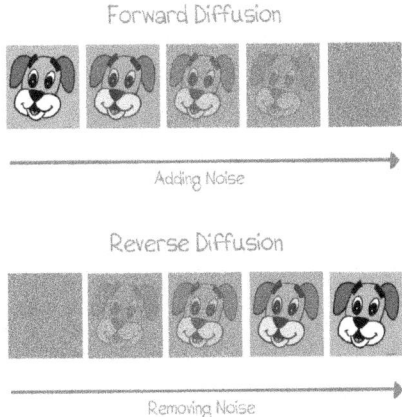

Figure 8.7. The forward process adds noise incrementally, while the reverse process removes it.

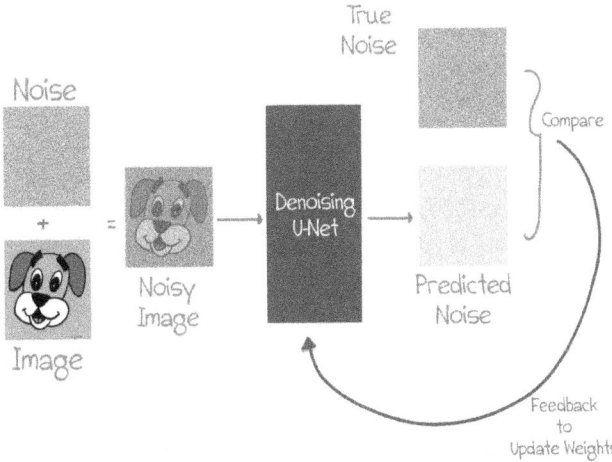

Figure 8.8. Training the model to predict the noise added to an image.

The Reverse Process

The reverse process is what we use in practice to generate images. As the name implies, the goal is to remove noise from the image until we have a noiseless image.

Now that training is complete, let's see how our model does on a few images it's not seen before. First, a simple example: we add a teensy bit of noise to an image of a dog and show the model this noisy image. It effortlessly removes the noise from this image to reveal the dog.

Next up, a harder example: we add quite a bit of noise to a tabby cat. We can still make out that it's a cat underneath all that noise. But only just. When the model sees this corrupted image, it does a pretty good job of denoising it. But some of the details of the original image have changed—the eyes are closed, the stripes are missing, and so on. After all, the model didn't see the original image without the noise. Thus, it makes a guess on how much noise to remove from each pixel of the image. That's why the details are either changed or missing.

Now, here's where the beauty of this method shines through. For the final test, we give the model an image of pure noise. This isn't an image of a cat or a dog where a truckload of noise has been added. This is just an image of pure noise. Nothing else.

What happens when we give this image to the model?

It tries to remove the noise to reveal the original image. The only problem—there's no original image, right? Doesn't matter. Since the model has been trained to think that there's always a cat or dog hiding behind a mountain of noise, it removes noise in a way to produce an image that actually resembles a cat or dog. So it makes sure that there are paws, eyes, ears, and so on. Thus, in this case, the model removes noise to reveal either a picture of a cat or a dog (Figure 8.9).

Crucially, we can't control what it generates (for now). All we can be sure of is that the result will be a cat or a dog.

So, to summarize, the model always assumes that there's an image hiding behind noise. What the image is depends on the training dataset. If we give it pure noise, it will remove the noise in such a way that the result is a meaningful image.

In other words, this model paints a picture by removing noise.

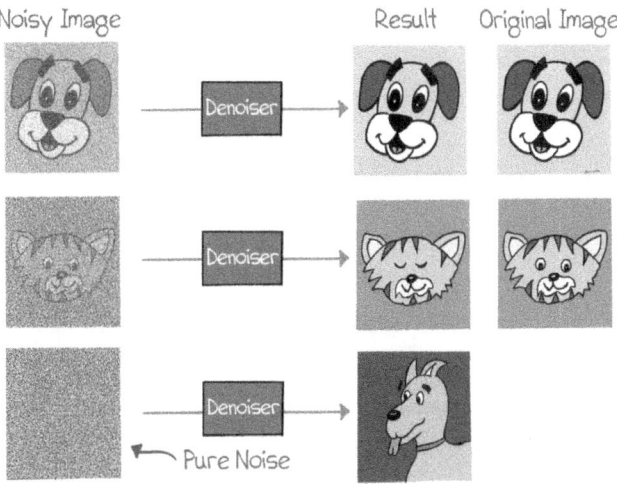

Figure 8.9. Our model always expects an image to be hiding behind the noise. What happens when we give it pure noise?

One Step or Many?

There might be many questions swimming in your head right now. However, if you've used one of these models before, there might be one question that burns more brightly than the others. If all the model does is remove noise from the image, why does it take so long to produce the final image?

These models don't denoise an image instantaneously. They denoise the image over a number of steps. At each step, a bit of noise is removed from the image. After this, the partially denoised image is fed back to the model. This process repeats until the image is fully noise free. Currently, researchers are focusing on ways to reduce the number of steps needed to denoise an image (Figure 8.10).[6]

Latent Speed

There's an elephant in the room we haven't addressed. It's a rather big elephant, too. So far, we've assumed that diffusion models take a noisy image as input. That used to be the case. There's a huge problem with using images directly. Nobody wants a teeny-weeny pixelated result

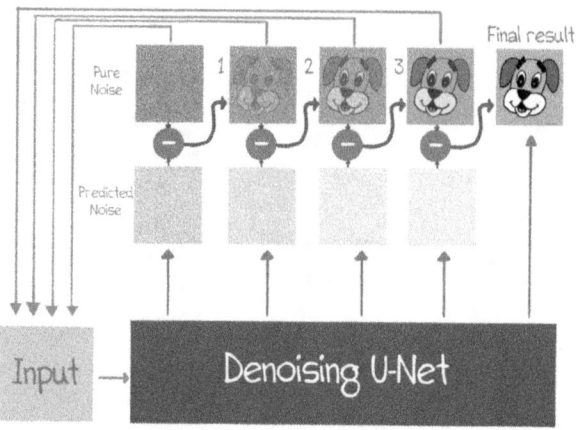

Figure 8.10. Denoising happens iteratively with each step bringing us closer to the final image.

from these models. Everyone wants a high-resolution image that they can proudly use as a screensaver, a book cover, or pass off as their own work of art.

A high-resolution image comes with a huge computational cost. Imagine you want a 1024 by 1024 image. That's 1,048,576 pixels, each with three values (one for red, green, and blue channels). Unless you're blessed with a server farm or have unlimited credits for cloud computing, you're not generating images that big anytime soon. You're also not training a model to produce said images anytime soon, either.

The solution to this problem is a return to latent space.

One of the innovations that Stable Diffusion[7] proposed was compressing the image first. Then, the denoising process could be done entirely on the compressed version. How do you compress an image?

Autoencoders!

We can train an autoencoder to learn a latent representation of the images in our dataset. Great. How do we do the denoising process now? Simple. Instead of adding noise to the image, we add noise to the latent representation of the image. The U-Net that previously worked on noisy images now removes noise from noisy latent vectors. Once the latent vector is denoised, the autoencoder's decoder can reconstruct the final image using this latent vector.

This innovation is so brilliant because this small change speeds up the diffusion process by several orders of magnitude. The latent space is much, much smaller than pixel space. So, it's significantly faster and more efficient to denoise in this space versus denoising in the pixel space (Figure 8.11).

So how does the training change? Not that much. The autoencoder's encoder compresses the image. We add noise to this compressed representation (a.k.a. the latent vector). The U-Net now guesses what the noise is on the latent vector. We compare its guess to the actual noise added. Rinse and repeat. The autoencoder's decoder reconstructs the image from the denoised latent vector.

Once the model is trained, we can give it random noise and let the U-Net denoise it into a latent code. This code can then be fed to the decoder, which will reconstruct an image from this code.

Creating What You Want

I lied earlier. There wasn't just one elephant in the room. There were two. We've addressed one of the above. Here's the other—How do

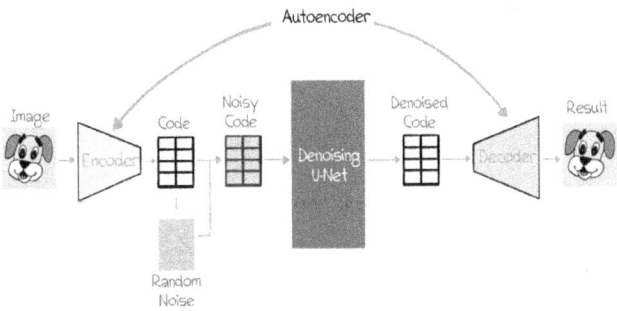

Figure 8.11. Making the denoising process faster through autoencoders.

you get the model to create the images that you want? So far, our model will create images similar to what it has seen in the training data. However, we have no control over what it generates. How do we address this?

Text prompts.

In addition to giving the model random noise, we also give it a description of what we want it to generate. This is called a prompt. The denoising U-Net can't interpret text directly, so we need a way to feed this information in a way that it can be understood. For this, we use a *text encoder*, which is often implemented using a Transformer model.

In diffusion models, a Transformer often serves as a text encoder, converting the text prompt into a numerical representation that the rest of the model can understand. It conveys the meaning of the prompt to the other parts of the model so that the image it generates matches the description provided. To achieve this, the Transformer is trained with a dataset containing images and captions. Each caption describes what the image is. In practice, these datasets are images scraped from the web along with their alt tags. That's why all the prompts we write don't read like conversational text but rather like cryptic shorthand. However, with the evolution of better datasets (which have descriptive captions), this won't be the case for long. Many modern diffusion models use pretrained language models as text encoders rather than training them from scratch on image-caption pairs. These pretrained models have already learned rich textual representations, which we know as embeddings.

Armed with these pairs of images and text, we can teach the Transformer to produce special text embeddings. Here's how. Say we have an image of a cow in a field. The caption that's associated with it reads, "Cow grazing in a field; sunshine; meadow." We ask the Transformer to produce two sets of embeddings. One for the image of the cow in the field and another for the caption. Now, we can take another caption that is completely unrelated to the image—"An astronaut taking a coffee break on the moon." We can ask our Transformer to produce a text embedding for this caption as well.

We now have an image embedding and two text embeddings. One of these text embeddings matches the image closely, while the other does not. Using a technique called contrastive learning, we can train the Transformer to bring the correct pair of image and text embeddings closer together and push the incorrect pair of image and text embeddings far apart.

How does it work?

We play a "match the pairs" game with the Transformer, where each image-text duo is a pair. A positive pair corresponds to the image and its correct caption (related text), and a negative pair consists of the image and an irrelevant caption (unrelated text). For every such pair, we ask the Transformer to decide whether the text matches the image. We then compare its guess with the actual label. If the guess is correct, the loss value decreases; if it's wrong, the loss value increases, providing a learning opportunity. Iterating this process refines the Transformer's ability to produce accurate text embeddings that align with image embeddings.

If we do this for a large number of image-text pairs, the Transformer learns the correct "text" representation of an image.

Thus, contrastive learning brings similar things together and pushes dissimilar things apart.

Once this Transformer has been trained, we can feed it prompts, and it will produce a text embedding that best represents the prompt. Our denoising U-Net can use these embeddings as guidance.[8] Huzzah!

So now, we can feed the U-Net a text embedding that represents the prompt and a random noise vector. The U-Net learns to use this text embedding to guide noise removal. Returning to our cats and dogs example, we'd now give a prompt like "Spotted cat sitting on a couch" along with a noisy latent vector. The denoiser would think, "Hmm, I need to remove noise so that what remains is a spotted cat on a couch."

This helps it generate an image that we want versus a random image. Thus, end-to-end, we provide a text prompt and receive an image matching the prompt. Internally, the prompt is converted to a text embedding. This, along with a noisy latent vector, is fed to the denoiser. The denoiser produces a denoised latent vector, which the autoencoder's decoder reconstructs into a beautiful image (Figure 8.12).

In practice, there's a lot more nuance and details to how these models work, but what we've covered so far captures the main ideas behind how they can generate incredible imagery. As these models get better and as the training data improves, the capabilities of these models will improve significantly, leading to a seismic shift in various creative media. Game developers, designers, and other creative professionals will be

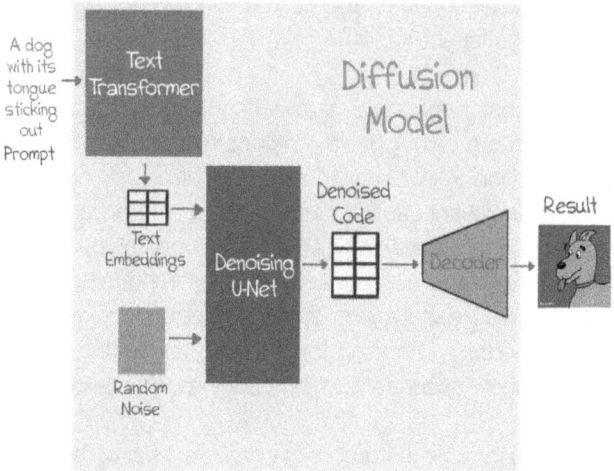

Figure 8.12. How the end-to-end image generation model looks under the hood.

able to increase their productivity and their project scope significantly. Creatives will only be limited by their imagination. But next, let's see how AI helps recommend things for us, whether it's music or items we'd like to purchase.

Chapter Summary

In this chapter, we learned about a collection of generative models. We discovered autoencoders are powerful tools for learning efficient codings of input data, enabling tasks such as dimensionality reduction, anomaly detection, and denoising. We also explored variational autoencoders (VAEs), which go beyond traditional autoencoders by modeling the underlying probability distribution of the data. This allows VAEs to generate new, original samples thanks to a structured latent space.

We saw GANs, where a generator and discriminator engage in an adversarial game. GANs can create realistic images but face challenges like mode collapse and training instability. Additionally, we saw how diffusion models took a different path. Instead of trying to create images directly, they learn by fixing increasingly messy versions of images—like learning to solve a puzzle by first scrambling it and then figuring out how to unscramble it. This method works remarkably well, especially when you can guide it with text descriptions like "Draw me a penguin wearing a top hat."

Speaking of text descriptions, we saw how Transformers help AI understand what we mean when we describe what we want to create. They bridge the gap between our words and visual ideas, making it possible to control AI art through natural language.

As we move into recommendation systems next, we'll see how these same ideas about understanding patterns help computers suggest things you might like—whether that's movies, music, or products.

Chapter 9
AI That Recommends Stuff

Since large language models and vision models catch all the limelight, it can be easy to think these are the only models used in practice. However, there exists a set of models that work silently behind the scenes, helping you without you even knowing they exist.

Browsing through a massive online catalog, you spot a pair of sneakers that's just your style. You'd like to see more options like this before purchasing. After all, you're a careful spender. Then, almost like magic, you're shown more sneakers, all of which you absolutely adore. A few guilty purchases later, you're streaming a movie on a lazy afternoon. It was pretty good, and once it's over, you see more movies and TV shows pop up on the screen. A lot of these new options look promising.

This isn't happening by magic, though—a recommendation system just guided you without you even realizing it.

Recommender systems (or recommenders for short) are everywhere, shaping our digital experiences. They're the reason you can find that perfect book in an online bookstore or that your social media feed seems to "know" what you want to see next.[1] These powerful systems sift through mountains of data to find and recommend items likely to pique your interest.

Over the course of this chapter, we'll look at the different types of recommender systems, how they work, and some practical challenges when building recommenders.

But first, what is a recommendation system?

Recommendations, Anyone?

Recommenders are a set of AI algorithms that understand your preferences based on past decisions and interactions. They are trained to learn this from data, including websites you've seen, links you clicked, purchases you made, and posts you "liked" on social media.

A good recommendation system can improve a business' revenue by several orders of magnitude.[2] Why? Think about it. We live in an attention-starved economy. We don't have time to wade through several web pages to find something we want. We want to find it instantly. If a website can show you things that are precisely tailored and personalized to your tastes, would you not spend more time (and money) there?

Not all recommenders are made equal. They come in different styles. Let's look at that next.

Types of Recommender Systems

Recommenders can be categorized into three broad flavors—collaborative filtering, content-based filtering, and hybrid systems. There are several recommendation algorithms, but almost all fall neatly into one of the three categories above.

Collaborative Filtering

Let's say we have three people: Sam, Evelyn, and Brian. Evelyn is friends with both Sam and Brian. Sam is a huge movie buff. He's binge-watched almost everything that his entire streaming catalog has to offer. One evening, over coffee, Sam laments that he has nothing left to watch and asks Evelyn if she's seen anything interesting lately. Evelyn recalls that her friend Brian loves movies, too. Like Sam, he loves comedy as well. She remembers Brian telling her about a new film, *Sharks Au Pain*, and how he couldn't stop laughing while watching it. She suggests this to Sam, who grins broadly on hearing the title. The next day, Sam tells

Evelyn that the movie was a rib-cracker and that he's never laughed so hard in his life (Figure 9.1).

You might wonder what on earth this has to do with recommenders. Evelyn just did collaborative filtering. Yep! Collaborative filtering methods recommend things to a user based on what other users with similar tastes prefer.

The name collaborative filtering comes from the fact that these methods use multiple users' past behavior to "collaboratively" filter out or recommend items to a target user. The idea behind this class of methods is based on a really simple insight. If two people like similar things, you can recommend what one likes to the other. Chances are the other person will enjoy the recommendation.

There are two subtypes within collaborative filtering. These are memory-based and model-based filtering methods.

Memory-Based Filtering

Let's look at memory-based methods first. These methods usually store lists of items each user has interacted with to generate new recommendations. Memory-based methods can be further subdivided

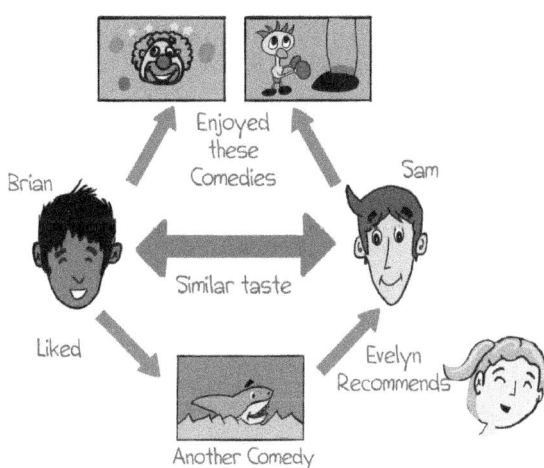

Figure 9.1. An overview of collaborative filtering.

into user-based filtering and item-based filtering.[3] User-based methods look for users who are similar to the target user and recommend items that these similar users like. The story of Sam and Evelyn above is an example of this.

Item-based methods are slightly different. In this case, instead of looking at user similarities, the system looks at the relationships between the items. This means that if a user likes a particular item, the system will recommend items similar to this item. So let's say that Sam ate at an Italian restaurant, "Cucina," and loved it. An item-based recommender would look at this and suggest other restaurants that were highly rated by users who loved Cucina. Memory-based systems employ sparse representations like one-hot encoding to keep track of user interactions.

Model-Based Filtering

As the name suggests, model-based systems use a model to predict and recommend items to a user. The model is trained on past user behaviors, items, and ratings. Once trained, the model can predict what a user likes or dislikes.

The key difference between memory-based and model-based systems is that the former uses the entire user-item relationship data directly. So, instead of operating directly on lists of items a user has interacted with, we learn a model based on this data. Thus, we use statistical methods to choose an item to recommend. In comparison, this makes memory-based methods simple and intuitive. So why do we need model-based methods, then? That's because memory-based methods suffer from a few limitations.

First, they can't handle sparse data well. If there's a user or item in the database with minimal information, memory-based systems will struggle to make accurate recommendations. Also, they can't scale to accommodate a large number of users or items. Why? We directly use lists of users and items. So, as this list grows, it becomes tricky to scale these systems to keep up. Finally, memory-based methods have difficulty dealing with new users or items because there's little to no data on them. This is called the cold start problem.

The cold start problem refers to the difficulty a recommendation system faces when making accurate recommendations for a new user or item. This is because the system has no previous data or behavior history to base its recommendations on.

Think of it this way: If you're a new user of a movie streaming platform, the system doesn't yet know your tastes and preferences. Similarly, if a new movie is added to the platform, the system has no user ratings or reviews to gauge its popularity. In both cases, the system faces a "cold start." It's like trying to start a car on a freezing winter day—it needs some time and the right conditions to get going properly!

Model-based systems, on the other hand, can handle sparse data and scale better than memory-based methods. They can also tackle the cold start problem more effectively, as they can infer the characteristics of users and items from related data.

However, model-based methods come with their own set of challenges. They use dense representations and can be more complex and computationally intensive, which can be a disadvantage when dealing with extremely large datasets. Also, they need to be updated regularly to accommodate new users or items, which can also be costly.

Ultimately, the choice between memory-based and model-based methods will depend on the specific requirements of the recommendation task at hand.

Content-Based Filtering

In content-based filtering, we switch our focus from user behavior to the specific qualities of each item. These systems use their information about each item to recommend new ones. Consider our movie-loving friend, Sam. If Sam watches and enjoys the movie *Sharks Au Pain*, a content-based filtering system would recommend movies to Sam that share similar characteristics with that film. This could be movies in the same genre, from the same director, starring the same actors, or having a similar plot or theme.

In other words, content-based filtering uses items' specific attributes or properties to suggest similar items. It doesn't need other users' data to make recommendations. It's all about matching the features of items to the preferences of the user (Figure 9.2).

The main advantage of content-based filtering is that it can handle the cold start problem better than collaborative filtering. As long as we have

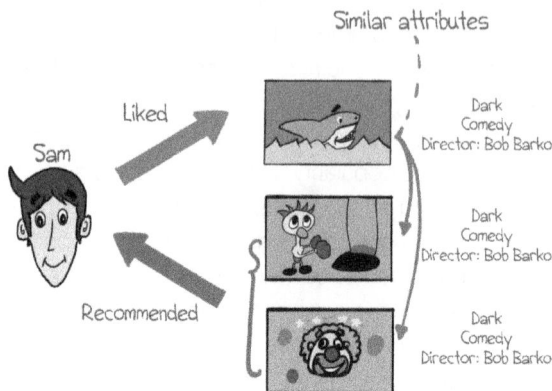

Figure 9.2. An overview of content-based filtering.

enough information about the item, we can make a recommendation even if no one else has interacted with it.

However, content-based filtering also has its limitations. First, it requires detailed and accurate information about the items. If this information is unavailable, limited, or inaccurate, the quality of the recommendations can be affected. Secondly, it may suggest only similar items, leading to a lack of diversity in the recommendations.

Hybrid Systems

A hybrid system combines the best of both worlds. It aims to leverage the strengths and mitigate the weaknesses of each method we've seen so far.

For instance, a hybrid system might use collaborative filtering to identify users who are similar to Sam and recommend movies that these users like. At the same time, it could use content-based filtering to suggest movies similar to the ones Sam enjoyed in the past. This way, it addresses the limitations of both systems.

Hybrid filtering methods often provide more accurate recommendations than collaborative or content-based filtering alone. They can deal with the cold start problem and offer a mix of expected and surprising recommendations, leading to a more engaging user experience.

Nevertheless, hybrid filtering also has some limitations. One is the complexity of designing and maintaining such systems, which combine multiple techniques. Also, data requirements can be substantial, as they need both user interaction data and detailed item information.

Entering the Matrix

We've seen the different types of recommenders, but how do they work under the hood? For that, we need to understand the user-item interaction matrix. This sounds like a mouthful, but don't worry. It's really simple once you understand how it works.

The user-item interaction matrix is a 2D grid. Each row represents a user. Each column represents an item. The value in each cell represents how much a user likes an item.

To make this clear, let's build a movie recommendation system for our friends Sam, Evelyn, and Brian. First, we need a row for each of them. Then, we need a column for various movies they have watched or haven't watched yet. For this, we need some movies. Let's go with *Sharks Au Pain*, a comedy, *The Soybean Vendetta*, an action movie, *Feline Fury*, another comedy, and *Love Is the King of the Game*, a romantic movie (Figure 9.3).

For every cell in this matrix, we either have a rating from 0 through 5 or a question mark. The higher the rating, the more the user liked the film. If a cell has a question mark, that means that the user hasn't watched the movie in question. This is where our recommender comes in. Its job is to figure out what the rating for these movies might be. Once it predicts a rating for the movie, it can then choose whether to recommend it to the user or not.

Thus, the recommender's job is to fill in the blanks and predict how likely a user is to enjoy a particular item given information about other related items (and users).

Ok, so now that we have this out of the way, let's look at how our recommender can solve this problem.

	Sharks Au Pain	The Soybean Vendetta	Feline Fury	Love is the King of the Game
Sam	?	3	5	?
Evelyn	?	5	?	4
Brian	5	?	?	5

Figure 9.3. The user-item interaction matrix.

Method 1: From Features to Ratings

First, let's look at how we can use content-based filtering to solve this. This approach starts with information about the users and the items and builds the matrix we saw above. Let's walk through an example to see how it does this.

We know that Sam loves comedy. He also loves action movies. But he hates romantic movies. So, we can create a matrix for Sam as follows. For each genre, we ask Sam to specify a rating between 0 and 5. The entries in this matrix are called user features. That's because these entries give us information about specific user preferences (in this case, Sam's).

We can also create a similar matrix for every movie on our list. If a movie falls into the romance and comedy genres, we will give it high values for those genres and low values for the other genres. For example, since the movie *Sharks Au Pain* is a comedy, it might have a score of 5 for comedy. But it would have a score of 0 for both romance and action since it doesn't fall under either of those genres.

The entries within this matrix are called item features, as they give us specific information about each item. To predict how much Sam will enjoy each of the movies, we have to examine how closely Sam's preferences align with the characteristics or genres of the movies. We can do this by multiplying Sam's preference values (user features) with the corresponding movie genre values (item features) for each movie (Figure 9.4).

The value we get from this calculation provides an estimate of how much Sam would appreciate the movie *Sharks Au Pain*. We can then use the same process for each of the other movies. By doing this for all the movies, we can predict which movie Sam is likely to enjoy the most (Figure 9.5).

This is a simple and intuitive process, right? We match what a user likes with the characteristics of each item to find the best items for the user. It's also a storage-efficient method. We just need to keep track of two smaller matrices instead of a giant table that has entries for all users and movies. Whenever we need to get the score for a particular user and movie, we compute the weighted sum as above, and we're good to go.

But, there are a few limitations. This approach assumes we have detailed preference information for each user and movie. What if a new user joins the service or a new movie gets added to the catalog? What do we do then? Do you recall taking a survey when you joined a new

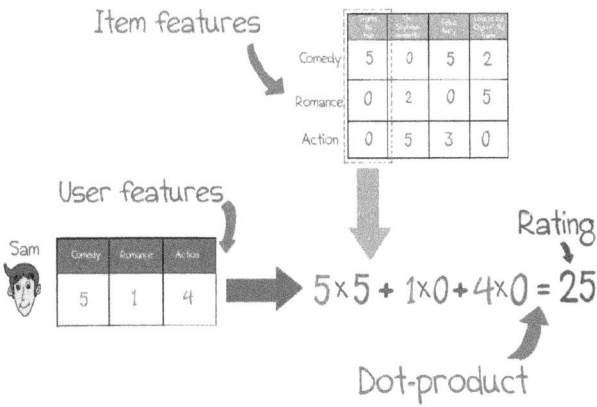

Figure 9.4. How the dot product is computed.

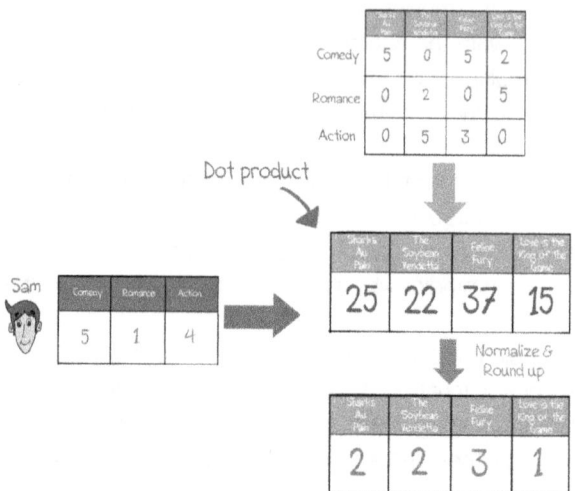

Figure 9.5. The dot product computes a score for each user-item pair, which we then normalize and round up.

streaming service? That survey is a way for the streaming service to find out what to recommend to you. How many of us patiently (and correctly) filled this survey out? Another limitation is that we specify the features here. For example, the movie genres are the features in our example above. But we could have so many other useful features like the cast, the director, the length of the movie, whether it has car chases, and so on.

Method 2: From Ratings to Features

This leads us to the collaborative filtering approach. As we saw in the previous section, collaborative filtering uses information from other users who have similar preferences as you to make recommendations.

Instead of starting with user features and item features, we start with the user-item interaction matrix itself. We need to figure out a way to break this large matrix into two smaller matrices—the user features matrix and the item features matrix.

If you're wondering if this is the reverse of what we did earlier, you're right. It is. Kind of. The key difference is that in this process, we don't know what the features will be. In the content filtering approach, we chose what features to use. In our example, these were the specific genres—action, romance, drama, and comedy.

In the collaborative filtering approach, however, we don't have names for the features we will find. They are learned from patterns in the data. That's why these features are also called latent factors.

Matrix Factorization

So, let's get back to the task at hand. We need to break the user-item interaction matrix into a user features matrix and an item features matrix so that when we multiply these two matrices, we should be able to recover the original user-item interaction matrix.

This process is called matrix factorization, and it's one of the most popular ways to build recommendation systems (Figure 9.6).

There are a number of ways to do matrix factorization. The two most commonly used approaches are gradient descent and weighted least squares.

We'll focus only on gradient descent here.

I'm sure you've noticed that the user-item interaction matrix we have is incomplete. So, we'll have to figure out what the user features and

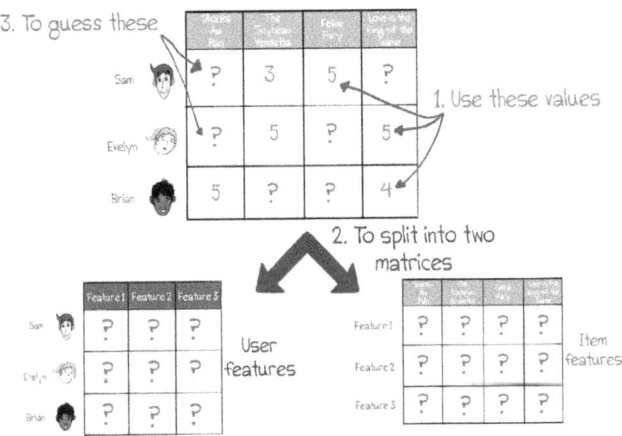

Figure 9.6. How matrix factorization works.

item features are from the partial information that's available. Then, using these two matrices, we can predict the missing values in the user-item interaction matrix.

Think of this process as solving a sudoku puzzle. There are specific numbers that go into each cell, but only one combination will fully satisfy every constraint in the puzzle. In this case, we need to fill two smaller matrices with numbers so that their product satisfies the constraints of the user-item matrix that we have.

I realize this is a lot to wrap your head around, so let's go step by step.

First, how do we factorize the user-item matrix? A naive approach would be to randomly guess the values of the user features and item features until we find the right combination. But this can take ages, especially if the number of users and items is large.

Can we solve this using machine learning instead? Yes, we can!

Recall that gradient descent helps us find the weights of a neural network so that the overall prediction error is minimized. We can do the same thing here. Instead of predicting a neural network's weights, we will try to predict the *known* values of the user features and item features. Gradient descent can help us find the values of these features so that the overall reconstruction error is minimized. If our model can accurately predict the known values in the user-item matrix, then it stands to reason that its predictions for the missing values would be reasonably accurate as well.

How does this work?

We can randomly initialize the user features and item features. Note that we only know how many features we want, but we don't know *what* they are. The number of features to use is a hyperparameter[4] that we choose.

With the random initialization at hand, we can multiply the user feature matrix and item feature matrix to get a *predicted* user-item interaction matrix. We then compare the values in this prediction with the actual user-item interaction matrix. Importantly, we can only compare the values that are available in the original matrix (Figure 9.7).

We can then take the difference between the actual values and predicted values to compute an error. We then use gradient descent to update the values of the user feature matrix and item feature matrix.

We repeat this cycle until the error is minimized.

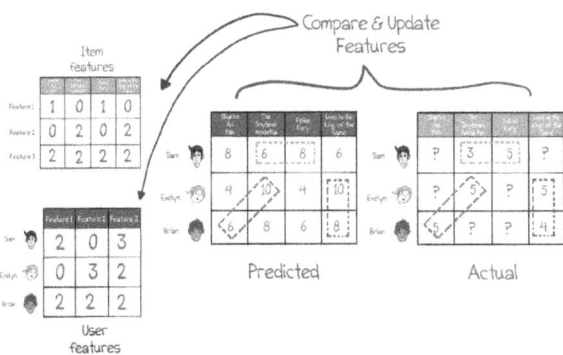

Figure 9.7. How are user and item features calculated? We use the available values in the user-item matrix to guess the user and item features. Once we've guessed reasonably well, we use the user and item features to complete the missing values in the user-item matrix.

The advantage of this approach is that we can discard the original user-item interaction matrix at the end of the process. Why? We can recover any value by simply multiplying the user feature matrix and item feature matrix. Thus, it can save space. Also, since the features are learned from the data, they are more robust and capture the connections between users and items much better. However, gradient descent can be slow if the user-item matrix is really large. This makes it tricky to scale. User-item interaction matrices are usually sparse since users only interact with a few items. Thus, predicting a large number of unknown values can lead to errors in the recommendation. These also struggle with the cold start problem, as we've seen before.

We've seen the traditional approach to recommendation systems. Next, let's look at how deep learning has exerted its influence in this domain.

Deep Learning and Recommendations

With the rise of big data and computation power, deep learning models have become increasingly popular for producing high-quality recommenders. Deep learning models are great at extracting robust features from data. This makes them fantastic backbones for recommendation systems. We've also seen the power of embeddings and how they model contextual information. Combine these two things, and you have a potent class of models that can be used in large-scale recommendation problems.

Training a Deep Learning Recommender

The simplest way to incorporate deep learning is to learn embeddings for the user and item features. With these embeddings, we can then recommend new items to a user based on how close their embeddings are to an item the user already enjoyed. Let's go back to our friend Sam for a minute. Since he likes *Sharks Au Pain*, the recommender might look at where this movie falls in embedding space. It will suggest other movies whose embeddings are very close to this movie's embedding. Chances are Sam might enjoy these recommendations.

For a more sophisticated approach, we could build a neural network recommender. During training, the network is trained on user-item interaction data. The model can be trained to produce a probability score that indicates how likely a user is to interact with an item. Since we use past data to train the model, we have ground truth information on whether the user really interacted with the item. Using our trusty approach of gradient descent and backpropagation, we can update the weights of the neural network to make it accurately predict whether a user will interact with a new item (Figure 9.8).

Using the Recommender

Once the network is trained, it's used in a two-step process to recommend items to a user—candidate generation followed by ranking.

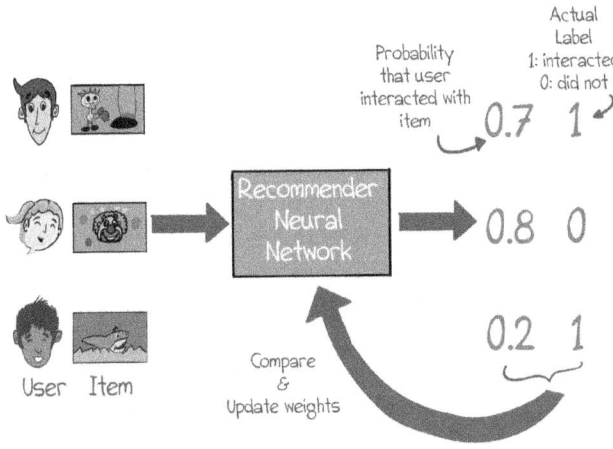

Figure 9.8. Training a deep neural network to predict user interactions.

Candidate Generation

A true recommendation system will have to deal with millions of items and users. Expecting it to produce probability scores for every item in the catalog is madness. We need to whittle the list of items down before using the neural network. This is where candidate generation comes in.

We take the user's query and then retrieve a pool of items the user will most likely interact with. Using the techniques we have covered so far, we retrieve the closest neighbors[5] to the user's query.

Ranking

Once the candidates have been identified, they are scored and ranked to produce a smaller set of items to present to the user. Typically, candidate generation and ranking are done by different models. Why? A real-world recommendation system could have multiple candidate generators. The ranking model would take in a diverse collection of candidates to rank them based on relevance. Since the ranking model deals with a much smaller set of items to evaluate, we could potentially use a more sophisticated model here. This is another reason why candidate generation and ranking models might be separate.

In some cases, there might be an additional re-ranking step before the final top items are presented to the user.

Think of this process like a funnel setup. We use a lightweight model at the top of the funnel to do a quick weed out of irrelevant items. Then we use a more complex model for ranking the remaining items, and finally, another model to re-rank them if needed. Thus, the complexity of the models we use increases further down the funnel. But, the number of items reduces from millions to thousands to hundreds to tens in each step (Figure 9.9).

Now that we've seen how deep learning recommendation models work in principle, let's briefly tour a few well-known architectures.

Popular Deep Learning Recommenders

There are many recommendation models out there. Here is a selection of four types that are worth checking out further.[6]

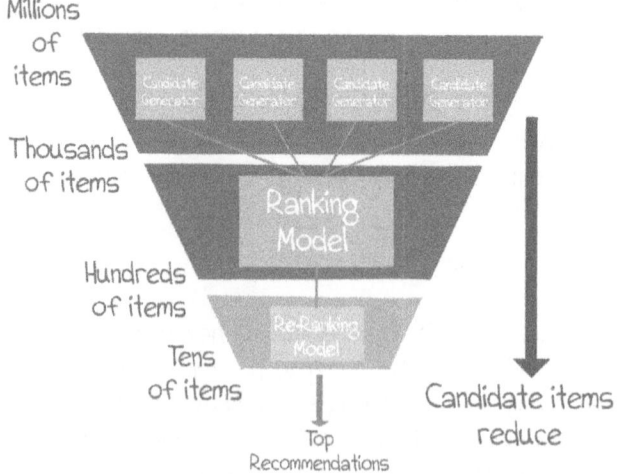

Figure 9.9. A funnel system helps us to rank and filter results. Notice how the number of recommendations reduces as we go deeper into the funnel.

- *Neural Collaborative Filtering*: This model is a twist on traditional collaborative filtering methods. Instead of simply measuring similarities, it uses a neural network to learn the complex and non-linear relationships between users and items. The hidden layers in the network can capture these complex patterns, making the recommendations more precise and personalized.
- *Wide and Deep Networks*: This is a two-part model. The "wide" part is a linear model that focuses on memorizing specific feature interactions. This helps the system remember frequently co-occurring user-item pairs. The "deep" part is a neural network that learns complex feature interactions, helping the system discover patterns and create better recommendations even for less common user-item pairs. This combination of "wide" and "deep" allows the model to make accurate recommendations while also maintaining diversity.
- *Deep and Cross Networks:* This model improves upon the Wide and Deep model by adding a "cross" component. The cross component specifically learns interactions between features. This makes the model even better at generating recommendations, especially when complex relationships exist among features.
- *Autoencoders*: We've already seen how autoencoders work. They are a great way to compress data. In recommendation systems, an autoencoder takes the user-item interaction matrix as input. Through a process of compression and reconstruction, it learns to recreate the original matrix. The beauty here is that in the process of recreating the matrix, it also fills in the missing values. Thus, it can predict unknown user-item interactions.

Bravo! We've covered a lot of ground. You now know a wide range of models and their applications. Next, it's time to roll up our sleeves and figure out how we can use machine learning for our own projects.

Chapter Summary

In this chapter, we learned that recommender systems are powerful AI algorithms that understand user preferences and provide personalized recommendations. Think about the last time you discovered your new favorite song or TV show. Chances are, a recommendation system played a part in that discovery. These AI systems have become the quiet guides of our digital lives, helping us navigate an overwhelming sea of content and choices.

They can be categorized into collaborative, content-based, and hybrid systems, each with strengths and limitations. We've seen how collaborative filtering learns from the crowd. If you and I like the same movies, maybe you'll enjoy other films I've rated highly. Content-based systems take a different route, looking at what makes items similar. If you love sci-fi books with complex characters, here are more books just like that. Hybrid systems combine the best of both approaches.

Matrix factorization is a fundamental technique in recommendation systems, helping to decompose the user-item interaction matrix into user and item feature matrices. Deep learning models have emerged as valuable tools for learning embeddings and modeling complex relationships. Popular deep learning recommender models include Neural Collaborative Filtering, Wide and Deep Networks, Deep and Cross Networks, and Autoencoders.

As these systems evolve, we're tackling fascinating challenges: protecting user privacy, explaining why recommendations are made, and solving the eternal question of how to recommend things to new users who haven't built up a history yet.

Recommendation systems are bridges connecting people with content they'll love, businesses with potential customers, and creators with their ideal audience. When done right, they open doors to discoveries we might never have made on our own.

Chapter 10
Building Intelligence
The Complete AI Project Guide

Every successful AI project starts with a story. Perhaps it's a medical center developing an AI system to help radiologists spot patterns in X-rays more quickly. Maybe it's a local farm using AI to optimize crop yields while using less water. Or it could be a small business creating a smarter customer service system. Behind each success are careful planning, thoughtful execution, and lessons learned from setbacks along the way.

You've learned what AI can do—from recognizing images to understanding language. Now, let's explore how organizations actually build these systems, what makes them succeed, and how to avoid common pitfalls that can derail even the most promising projects.

Planning, Building, and Launching AI Projects

Imagine you're about to build a house. You'd start with blueprints, not bricks. You'd carefully consider the foundation, materials, and whether you really need a house or if a simple renovation would do. Most importantly, you'd make sure it fits your needs and budget. AI projects follow a surprisingly similar path, though they combine both established best practices and rapidly evolving technologies. Just as a poorly planned house can collapse, an AI project without proper planning can crumble—but the costs can be far higher. So, let's dive deeper into each phase and understand how we can build successful AI projects.

Planning

While AI projects traditionally required massive investments in computing power and specialized talent, today's landscape offers more accessible options—from pretrained models to cloud services. However, the true costs often lie in data preparation, testing, and ongoing maintenance. A misstep can be costly both in terms of money and time (several months' worth sometimes). Thus, planning is the most crucial step for AI projects. In this phase, we ideate, scope, and define the problem we want to solve. We must do much more than just have a good idea.

Before you embark on an AI project, consider whether AI is transforming the product (or service) or if it's a buzzword feature tacked on to make the product feel hip.

This distinction separates truly AI-native solutions from superficial applications.

The key question isn't "How can we add AI to our product?" but rather, "How can we build our product around AI?"

Building AI-native solutions demands more than just an investment in technology. It requires a cultural shift within the organization. Teams need to foster a mindset of continual learning and adaptation while being mindful of ethical considerations and responsible AI practices.

During the planning phase, our goal is to not think of the models to use or the datasets first. It's to think about the users first. Define the problem the user is facing, and then work back from there. If you disregard the user and focus on the model with a hypothetical promise of 10× improvements in performance, you're guaranteed a 10× acceleration rate to failure.

Once you clearly state the problem and the user's requirements, consider the problem type. Is it a classification problem, regression problem, recommendation problem, or something else?

This will clarify what data to use, how to collect and process it, and your modeling options. You might discover that you can achieve your goals with more straightforward machine learning approaches or that you can leverage existing pretrained models rather than building everything from scratch.

The choice of modeling options and data, in turn, gives you clarity on the computation power you'll need, the storage options you'll have to consider, and so on. This includes deciding whether to run models locally or in the cloud and how to handle data securely and responsibly.

Planning also includes identifying the metrics that will be used to measure the project's success. In many large-scale systems, the AI component might be one part of the system. Understanding how the AI component interacts with other parts of your system is crucial—from data pipelines to user interfaces. While model accuracy is important, real success often depends on broader metrics like user satisfaction, system reliability, and business impact.

Taking time to plan thoroughly pays dividends throughout the project. Good planning helps you anticipate challenges, from data privacy concerns to system scalability, before problems become costly.

Building

Now, it's time to put on the builder's helmet. Modern AI development often starts by evaluating existing solutions and datasets before jumping into data collection. When you do need to collect data, it must be done ethically and systematically.

The next step is preparing your data—transforming it into a format that AI models can learn from effectively. This might mean extracting specific features from text, images, or numerical data. While the planning phase gives you clues on what models might work, the actual choice largely depends on the specific problem at hand and the nature of the data. After choosing an approach, the process of training and refining the model begins. This involves careful testing and adjustment to ensure the model performs reliably, not just in controlled tests but in real-world conditions.

The final step of the building phase is integration. This is to ensure that your AI model works seamlessly with other system components. We'll be looking at the build phase in much more depth later.

Launching

Launching an AI system is more than just flipping a switch. It's a careful process of rolling out the system to real users, often starting with a small pilot group before wider deployment. This is when theory meets reality—when your system faces real-world data and user interactions.

But the work's not done just yet! Success requires ongoing attention: monitoring technical metrics, user feedback, and system impact. AI systems can become less effective over time as real-world conditions change, so you need processes for detecting and addressing performance issues quickly. For example, a 2019 customer service AI bot would be confused by questions about curbside pickup or social distancing. You need ways to spot these problems quickly and update your system, typically by retraining it with newer data.

Since building AI systems is challenging, we must have a diverse team combining technical expertise, domain knowledge, and user empathy. It's not about individual brilliance but about collaborative problem-solving and continuous learning (Figure 10.1).

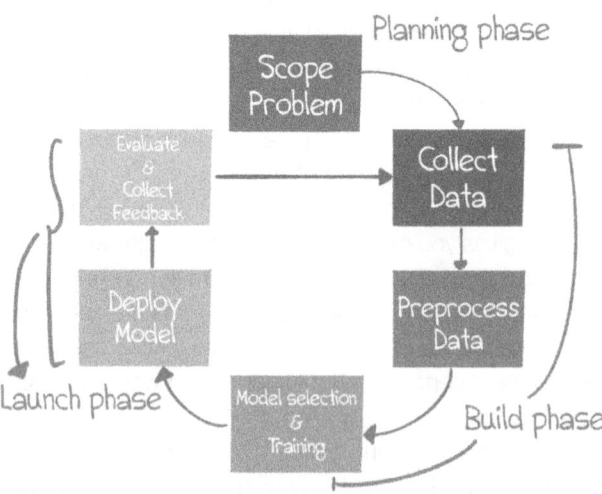

Figure 10.1. The AI project life cycle.

The AI Team

Naturally, an AI project requires a cross-functional team. While there are many other roles like UX engineers, full-stack engineers, and so on, the ones listed below are at the core of an AI project.

Research Scientist

This role typically requires a PhD and focuses on pushing the boundaries of what AI can do. While some exceptional engineers without PhDs have become research scientists through groundbreaking work and published research, this path is rare. Think of research scientists as the architects who design entirely new types of AI systems rather than building with existing tools.

Research Engineer

This bridging role exists in larger AI companies, turning research scientists' theoretical ideas into working prototypes. While some companies use this title interchangeably with research scientist, the key difference is that Research Engineers focus on proving whether new AI approaches can work in practice. They build experimental systems that might become tomorrow's standard tools.

Machine Learning Engineer (MLE)

MLEs are the builders who turn AI ideas into reliable systems that solve real business problems. They combine software engineering expertise with machine learning knowledge to create AI systems that work at scale. For example, an MLE might take a customer service AI from handling 100 test conversations to reliably processing millions of real customer interactions.

Data Scientist

Data Scientists dig through data to find patterns and insights that shape business decisions. Unlike MLEs who build systems to solve known problems, data scientists often figure out what problems to solve in the first place. For example, a data scientist might discover that weather patterns strongly influence customer buying behavior, leading to an AI system that automatically adjusts inventory based on weather forecasts.

Data Engineer

Data Engineers build and maintain the foundation that AI systems run on: the data infrastructure. They create the pipelines that collect, clean, and organize data, ensuring that it's reliable and accessible. Without data engineers, even the best AI models would struggle with messy, inconsistent, or slow data. For instance, they might build systems that can process millions of customer interactions in real-time while ensuring data quality and privacy.

ML Operations (MLOps) Engineer

MLOps engineers specialize in building and maintaining the infrastructure of AI systems. They ensure models can be deployed quickly, monitored effectively, and updated seamlessly. Think of them as combining DevOps expertise with ML knowledge. They're the ones who make sure your AI system runs reliably 24/7 and can handle real-world traffic.

Prompt Engineer

Prompt engineers are specialists who get the best results from large language models and other AI systems through careful input design. They bridge the gap between what users want to accomplish and how AI systems need to be instructed. This relatively new role has become increasingly important as organizations build applications on top of foundation models.

AI Product Manager

AI product managers combine product thinking with an understanding of AI capabilities and limitations. They need to manage unique aspects of AI products like data strategy, model performance metrics, and ethical considerations. Unlike traditional PMs, they must balance technical feasibility with the sometimes unpredictable nature of AI systems.

Team Structure and Scaling

The size and composition of your AI team evolve with your project's scope and maturity. Most successful projects start small with a machine learning engineer to build the AI systems, a data engineer to manage data pipelines, and an AI product manager to guide development. As projects grow, teams typically expand to include specialists like MLOps engineers for robust deployment, prompt engineers for working with foundation models, and data scientists for deeper analysis.

At the enterprise level, you might see multiple teams with research scientists exploring novel approaches, AI ethics and governance specialists, and platform teams supporting various AI products. But remember, starting lean and growing based on concrete needs is better than trying to build a "perfect" team from day one.

Next, let's look at what these teams build: the lifecycle of an AI model. From initial concept to deployment and maintenance, each stage requires careful attention and brings its own challenges.

The Lifecycle of an AI Model

Every AI model follows a journey from idea to reality, similar to how a product moves from design to store shelves. Each stage requires different team members to work together to solve specific challenges.

Data Collection and Cleaning

Data collection is where your data engineers and data scientists first shine. They need to gather the right information to teach your AI system. This might come from your existing product, like customer purchase history, public datasets like weather records, or real-time sources like social media feeds. Getting this right is crucial. An AI model can only be as good as the data it learns from.

But raw data is rarely perfect. It's like a diamond in the rough—valuable but needs polishing. Your data engineers spend considerable time cleaning this data: filling in missing information (like incomplete customer profiles), removing duplicates (like repeated transactions), and handling unusual cases (like impossibly high prices that might be errors). This clean, reliable data becomes the foundation that machine learning engineers will build upon.

Raw Data and Features

Even clean data must be transformed into something AI models can learn from effectively. Imagine a house price prediction system: your raw data includes square footage, number of bedrooms, and zip code. But just like a chef doesn't just throw ingredients in a pot, your MLEs don't use this raw data directly. They combine and transform this information into more meaningful insights: price per square foot in a neighborhood, how much larger or smaller a house is compared to its neighbors, or whether the number of bedrooms is unusual for that area. These new "features" help the AI understand the housing market better than it could from raw numbers alone.

The Art of Feature Engineering

Feature engineering is the process of selecting, creating, or transforming features to improve the performance of your AI models. This is where data scientists and MLEs combine their expertise. Good feature engineering is often what separates successful projects from failures. It's not just about having data but also about having the right view of that data.

This process plays a crucial role in determining the performance of the model. Even the most advanced AI algorithms can deliver poor results if the features are not well-engineered. For example, in an AI system predicting customer behavior, knowing someone's total purchases might be less useful than knowing if their purchasing frequency is increasing or decreasing. Data scientists might create new features that capture these trends, while MLEs ensure these calculations can happen quickly enough for real-world use.

Feature engineering isn't a one-and-done process. As your system encounters real users and real problems, you'll often discover new ways to look at your data that make your AI more effective. This is where the iterative nature of AI development becomes apparent. Each customer interaction contributes insights that lead to better features.

Model Selection and Hyperparameter Tuning

With good features in place, machine learning engineers focus on choosing and configuring the right AI approach. Each type of AI model has its strengths and costs.

This is where collaboration between MLEs and MLOps engineers becomes crucial. While MLEs experiment with different models, trying dozens or hundreds of variations, MLOps engineers build systems to track these experiments, manage computing resources, and ensure results are reproducible. To make sense of all these experiments, AI teams start with a baseline. A baseline model is the simplest or most naive strategy you adopt to solve your problem.

This could be a model that always predicts the most common class in your dataset or even a more complex one like logistic regression or a decision tree model.

But here's why a good baseline is more than just a beginner's step:

- *Realistic Expectations*: A baseline gives you an idea of the minimum performance your model should be able to achieve. This is important because it sets a practical floor for what you can expect from your more complex models. If your complex model is performing worse than your baseline, you know there's a problem that needs addressing.

- *Benchmarking*: It provides a reference point to compare how well other models are doing. Without this comparison point, measuring progress or the degree of improvement a more sophisticated model provides is hard.

- *Insight into the Dataset*: Simple baseline models can often reveal much about your data. For example, if a naive model (like always predicting the most common class) performs surprisingly well, it could indicate a class imbalance in your data.

- *Time and Resource Management*: If a simple baseline model already provides acceptable performance, it might be unnecessary to pursue more complex models, saving you time and computational resources.

- *Troubleshooting*: The baseline can be a debugging tool if more complex models aren't improving accuracy. The comparison between the baseline and more sophisticated models can give you insights into what could be going wrong.

So, a good baseline is like a reality check, a point of reference, and a wise old guide all rolled into one. It's a critical component in developing an effective AI solution.

Once promising models are identified, MLEs and MLOps engineers work together to optimize them. MLEs focus on adjusting model settings (remember hyperparameters from previous chapters?) to improve performance, while MLOps engineers build automated systems to test thousands of combinations efficiently. This collaboration helps find the best configuration while keeping computing costs under control. A 1 percent improvement might sound small, but it can have a massive impact in production systems handling millions of predictions.

Cross-Validation

Before any model goes to production, we need to be confident it will perform reliably. This is where cross-validation comes in. This is a systematic way of testing your model's performance. MLEs and MLOps engineers might work together here with MLEs designing the validation strategy, while MLOps engineers ensure these tests are automated, reproducible, and efficiently tracked.

The main purpose of CV is to prevent overfitting, which is when the model blindly memorizes the training data, resulting in poor performance on unseen data (Figure 10.2).

Cross-validation is like a dress rehearsal before opening night at Broadway. It helps predict how your AI will perform in the real world. Using automated tests that run continuously, we can catch potential problems before they affect users. While there are several validation strategies to choose from, the key is picking one that matches your

Building Intelligence

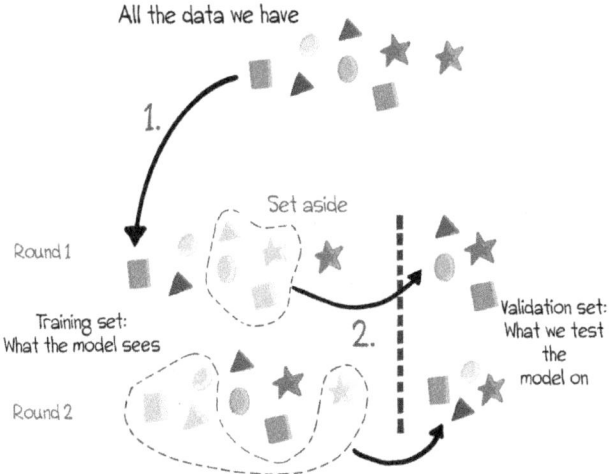

Figure 10.2. Cross-validation helps us predict how well the model will perform on unseen data.

data type and business needs. For example, if you're predicting future events, you need special validation approaches that respect time order.

Deployment

After going through all these steps, the next step is deployment. This stage is where your AI project really comes to life. Here are a few things that happen during deployment:

- *Production Readiness:* MLEs and MLOps engineers transform research code into production systems, adding monitoring, failsafes, and performance optimizations.
- *Infrastructure Decisions:* The team chooses where to run the model based on needs like speed, cost, and scale—from cloud services to edge devices.
- *System Integration:* MLEs and MLOps engineers work together to connect the AI system with existing company software, ensuring smooth data flow and quick predictions.

- *Performance Tracking:* MLOps engineers set up dashboards and alerts to monitor everything from prediction accuracy to system health.

- *User Testing:* Product managers and MLEs gather feedback from real users, while MLOps engineers might track technical metrics to ensure the system meets both user needs and technical requirements.

Monitoring and Updating

Launching your AI system is just the beginning of its lifecycle. This is where the full team comes together, each playing a crucial role in keeping the system healthy and improving it over time. MLOps engineers build the monitoring infrastructure, data scientists and MLEs interpret the results, and product managers gather user feedback.

Models can "drift" over time as data and circumstances change, becoming less accurate as the world changes around them. For example, a product recommendation system trained before the 2020 pandemic might have failed to adapt to new shopping patterns. If the model's performance starts to degrade or new data becomes available, it may be necessary to retrain or fine-tune the model. Sometimes, you may need to return to the feature engineering or data collection stage.

Modern AI systems need both technical and business monitoring. MLOps engineers need to track system health metrics like prediction speed, error rates, and computing costs. Meanwhile, product managers and data scientists monitor business metrics and user feedback. For example, your AI might be making technically accurate predictions, but the system isn't truly successful if users find it hard to act on.

The lifecycle of an AI model is truly circular. Insights from monitoring often spark new ideas for features, data collection, or model improvements. This is why having a cross-functional team is so crucial. Data Engineers might spot data quality issues, MLEs might identify better modeling approaches, and product managers might uncover new user needs. Each insight can trigger another round of development, helping your AI system grow more valuable over time. This continuous improvement cycle, supported by robust MLOps practices, transforms a promising AI project into a reliable, production-grade system that delivers real business value.

As we've seen how AI systems evolve from idea to reality, the next question becomes crucial: how do we measure success? Let's explore how different teams evaluate their work and ensure they deliver real value.

Evaluating AI Project Success: Metrics and KPIs

An AI project's success is based on more than just whether the model was built. It's also about evaluating if the solution added value to the business and met the objectives outlined at the project's onset. This is where metrics and Key Performance Indicators (KPIs) come in. They help gauge the project's success in a quantifiable manner.

Metrics

These quantifiable measures can help assess and compare the performance of processes or models. Machine learning and MLOps engineers track detailed performance metrics like model accuracy, prediction speed, and system reliability. Data Engineers monitor data pipeline efficiency and data quality scores. These technical metrics help the team spot problems quickly and make informed decisions about system improvements. In addition to these, MLOps engineers and product managers also track broader system metrics: How much does each prediction cost? How often does the system need human intervention? How quickly can we update the model when needed? These metrics help optimize the system's efficiency and cost-effectiveness.

KPIs

While your technical team focuses on metrics like model accuracy, product managers and business stakeholders need to track how the AI system impacts business goals. For a customer service AI, this might mean:

- Reduction in response times;
- Customer satisfaction scores;
- Cost savings compared to traditional solutions;
- Revenue impact.

These KPIs help justify the investment in AI and guide future development priorities. Your MLOps dashboard might show 99 percent uptime and lightning-fast predictions, but if customer satisfaction drops, something's wrong. Success means aligning technical excellence with business value. This is why modern AI teams need strong collaboration between technical experts and business stakeholders.

Ethics and Bias in AI: A Team Responsibility

Ethics in AI isn't a checkbox to be ticked but woven into every team member's daily work. Data engineers start the ethical pipeline by ensuring data collection respects privacy and consent, carefully documenting data sources and potential biases. Data scientists and MLEs then build on this foundation, incorporating fairness metrics into their model evaluation process and designing systems that detect and mitigate bias. Meanwhile, MLOps engineers create monitoring systems to track model behavior in production, ensuring the system remains fair as it encounters real-world data.

Understanding and identifying bias requires constant vigilance. AI systems can subtly amplify existing societal biases or create new ones. For instance, a loan approval system might discriminate against certain neighborhoods not because it was programmed to do so but because it learned from historical lending data that reflects decades of discriminatory practices. A facial recognition system might perform poorly for certain demographics simply because its training data wasn't diverse enough. These aren't theoretical problems but real challenges that AI teams face daily.

Mitigating these biases requires a coordinated effort across the entire team. The data team works to audit data sources for representation gaps and documents known biases in datasets. Sometimes, they might even create synthetic data to balance underrepresented groups. Engineers implement fairness metrics in model evaluation and build automated bias detection into their deployment pipelines. For high-risk decisions, they create fallback systems and human review processes. Product teams ensure these technical safeguards translate into fair user experiences by conducting research across diverse groups and designing inclusive interfaces.

Responsible AI practices must be implemented at every phase of development and deployment. During planning, teams must conduct ethical impact assessments and establish data governance frameworks. In development, they should create detailed documentation of model limitations and assumptions and build features explaining the system's decisions. Once in production, they need to continuously monitor for emerging biases or performance disparities across different user groups.

This commitment to ethical AI requires both technical rigor and human judgment. Teams need to regularly review their systems' behavior for technical performance, fairness, and societal impact. They must be ready to adjust or rebuild systems that show concerning patterns, even if those systems meet their technical performance metrics. This might mean accepting lower accuracy in exchange for more equitable performance across different groups or adding additional review steps for high-stakes decisions.

The goal isn't to create perfect AI systems—that's likely impossible. Instead, the aim is to build systems that are transparently imperfect, where we understand and can explain their limitations, biases, and failure modes. This transparency allows users to make informed decisions about when and how to rely on AI systems and helps teams continuously improve their systems' fairness and reliability.

Responsible AI Deployment: Guidelines and Recommendations

Deploying AI responsibly means turning ethical ideals into everyday actions. In production, this starts with radical transparency. Every AI system needs clear documentation and honesty about its strengths and limitations. It's not enough to showcase impressive accuracy numbers. We must be upfront about what the system might get wrong and who could be affected. Monitoring dashboards should make issues visible before they become problems, tracking everything from technical hiccups to fairness concerns.

Privacy and security features are foundational requirements. Modern AI systems need sophisticated safeguards: strict data access controls, robust anonymization, and automatic data cleanup policies. Consider collecting user data like borrowing someone's personal belongings—take only what you absolutely need, protect it carefully, and return it (or delete it) when you're done. When gathering feedback to improve the system, resist the temptation to collect extra data just because you can.

Real-world deployment means expecting the unexpected. Every AI system will eventually face situations it wasn't trained for. The question is how gracefully it handles them. Critical systems need clear escalation paths: Who gets notified when something looks wrong? What backup systems kick in? When do humans need to take over? These are core design decisions that separate robust systems from risky ones.

Environmental impact has moved from an afterthought to an essential consideration. Every training run and every prediction consumes energy. Modern deployments must balance performance against power consumption, sometimes choosing simpler models that achieve similar results with smaller carbon footprints. Do you really need that extra 1 percent accuracy if it doubles your energy usage?

Maintaining standards over time is perhaps the greatest challenge. AI systems can subtly drift off course as the world around them changes. Yesterday's fairness might become tomorrow's bias. Regular impact assessments shouldn't be considered bureaucratic overhead but essential maintenance, like checking your car's brakes. User feedback often reveals problems that metrics miss, especially when it comes from people your system is supposed to help.

This commitment to responsible AI requires courage at every level. Sometimes, it means telling stakeholders that their timeline isn't realistic or that their favorite feature creates unfair bias. It means giving teams the authority to raise concerns and the resources to fix problems. Most importantly, it means accepting that responsible AI deployment is a journey without end. There's always room for improvement, new challenges to address, and better ways to serve and protect users.

The future of AI will be shaped by how well we handle these responsibilities today. Every deployment sets precedents, builds trust, or erodes it, and shows what's possible when we prioritize doing things right over doing them fast. The technology is powerful—our challenge is keeping it pointed in the right direction.

Building for Tomorrow: The Road Ahead

A profound transformation reshapes the landscape as we close this chapter on building and deploying AI systems. The rise of open-source AI has turned what was once proprietary knowledge into public infrastructure. Tools and models that would have cost millions to develop are now freely available, letting small teams tackle problems that once required tech giants. This democratization isn't just about access to code—it's about sharing knowledge, techniques, and lessons learned across the global AI community.

Foundation models have become the new building blocks of AI development. Instead of starting from scratch, teams can now build on these powerful pretrained models, adapting them to specific needs. Complex AI capabilities can be accessed through APIs with just a few lines of code, letting developers focus on solving specific problems rather than understanding the intricacies of model architecture. This accessibility sparks innovation across industries as organizations of all sizes experiment with AI-enhanced products and services.

Yet this democratization brings new challenges. As AI tools become more accessible, the difference between building AI systems and building them well becomes crucial. Understanding responsible development, knowing how to evaluate risks, and building robust systems are skills that become more important, not less. The future belongs not to those who can simply use AI tools but to those who can use them wisely.

We're in a unique moment in technological history—AI is perhaps the first major technology being democratized even as it's being developed. There's no complete instruction manual because we're writing it together as we go, learning and adapting in real-time. While concerns about job displacement are real, history suggests that technological revolutions often create more opportunities than they eliminate. The key is to ensure we're prepared for this transition, focusing on upskilling and reimagining roles rather than replacing them.

The future of AI belongs not just to those who can build it but to those who can envision new ways to use it wisely and ethically. Whether you're a developer, business leader, or someone curious about AI's potential, you have a part to play in shaping how this technology evolves. As we dive deeper into specific AI technologies in the coming chapters, remember—we're not just passive observers in this transformation; we're all active participants in writing the next chapter of human progress.

Chapter Summary

In this chapter, we explored the full journey of bringing AI projects to life. We started by demystifying the planning process to ensure that AI genuinely solves user problems rather than serving as a technological garnish. We examined how modern AI teams function, from specialized roles like Research Scientists and MLEs to newer positions like MLOps Engineers and Prompt Engineers. This reflects how the field has evolved with the rise of foundation models and automated tools.

We traced an AI model's lifecycle from conception to deployment, examining critical stages like data preparation, feature engineering, and model selection. We emphasized that deployment isn't a finish line but a starting point—modern AI systems require constant monitoring, updating, and refinement as they encounter real-world challenges. We explored how cross-validation and careful testing help build reliable systems that perform well beyond controlled environments.

Success metrics evolved beyond technical accuracy to encompass business KPIs and broader societal impacts. We dove deep into responsible AI deployment, examining how teams can build systems that are not just powerful but also transparent, fair, and accountable. Discussing bias and ethics, we emphasized practical steps teams can take to build more equitable systems.

Perhaps most importantly, we explored how AI development is being democratized through open-source tools, foundation models, and accessible APIs. While this creates exciting opportunities, it also heightens the importance of understanding how to build AI systems well. As we write the manual for this transformative technology together, success lies in technical excellence and building systems that genuinely benefit humanity while preparing for the changes ahead.

Closing Thoughts

Dear Reader,

We've traversed the landscape of artificial intelligence together, from the fundamental principles of machine learning to the intricate architectures of deep neural networks. We've watched computers learn to see, speak, and understand. We've explored how AI shapes the movies we watch and the products we discover. And finally, we've learned how to bring these powerful ideas to life through thoughtful planning and responsible deployment.

But this book is just the beginning of your journey.

We stand at a unique moment in human history. Artificial Intelligence is a fundamental shift in how we solve problems, create value, and understand ourselves. The tools we've explored together are transforming industries, reshaping societies, and opening possibilities that were science fiction just a few years ago.

You now hold some of the most powerful tools humanity has ever created. With foundation models, open-source frameworks, and cloud APIs, you can access capabilities that once required massive teams and budgets. But with this power comes profound responsibility. As you build, remember that every line of code, every model deployed, and every system launched has the potential to impact lives—for better or worse.

The future of AI isn't just about algorithms and architectures. It's about wisdom in application, creativity in solution-finding, and courage in addressing challenges. It's about building systems that amplify human potential rather than diminish it, that unite rather than divide, that elevate rather than merely automate.

Keep learning, for AI never stands still. Today's cutting-edge is tomorrow's baseline. Join communities, participate in competitions, experiment with new tools, and most importantly—build. Build with purpose, build with care, build with vision.

I'd love to hear about your journey. Share your thoughts, discoveries, and creations with me at sairam@artofsaience.com, @Sairam Sundaresan on LinkedIn, or @DSaience on X. Join the "Gradient Ascent" community at newsletter.artofsaience.com, where we continue to explore the frontiers of AI together.

Remember: You're not just learning about AI—you're becoming part of its story. Every great innovation started with someone like you, armed with knowledge and driven by curiosity, asking, "What if?"

The future is not something that happens to us. It's something we create: one decision, one model, one project at a time. You now have the tools to shape that future.

Make it count. Make it meaningful. Make amazing happen.

The adventure begins now.

Notes

Chapter 1

1. Atleast at the time of writing, that is.
2. Ironically, history repeats itself today. Some of us with lesser compute resources have to wait weeks for results in some cases. This time though, we know these methods work. Hence the patience.
3. Olga Russakovsky, Jia Deng, Hao Su, Jonathan Krause, Sanjeev Satheesh, Sean Ma, Zhiheng Huang et al. "ImageNet Large Scale Visual Recognition Challenge." *ArXiv*, (2014). Accessed December 5, 2024. https://arxiv.org/abs/1409.0575.
4. Top-5 error rate refers to the fraction of times a model didn't include the correct answer in its top five guesses.
5. Heck, I did it myself in the section above.
6. This book will cover techniques in machine learning and deep learning. The field of AI is wider than Jupiter and covering everything in it will take a few books. Ok, perhaps I'm exaggerating a bit. It's definitely wider than Pluto.
7. Except when greeting you or hunting for treats on the kitchen counter.
8. As of this writing.
9. Deep learning-based approaches that is.
10. We can "transfer" the knowledge of a trained model and adapt it for our task. This process, called transfer learning requires significantly lesser data BUT still requires high-quality samples. Additionally, there has also been research into data-efficient methods of training these models called "few-shot" learning. That's for another day.
11. No cockroaches were harmed in the making of this book.

Chapter 2

1. The baker wants to automate things and cut costs to tackle macroeconomic headwinds.
2. After all, this is your family's honor we're talking about.
3. She offers some freshly baked muffins as a thank you, but you politely refuse. The accusation still smarts.
4. Tech isn't the only sector affected by macroeconomic headwinds it seems.
5. These dance teachers can be mean.
6. Note that the word model in the machine learning community can mean the process of finding patterns in the data ("I can model the data") or the type of AI system ("This model was great for tagging movie reviews."). We're a confusing bunch. I know.
7. It's quite possible that the kid is a prodigy. But, I'm taking my chances.

Chapter 3

1. Think lines in two dimensions, planes in three dimensions and if you're really interested in much higher dimensions, hyperplanes.
2. For the sake of argument, assume that this is happening in the early 1990s when real-estate apps were non-existent.
3. The name is derived from the Greek letter Sigma.
4. Note that there are other metrics like the area under the curve which the reader is encouraged to explore.
5. Unlike real trees, decision trees are not green and don't perform photosynthesis. However, they do have roots, branches, and leaves.
6. A node with no further branches flowing down from it.
7. Explaining these ideas requires some math, and I'd encourage you to explore them yourself if you're interested.
8. Like other models, we can evaluate our decision tree using metrics like accuracy, precision, recall, and the F1-score. The best metric, as always, depends on the task.
9. There are other metrics like the Manhattan distance or Cosine similarity but I leave those to you to explore.

Chapter 4

1. Wikipedia. 2024. "Artificial Neuron." *Wikimedia Foundation*. Last modified September 26, 2024. https://en.wikipedia.org/wiki/Artificial_neuron.
2. Boolean functions are a way of combining simple true/false values to get a single true/false result.
3. Wikipedia. 2024. "Perceptron." *Wikimedia Foundation*. Last modified October 9, 2024. https://en.wikipedia.org/wiki/Perceptron.
4. In later evolutions of the Perceptron, a bias term was added as shown in the figure. The model would compute a weighted sum of the inputs, add the bias term, and then take the threshold.
5. The most common Boolean functions are AND, OR, NOT, and XOR. Wikipedia. 2024. "Boolean Function." *Wikimedia Foundation*. Last modified April 15, 2024. https://en.wikipedia.org/wiki/Boolean_function.
6. For classification problems, the output layer produces probability scores for each class. If we just have two classes, then a single neuron is sufficient. Why? Let's assume our neuron outputs the probability that the image is that of a cat. If this score is low, then it implies that the output is more likely to be a dog, right?
7. This is an extension of the sigmoid activation to classification problems that have multiple categories. The sigmoid activation is used for binary classification problems but can be extended into multi-class problems. The Softmax is a better way to do this.
8. The details are beyond the scope of this book, but it's really worth learning if you're interested.
9. Math alert, but visualize this as the way to compute the steepness of the terrain.
10. In real life, that's not always the case. Imbalanced datasets are very common and need to be addressed properly. This is left as an exploration for you, the reader.

Chapter 5

1. I feel like a dinosaur when I hear new slang. Don't you?
2. Clearly, feeding my then infant has left scars.
3. Wikipedia. 2024. "Word2vec." *Wikimedia Foundation*. Last modified November 16, 2024. https://en.wikipedia.org/wiki/Word2vec.

4 Recall that dense or fully connected neural networks consist entirely of linear layers and activation functions.

Chapter 6

1 Ashish Vaswani, Noam Shazeer, Niki Parmar, Jakob Uszkoreit, Llion Jones, Aidan N. Gomez, Lukasz Kaiser, and Illia Polosukhin. "Attention Is All You Need." *ArXiv*, (2017). Accessed November 26, 2024. https://arxiv.org/abs/1706.03762.

2 We compute the dot product between Q and K to compute the first score and then scale it. Hence the name scaled dot-product attention.

3 For example if our vocabulary has twenty-six words and our output sentence has five words, the decoder would have a list of five items. Each item in this list would have twenty-six entries. We would generate probability scores for each of these entries.

4 Note that there are better strategies for doing this, like Beam search, but discussing those is beyond the scope of this book.

5 In case you're wondering, this is exactly the same as one-hot encoding which we saw earlier.

6 At least billions. LLMs nowadays are reaching beyond the trillion parameter barrier.

7 Yes, there's a strong connection to Sesame Street with the naming of a lot of these models.

8 Take that Peter Piper picked a peck of pickled peppers

9 This pioneering technique was introduced in the ULMFit paper — The model itself was an LSTM based language model. Jeremy Howard, and Sebastian Ruder. "Universal Language Model Fine-tuning for Text Classification." *ArXiv*, (2018). Accessed November 27, 2024. https://arxiv.org/abs/1801.06146.

10 Wikipedia. 2024. "Proximal Policy Optimization." *Wikimedia Foundation*. Last modified November 12, 2024. https://en.wikipedia.org/wiki/Proximal_policy_optimization.

11 Wayne X. Zhao, Kun Zhou, Junyi Li, Tianyi Tang, Xiaolei Wang, Yupeng Hou, Yingqian Min et al. "A Survey of Large Language Models." *ArXiv*, (2023). Accessed November 28, 2024. https://arxiv.org/abs/2303.18223.

Chapter 7

1. Note that category and class are interchangeable here. As you might have seen so far, a lot of terms are used interchangeably. There are people who shake their fists at this. I, for one, am not one of them.
2. No, it isn't one from Old MacDonald's farm.
3. Recall that transfer learning is the idea of "transferring" the knowledge a model has gained by solving a different problem over to the problem you want it to solve. In this case, we could take a model that can already recognize thousands of object classes and fine-tune it to recognize the faces of people and pets we care about. This requires significantly less data and time!
4. Note that in practice, it's best to use one of the preexisting architectures. Researchers have spent years bashing their heads to perfect them. No reason why you need to as well. Unless, you'd like to.
5. In practice, we use much smaller images by creating a lower-res version of the actual pictures. Even still, computationally, linear layers for very large inputs are still prohibitive.
6. One-dimensional and higher-dimensional convolution layers exist and are used in practice. For brevity, I'm focusing just on the 2D ones.
7. There are a few more, including padding, which I omit for the sake of clarity.
8. Since these kernels "filter" out a specific type of feature from the input, they are also called filters.
9. Abolfazl Younesi, Mohsen Ansari, MohammadAmin Fazli, Alireza Ejlali, Muhammad Shafique, and Jörg Henkel. "A Comprehensive Survey of Convolutions in Deep Learning: Applications, Challenges, and Future Trends." *ArXiv*, (2024). Accessed October 26, 2024. https://arxiv.org/abs/2402.15490.
10. Tsung Lin, Michael Maire, Serge Belongie, Lubomir Bourdev, Ross Girshick, James Hays, Pietro Perona, Deva Ramanan, C. L. Zitnick, and Piotr Dollár. "Microsoft COCO: Common Objects In Context." *ArXiv*, (2014). Accessed October 26, 2024. https://arxiv.org/abs/1405.0312.
11. The details of this are more nuanced and depend on the specific neural network architecture. For now, we'll wave a magic wand and assume that we've accounted for these conditions.
12. Zhongxia Zou, Koyan Chon, Zhonwei Shi, Yuhong Guo, and Jieping Ye. "Object Detection in 20 Years: A Survey." *ArXiv*, (2019). Accessed October 26, 2024. https://arxiv.org/abs/1905.05055.
13. Shervin Minaee, Yuri Boykov, Fatih Porikli, Antonio Plaza, Nasser Kehtarnavaz, and Demetri Terzopoulos. "Image Segmentation Using Deep

Learning: A Survey." *ArXiv*, (2020). Accessed October 26, 2024. https://arxiv.org/abs/2001.05566.

14 Alexey Dosovitskiy, Lucas Beyer, Alexander Kolesnikov, Dirk Weissenborn, Xiaohua Zhai, Thomas Unterthiner, Mostafa Dehghani et al. "An Image Is Worth 16x16 Words: Transformers for Image Recognition at Scale." *ArXiv*, (2020). Accessed October 26, 2024. https://arxiv.org/abs/2010.11929.

Chapter 8

1 In reality, these models can create more than just images.
2 In some implementations, the generator receives multiple updates for each discriminator update. This is because generation is a harder problem to solve.
3 Guillermo Iglesias, and Edgar Talavera. "A Survey on GANs for Computer Vision: Recent Research, Analysis and Taxonomy." *ArXiv*, (2022). Accessed October 26, 2024. https://doi.org/10.1016/j.cosrev.2023.100553.
4 Physics and Thermodynamics experts please close your eyes. I feel your pain.
5 Florinel Croitoru, Vlad Hondru, Radu T. Ionescu, and Mubarak Shah. "Diffusion Models in Vision: A Survey." *ArXiv*, (2022). Accessed October 26, 2024. https://doi.org/10.1109/TPAMI.2023.3261988.
6 At the time of writing, the number of steps is still greater than one. When you read this, you might be chuckling at the woefully outdated nature of information here. Such is the pace of AI.
7 Robin Rombach, Andreas Blattmann, Dominik Lorenz, Patrick Esser, and Björn Ommer. "High-Resolution Image Synthesis with Latent Diffusion Models." *ArXiv*, (2021). Accessed October 26, 2024. https://arxiv.org/abs/2112.10752.
8 The U-Net uses a mechanism called cross-attention to understand specific aspects of the text but covering that is beyond the scope of this book.

Chapter 9

1 More funny dog videos please.
2 Netflix hosted a competition with a grand prize of $1 Million—the winning entry had to be at least 10 percent more accurate than their in-house

system. Wikipedia. 2024. "Netflix Prize." *Wikimedia Foundation*. Last modified February 28, 2024. https://en.wikipedia.org/wiki/Netflix_Prize.

3 I sincerely apologize for the number of categories. After all, this is a chapter on recommendation systems, and where would we be without a whole bunch of them?

4 Remember that hyperparameters are the settings of a machine learning algorithm that are tuned before the learning process begins. They are different from parameters, which are learned during the training process. Essentially, hyperparameters are the knobs and dials you adjust to set up your machine learning algorithm and can significantly impact the performance of the model.

5 In really large-scale recommenders, the nearest neighbors are precomputed and cached. This saves time and computation, allowing the recommender to process many user requests at once.

6 Shuai Zhang, Lina Yao, Aixin Sun, and Yi Tay. "Deep Learning Based Recommender System: A Survey and New Perspectives." *ArXiv*, (2017). Accessed November 13, 2024. https://doi.org/10.1145/3285029.

Index

accessibility 122, 219
accuracy 1, 13, 17, 29, 46, 54, 76, 118, 125, 139, 151, 164, 205, 212, 214, 215, 217, 218, 220, 226
actions 6, 23–5, 218
activation functions 65–8, 77, 139, 228
activation layers 133, 138, 139
agent 23, 24, 38
AI product manager 208, 209
AI projects x, 203, 204, 220
AI team 207, 209
AI-native solutions 204
AlexNet 3, 125
algorithms viii, ix, 11, 15, 37, 39, 41, 43, 45, 47, 49, 51–3, 55, 57–9, 61, 126, 148, 186, 201, 210, 223
alignment 121, 122
AlphaFold 1
alt tags 180
anomaly detection 16, 160, 182
APIs 219, 221, 223
artificial general intelligence 4
artificial intelligence (AI) viii, 1, 4, 10, 62, 97, 100, 223
artificial narrow intelligence 4
artificial neural networks 6, 10, 58, 61
artificial neurons 6, 61, 63, 64, 76
attention mechanism 107, 122

attention scores 104
Autoencoders 157, 160–4, 178, 179, 182, 201, 202
autofocus system 142
Automation 8, 9
auto-regressive language modeling 113
average pooling 137

backpropagation 69–71, 73–5, 77, 94, 109, 132, 143, 151, 164–6, 174, 198
bag of words 83–5
baseline models 211
batch gradient descent 73
bias 9, 39, 41, 63, 68, 70–2, 216–19, 221, 227
bias detection 217
bias term 63, 72, 227
Bidirectional Encoder Representations for Transformers (BERT) 114, 121, 154
big data 198
BigGAN 171
binary classification 62, 130, 227
biological neurons 61, 62
Boolean functions 227
Boolean variables 62
building phase 205
business metrics 214
business value 215, 216

candidate generation 199, 200
CAPTCHA 1
cell state 95, 96
centroids 56–8
chain rule 70, 164
chatbots 4, 90
ChatGPT 6, 90, 120
classification 4, 43–7, 51, 52, 59, 62, 129–31, 140, 143, 149, 153, 155, 204, 227, 228
classification problems 47, 51, 130, 227
classification task 143
Claude 121, 123
cloud services 204, 213
cluster assignment 56
clustering 14, 15, 17, 37, 55, 57–9
clustering algorithms 37
Codex 121
coefficients 39, 41
cold start problem 188–90, 197
collaborative filtering 186, 187, 189, 190, 194, 195, 201, 202
complex patterns 10, 138, 155, 201
compression 158, 159, 201
computational cost 178
computational resources 116, 212
computer vision ix, x, 106, 126, 155, 230
computing power 3, 204
constitutional AI 121
content-based filtering 186, 189, 190, 192
continuous improvement 214
contrastive learning 180, 181
ConvNext 139
convolutional layers 135–9, 150
convolutional neural networks (CNNs) 137, 147, 153, 155

convolutions 22, 134, 136, 137, 150
corpus 17, 19, 20, 80, 81, 86, 88
cosine similarity 89, 226
cost-effectiveness 9, 10
cross attention 107
cross component 201
cross-entropy loss 144
cross-validation 212, 213, 220
crowdsourcing 1
customer segmentation 55, 59
CycleGAN 171

DALL-E 157
data cleaning 209
data collection 1, 205, 209, 214, 216
data engineer 208, 209
data governance 217
data imbalance 29
data mining IV
data pipelines 205, 209
data preparation 204, 220
data quality 35, 43, 208, 214, 215
data science 4, 6, 7
data scientist 30, 207, 208
datasets 3, 17, 26, 27, 29, 32, 35, 52, 54, 77, 112, 113, 115, 116, 141, 180, 189, 204, 205, 209, 217, 227
decision trees 37, 47–55, 59, 226
decoder 101, 107–9, 111, 112, 158–60, 162, 165, 166, 168, 179, 181, 228
decoder-based models 114
deep and cross networks 201, 202
deep learning ix, x, 4, 6, 7, 10, 31, 37, 58, 59, 64, 76, 126, 197, 198, 200, 202, 225, 229, 231

DeepLab   152
democratization   219
denoising   160, 176, 178–82
  process   178, 179
dense layer/s   64, 65
dense representations   189
dependent variables   38
diffusion models   171–3, 177, 180, 182, 230
digital experiences   185
dimensionality reduction   14, 15, 160, 182
Direct Preference Optimization (DPO)   120
discrimination   9
discriminator   166–71, 182, 230
disinformation   117
diversity   54, 171, 190, 201
dot product   193, 194, 228

edge devices   213
efficiency   121, 137, 215
EfficientNet   139
embeddings   86–92, 97, 103, 153, 180, 181, 198, 202
emergent abilities   110
encoder   101–3, 106, 107, 109, 111, 112, 158–60, 162, 165, 179, 180
ensemble learning   52
Entropy   49
environment   9, 24
environmental impact   122, 218
epochs   74, 75
ethics   8, 9, 209, 216, 221
ethics in AI   216
Euclidean distance   57
evaluation metrics   42
exploding gradient problem   94
exploitation   24, 25
exploration   24, 25, 76, 97, 227

F1-Score   47, 226
facial recognition   4, 216
failure modes   217

fairness metrics   216, 217
false negative   46, 146
false positive/s   46, 146
Fast/ Faster RCNN   147
feature/s   3, 7, 30, 31, 34, 39, 41, 42, 44, 45, 47, 50–2, 54, 59, 72, 107,. 126, 128, 131, 134–6, 138, 143, 149, 150, 159, 160, 164, 189, 192–8, 201, 205, 210, 211, 214, 217, 218
  engineering   30, 31, 35, 210, 211, 214, 220
  interactions   201
  matrices   202
  selection   30, 52, 54
Feature Pyramid Networks (FPN)   147
feedback   13, 22–4, 27, 34, 93, 116–21, 132, 160, 164, 168, 170, 206, 214, 218
feed-forward layers   107
few-shot learning   111, 121, 122
filters   2, 4, 29, 79, 134–7, 229
fine-tuning   113, 115–18, 122, 228
floating point numbers   86, 87
forget gate   95
forward process   173, 175
forward propagation   68, 77
foundation models   115, 208, 209, 219–21, 223
funnel system   200

Gated Recurrent Units (GRU)   95
gating mechanism   95
Gemini   121, 123
Generalizability   31
generalization   25, 35, 52, 164
generative adversarial networks (GANs)   166–8, 170, 171, 182, 230
generative models   152, 155, 157, 159, 161, 163, 165–7, 169, 171–3, 175, 177, 179, 181–3

Generative Pretrained Transformer (GPT)   111, 114
generator   19, 166–71, 182, 230
Gini impurity   49
google   80, 87, 101
gradient descent   41, 69–75, 77, 132, 143, 151, 174, 195–8
gradients   70, 71, 74, 94, 96, 164, 165
Graphical Processing Units (GPUs)   3
ground truth   109, 145, 151, 198
guidance   59, 181

harmonic mean   47
hidden layers   63–5, 72, 201
hidden state   93, 95
hidden units   72
human preferences   117–20, 122
human review processes   217
hybrid systems   186, 190, 202
hyperbolic tangent   67
hyperparameter tuning   211
hyperparameters   72, 171, 212, 231

image classification   129–31, 140, 153
image embeddings   181
image generation   155, 182
image inpainting   149
image segmentation   129, 130, 148, 152, 155, 174, 229
image tokens   153
image-caption pairs   180
ImageNet   3, 225
imbalanced data   29, 35
impact assessments   217, 218
independent variables   38
inference time   34
Infrastructure decisions   213
initialization   55, 196
innovation   8, 121, 123, 179, 219, 224
input embeddings   103

input gate   95
input layer   63, 65, 68, 72
instance segmentation   151
instance-based systems   25–6, 34
instruction tuning   115, 116, 122
insufficient data   9, 29, 34, 35
interaction data   191, 198
Intersection over Union (IOU)   144, 151
irrelevant data   30
item features   192–8
item-based filtering   188

job displacement   220

kernels   134, 135, 229
key (K)   104
KL divergence   163, 164
K-means clustering   55, 58, 59
KPIs   215, 216, 220
Kullback-Leibler divergence   163

labeled data   16, 18, 20, 55, 131, 141
large language models (LLMs)   37, 99, 101, 103, 105, 107, 109–12, 113, 115–116, 119–22, 123, 185, 208, 228
latent diffusion   230
latent factors   195
latent space   158–60, 162, 164, 168, 178, 179, 182
layer normalization   106, 107
leaf node   48, 50, 51
learning rate   74, 75
least squares method   41
Lemmatization   81, 82
Li, Fei Fei   3
linear combination   67
linear layers   66, 67, 107, 133, 134, 137, 228, 229
linear models   38

linear regression   38–40, 42–7, 59
linear transformation   66
Llama   121
local minima   73
logistic regression   43–7, 59, 63, 211
Long Short-Term Memory (LSTM)   95
loss function   70, 71, 74, 75, 109, 143, 144, 151, 163, 164, 168

McCulloch, Warren   2, 62
machine learning   viii, ix, 4–7, 10, 11, 13, 25, 28–30, 34, 35, 38, 43, 49, 52, 58, 59, 72, 79, 83, 86, 158, 166, 172, 196, 201, 205, 207, 209–11, 215, 223, 225, 226, 231, 232
machine learning engineer   207, 209
machine vision   125, 127, 129, 131, 133, 135, 137, 139, 141, 143, 145, 147, 149, 151, 153, 155
map   13, 38, 103, 138, 145, 147, 149–51, 174
Mask R-CNN   152
MASK token   154
masked image modeling   154, 155
masked language modeling   114, 154
masked self-attention   108
mathematical model   2, 26
mathematical space   87
matrix factorization   195, 202
max pooling   137
mean   5, 6, 9, 14, 42, 47, 58, 74, 137, 139, 144–7, 160, 162, 165, 183, 205, 216, 217, 226

mean absolute error   42
mean Average Precision (mAP)   145, 147
mean squared error   42, 144
memory-based filtering   187
Midjourney   6, 157, 173
mini-batch gradient descent   73
mini-batch size   74
missing data   30, 35
missing values   52, 196, 197, 201
Mistral   121
ML Operations (MLOps)   208, 209, 211–16, 220
  engineer   208
mode collapse   170, 171, 182
model accuracy   205, 215
model selection   35, 211, 220
model-based filtering   187, 188
model-based systems   26–8, 34, 188, 189
monitoring dashboards   218
MS-COCO   141
multiclass classification   130
multidimensional space   87
multi-head attention   105, 106
Multi-Layer Perceptron (MLP)   62
multilabel classification   131
multimodal capabilities   121

n-grams   83
natural language processing (NLP)   ix, 79
network architecture   229
network parameters   71
network training   74, 76
neural collaborative filtering   201, 202
neural networks   ix, x, 2, 3, 6, 7, 10, 31, 58, 61–9, 71, 73, 75–7, 92, 94, 97, 133, 134, 137, 141–3, 151, 159, 165, 166, 174, 223, 228
neurons   2, 6, 61–6, 68, 72, 76
next sentence prediction   114

node impurity   49
noise in data   16
noise removal   181
non-linear relationships   201
Nonlinearities   66–67

object detection   129, 130, 140–2, 144, 148, 229
one-hot encoding   85, 86, 188, 228
optimization   35, 119, 120, 228
outliers   30, 31, 42, 52, 58
output gate   95
output layer   64, 65, 68, 72, 143, 227
overfitting   33–5, 51, 137, 164, 212

PaLM   121
panoptic segmentation   151, 155
parallel processing   3, 100
parameters   27, 51, 71, 72, 77, 87, 110, 112, 116, 121, 137, 231
patches   152–5
pattern recognition   122
penalty   23, 24
Perceptron   62, 63, 66, 76, 227
performance metrics   208, 215, 217
petabyte-scale datasets   113
photo tagging   131, 132, 134, 136, 138
Pitts, Walter   2
pixel accuracy   151
pixel space   179
planning phase   204, 205
policy   23, 24, 119, 228
pooling layers   137–9
positional embeddings   153
positional encoding   103
precision   47, 77, 82, 145–7, 226
prediction accuracy   214, 215
prediction error   196
prediction speed   214, 215

preprocessing   80, 82, 83
pretext task   21
pretrained models   29, 180, 204, 205, 219
Pretraining   112–17, 122
privacy   8–10, 202, 205, 208, 216, 218
probability   ix, 44, 45, 63, 68, 72, 104, 108, 109, 138, 139, 162, 182, 198, 199, 227, 228
probability distribution   109, 162, 182
probability scores   104, 138, 139, 199, 227, 228
production readiness   213
prompt engineer   208
Proximal Policy Optimization (PPO)   119

query (Q)   104

R-squared   42, 43
random assignment   83, 84
random forests   52–5, 59
ranking   118, 198–200
raw data   14, 30, 31, 210
RCNN   147
Recall   15, 47, 72, 87, 104, 107, 133, 145–7, 168, 193, 196, 226, 228, 229
recommendation problems   198
recommendation systems   4, 91, 183, 195, 197, 198, 201, 202, 231
recommender systems   185, 186, 201
reconstruction   159, 160, 163, 164, 196, 201
reconstruction error   163, 196
reconstruction loss   160, 163, 164
rectified linear unit   67
Recurrent Neural Networks (RNNs)   92

regression 38–40, 42–7, 51–3, 59, 63, 143, 204, 211
regression problems 51, 53
regression task 143
regularization 34
reinforcement learning 11, 21, 23, 24, 34, 117–20
Reinforcement Learning with AI Feedback (RLAIF) 120
Reinforcement Learning with Human Feedback (RLHF) 117
Rectified Linear Unit (ReLU) 67
reparameterization trick 165
representation gaps 217
re-ranking 200
research engineer 207
research scientist 207
residual connections 106, 122
Residual Neural Network 139
residuals 39–41
ResNet 139
response times 216
responsible AI 204, 217–19, 221
RetinaNet 147
retraining 206
revenue impact 216
reverse process 173, 175, 176
reward modeling 118
rewards 23–5, 34, 57, 119
risk assessment 50
root node 48
Rosenblatt, Frank 62
rule-based systems 5, 6

scalability 205
search engines 90
Security 8, 10, 16, 95, 218
segmentation map 149–51, 174
self-attention 103–5, 107–9, 111, 122
self-supervised learning 11, 18, 20, 21, 34
semantic segmentation 151

semi-supervised learning 11, 16–18, 34, 132
sentiment analysis 81
sequence models 91
sequence-to-sequence models 110
sigmoid function 45, 63
silhouette score 58
similarity measures 26
single-stage detectors 147
skip connections 106
slope 39, 45, 70, 71
softmax 67, 104, 108, 109, 227
softmax function 104
spam detection 59
spam filtering 1, 46
spam filters 2, 4, 79
sparse data 188, 189
sparse representations 188
specialized models 121, 122
speech recognition 8, 17, 66
SqueezeNet 139
SSD 147
Stable Diffusion 157, 173
standard deviation 162, 165
state 16, 24, 93, 95, 168, 170, 204
stemming 81, 82
step function 62–4, 66
stochastic gradient descent 73
StyleGAN 171
stop words 81, 84
subwords 80
supervised fine-tuning 117, 118
supervised learning 11–14, 17, 34, 132
synthetic data 217
system health 214
system integration 213
system reliability 205, 215

Tanh 67
target task 21

team structure 209
technical metrics 206, 214, 215
test set 32
text embeddings 180, 181
text encoder 180
text prompts 180
threshold 45, 62, 145–7, 227
tokenization 80, 81, 97, 103
tokens 109, 116, 152, 153
training data 8, 9, 13, 34, 35, 51, 52, 76, 114–16, 141, 143, 153, 164, 166, 180, 181, 212, 216
training instability 171, 182
training process 11, 72, 103, 104, 112, 114, 117, 135, 163, 168, 171, 231
training stability 106
transfer learning 21, 132, 225, 229
transformers 96, 99, 101, 103, 105, 107, 109–11, 113, 115, 117, 119, 121, 123, 147, 152–5, 183, 230
translation services 79
transparency 217, 218
transposed convolutional layers 150
trial and error 23, 25
true positives 146, 147
two-stage detectors 147

U-Net 152, 178–81, 230
U-Nets 174
underfitting 33, 35, 51
unlabeled data 20, 34
unsupervised learning 11, 14, 15, 17, 20, 34, 55
upsampling 150

upskilling 220
user behavior 189
user experience 191
user features 192–6
user preferences 192, 201
user satisfaction 205
user-based filtering 188
user-item interaction matrix 191, 192, 194–7, 201, 202
user-item pairs 201

variational autoencoders (VAEs) 162–6, 171, 182
validation set 32, 35, 76
value (V) 104
vanishing gradient problem 96
variational autoencoders 161, 182
vectors 86, 87, 89, 107, 178
virtual assistants 79
Vision Transformer (ViT) 155
vocabulary 21, 85, 86, 108, 228

weighted least squares 195
weighted sum 62, 63, 66, 68, 109, 193, 227
weight-sharing 136
weights 62, 63, 68–75, 87, 94, 104, 106, 109, 134–7, 153, 160, 165, 168–71, 174, 196, 198
wide and deep networks 201, 202
word vectors 89
Word2Vec 87, 227

XOR 62, 227

YOLO 147

About the Author

Sairam Sundaresan is an AI Engineering Leader with over fourteen years of experience in the tech industry. He currently spearheads advanced AI projects at Valeo, managing a large team of researchers developing autonomous vehicle perception systems. Previously at Intel Labs, he pioneered research in deep learning algorithms, focusing on algorithm-hardware co-design and multimodal models that pushed the boundaries of AI efficiency.

He began his career at Qualcomm as Senior Machine Learning Engineer. Sairam's work on the development of Qualcomm's FastCV library, Touch to Track, and real-time 3D reconstruction on mobile devices earned significant recognition and was featured in Forbes. Some of this technology found its way into consumer devices.

His research work has earned him several patents and led to numerous publications.

An educator at heart, Sairam has served as Machine Learning Lead and Mentor at the Frontier Development Lab since 2019. During this time, he has led projects on understanding the Sun, focusing on starspots, solar wind, and reconstructing its surface. The teams he mentored have achieved significant recognition, with their work accepted at high-profile conferences such as NeurIPS.

Driven by a passion to make AI accessible, Sairam created "Gradient Ascent," a weekly newsletter to demystify AI even for non-technical audiences. His skill at breaking down complex jargon has enabled a wide range of people to engage with the world of AI, from product managers at top tech companies to CEOs and analysts at premier VC funds.

Sairam is an alumnus of the University of Michigan, Ann Arbor, from where he holds a master's degree in Electrical Engineering. There, he specialized in Computer Vision and Signal Processing. This academic foundation underpins his work, enabling him to integrate practical applications with a robust understanding of theoretical principles.

Outside the lab, Sairam is an award-winning nature photographer, illustrator, and writer. These perspectives enhance his problem-solving approach and fuel his creativity.